2901-

STRATEGIC COST MANAGEMENT

425

Dr. P.K. Bandgar

M.Com., Ph.D., FICWA,

Director, Oriental Institute of Management,
Sector 12, Vashi,
Navi Mumbai-400703.

HPH

Himalaya Publishing House

MUMBAI • NEW DELHI • NAGPUR • BENGALURU • HYDERABAD • CHENNAI • PUNE • LUCKNOW • AHMEDABAD • ERNAKULAM • BHUBANESWAR • INDORE • KOLKATA • GUWAHATI

First Edition : 2013

Published by : Mrs. Meena Pandey for **Himalaya Publishing House Pvt. Ltd.,**
"Ramdoot", Dr. Bhalerao Marg, Girgaon, **Mumbai - 400 004.**
Phone: 022-23860170/23863863, Fax: 022-23877178
E-mail: himpub@vsnl.com; Website: www.himpub.com

Branch Offices :

New Delhi : "Pooja Apartments", 4-B, Murari Lal Street, Ansari Road, Darya Ganj, New Delhi - 110 002. Phone: 011-23270392, 23278631; Fax: 011-23256286

Nagpur : Kundanlal Chandak Industrial Estate, Ghat Road, Nagpur - 440 018. Phone: 0712-2738731, 3296733; Telefax: 0712-2721216

Bengaluru : No. 16/1 (Old 12/1), 1st Floor, Next to Hotel Highlands, Madhava Nagar, Race Course Road, Bengaluru - 560 001. Phone: 080-22286611, 22385461, 4113 8821, 22281541

Hyderabad : No. 3-4-184, Lingampally, Besides Raghavendra Swamy Matham, Kachiguda, Hyderabad - 500 027. Phone: 040-27560041, 27550139

Chennai : 8/2 Madley 2nd street, T. Nagar, Chennai - 600 017. Mobile: 09320490962

Pune : First Floor, "Laksha" Apartment, No. 527, Mehunpura, Shaniwarpeth (Near Prabhat Theatre), Pune - 411 030. Phone: 020-24496323/24496333; Mobile: 09370579333

Lucknow : House No 731, Shekhupura Colony, Near B.D. Convent School, Aliganj, Lucknow - 226 022. Mobile: 09307501549

Ahmedabad : 114, "SHAIL", 1st Floor, Opp. Madhu Sudan House, C.G. Road, Navrang Pura, Ahmedabad - 380 009. Phone: 079-26560126; Mobile: 09377088847

Ernakulam : 39/104 A, Lakshmi Apartment, Karikkamuri Cross Rd., Ernakulam, Cochin - 622011, Kerala. Phone: 0484-2378012, 2378016; Mobile: 09387122121

Bhubaneswar : 5 Station Square, Bhubaneswar - 751 001 (Odisha). Phone: 0674-2532129, Mobile: 09338746007

Indore : Kesardeep Avenue Extension, 73, Narayan Bagh, Flat No. 302, IIIrd Floor, Near Humpty Dumpty School, Indore - 452 007 (M.P.). Mobile: 09303399304

Kolkata : 108/4, Beliaghata Main Road, Near ID Hospital, Opp. SBI Bank, Kolkata - 700 010, Phone: 033-32449649, Mobile: 7439040301

Guwahati : House No. 15, Behind Pragjyotish College, Near Sharma Printing Press, P.O. Bharalumukh, Guwahati - 781009, (Assam). Mobile: 09883055590, 08486355289, 7439040301

DTP by : HPH, Editorial Office, Bhandup **(Pooja S.)**

Printed at : M/S Sri Sai Art Printer Hyderabad. On behalf of HPH

Preface

It is a matter of great privilege for me to place before the esteemed readers the first edition of the book **"Strategic Cost Management."** At the beginning of the twenty-first century, changes in the business environment have profoundly affected cost accounting and cost management. These changes are an increased emphasis on providing value to two customers, globalisation of markets, growth of services industry and awareness of ethical and environmental business practices. Therefore, the new cost management system can be more accurately referred to as an activity and strategic based cost management system.

The book covers lucid presentation, tailor-made approach comprehensive text with plenty of illustrations and has several additional welcome features. The book covers the course contents of the students preparing for MBA/MMS of the University of Mumbai and other Universities in India and M.Com., CA, CS and ICWA and other professional examinations. I am confident that with all these features the students and faculties will find this book all the more useful and rewarding for them. This book is dedicated to Lord Ganesha who is a constant source of energy and involves in serving the students and teacher community. Constructive and helpful suggestions for improvement in this book will be gratefully acknowledged.

I am very much thankful to Dr. M.G Shivhatti, Director General, Oriental Institute of Management and Dr. Rashmi Soni, Dean, Academics, OIM, Navi Mumbai for their inspiration and support while writing this book.

I am very much thankful to Mr. S.K. Srivastava, Mr. S.K. Patil, Nimisha Kadam and all staff members of Himalaya Publishing House Pvt. Ltd., Bhandup, Mumbai for their personal involvement in the publication of the book.

01.06.2013 **Dr. P.K. Bandgar**

Syllabus

1. Cost-Benefit Analysis: With Reference to Strategic Business Decision Making – Qualitative and Quantitative Aspects.
2. Different Aspects of Strategic Cost Management:
   - Value Analysis and Value Engineering,
   - Wastage Control,
   - Disposal Management,
   - Business Process Reengineering,
   - Total Quality Management
   - Total Productive Maintenance,
   - Energy Audit,
   - Control of Total Distribution Cost and Supply Cost,
   - Cost Reduction,
   - Product Life Cycle Costing etc.
3. Activity Based Costing
   - Target Costing
4. Value Chain Analysis and Long-term Cost Management
5. Objective Based Costing
6. Balance Scorecard Concept
7. Cost Audit and Management Audit under Companies Act with Reference to Strategic Assessment of Cost and Managerial Performances
8. Strategic Cost-Benefit Analysis of Different Business Restructuring Propositions.
9. Entrepreneurial Approach to Cost Management, with Reference to Core Competencies, Strategic Advantages and Long-term Perspective of Cost Management

Reference Text:

1. Strategic Cost Management – Dr. Govindaraja
2. Strategic Financial Management – Dr. Girish Jakhotiya

Detailed Contents

1. Cost Analysis for Strategic Business Decisions **1 – 28**

1.1 Introduction 1.2 Strategic Cost Management 1.3 Cost Leadership Strategy 1.4 Strategic Business Plans 1.5 Strategic Cost Management Programme 1.6 Importance of Strategic Cost Management 1.7 Cost-Benefit Analysis 1.8 Illustrations 1.9 Exercises

2. Different Aspects of Strategic Cost Management **29 – 66**

2.1 Introduction 2.2 Value Analysis and Value Engineering 2.3 Wastage Control 2.4 Disposal Management 2.5 Business Process Reengineering 2.6 Total Quality Management 2.7 Total Productive Maintenance 2.8 Energy Audit 2.9 Control of Total Distribution Cost and Supply Cost 2.10 Cost Reduction 2.11 Product Life Cycle Costing 2.12 Exercises

3. Activity Based Costing **67 – 102**

3.1 Introduction 3.2 Activity Based Costing 3.3 Identifying Activities 3.4 Development of ABC 3.5 Activity Based Costing Procedure 3.6 Benefits of Activity Based Costing 3.7 Implementation of Activity Based Costing System 3.8 Activity Based Costing in Service Sector 3.9 Activity Based Management 3.10 Limitations of Activity Based Costing 3.11 Illustrations 3.12 Target Costing 3.13 Exercises

4. Value Chain Analysis and Long-term Cost Management **103 – 131**

4.1 Introduction 4.2 Value Analysis 4.3 Value Chain Analysis 4.4 Exploiting Internal Linkages 4.5 Exploiting Supplier Linkages 4.6 Exploiting Customer Linkages 4.7 Value Chain Framework 4.8 Organisation Activities and Cost Drivers 4.9 Operational Activities and Cost Drivers 4.10 Value Chain Analysis – Traditional Cost Management 4.11 The Role of Management Accountant 4.12 Long-term Cost Management 4.13 Exercises

5. Objective Based Costing **132 – 147**

5.1 Introduction 5.2 Meaning of Activity Based Management 5.3 Process Value Analysis 5.4 Kaizen Standards 5.5 Benchmarking 5.6 Activity Based Management 5.7 Exercises

6. Balance Scorecard Concept **148 – 164**

6.1 Introduction 6.2 Balanced Scorecard 6.3 Four Basic Business Perspectives 6.4 Components and Measures of Performance 6.5 Evaluation of Responsibility Center 6.6 Exercises

7. Audit 165 – 176

7.1 Introduction 7.2 Definition of Auditing 7.3 Compulsory Audit 7.4 The Auditor 7.5 Internal Audit 7.6 Cost Audit 7.7 Efficiency Audit 7.8 Management Audit 7.9 Strategic Assessment of Cost and Managerial Performances 7.10 Exercises

8. Strategic Cost-Benefit Analysis 177 – 200

8.1 Introduction 8.2 Strategic Cost-Benefit Analysis 8.3 Entrepreneurial Approach to Cost Management 8.4 Strategic Advantages 8.5 Long-term Perspectives of Cost Management 8.6 Exercises

9. Abbreviations 201 – 202

Chapter 1

Cost Analysis for Strategic Business Decisions

STRUCTURE:

1.1 Introduction

1.2 Strategic Cost Management

1.3 Cost Leadership Strategy

1.4 Strategic Business Plans

1.5 Strategic Cost Management Programme

1.6 Importance of Strategic Cost Management

1.7 Cost-Benefit Analysis

1.8 Illustrations

1.9 Exercises

1.1 INTRODUCTION

The Indian economic environment has been going through a sea change. This is being brought about by government's economic policies of liberalisation. The new environment offers more opportunities for growth of business and economy. But it has been bringing in much more competition. Costs have once more become relevant for Indian managements. The recent Indian economic changes can be summarised as a shift from a 'regulatory' to a 'business' environment. It is consequently moving from a seller's market to a buyer's market. The dimension of cost which was secondary in most business has once again become relevant. The liberalisation process has been accentuated since 1991. Most industries do not require a licence to enter. Direct taxes, excise and customs duties are being progressively reduced. Money and capital market are free subject only to SEBI regulations. Infrastructure sectors of power, telecom, oil, gas roads and ports are 'now open' for Indian and foreign private investment. Foreign investment is not just 'allowed' but actively encouraged. The central aim of liberalisation is to relaunch the sluggish Indian economy on a higher growth path.

Multilateral, bilateral and independent research agencies worldwide are looking upon India as an emerging market, an Asian tiger, a locomotive economy and an economic superpower of the 21st century. This opens up enormous opportunities of growth for Indian companies. However, the opportunities also attract severe competition. In most industries, the existing players are planning expansion. Many companies are also attracting new players, Indian, foreign or joint ventures. Multinational corporations with majority or substantial holdings are bringing in latest technology, brand names and funds. Imports of capital goods, intermediates and raw materials are a more immediate threat. Mergers and Acquisitions (M & A) are also creating bigger competitions with economies of scale and scope.

In the liberalised, competitive economy, costs have once again become relevant. If a firm is to optimise its performance and not just satisfice, it should have been constantly searching for improvements in all areas including costs. Those who have been involved in export markets have been worried about costs. The new savage competition is forcing cost consciousness on Indian businesses.

It is useful to recall the elegant three step model for managing costs, i.e., cost information, control and reduction. The cost information should be disseminated not as a complaint or criticism but as a stimulus to innovation, ingenuity and improvisation at worker, supervisor and executives. When the ground is prepared with cost information, management can take the next step of reviving or introducing a cost control system and process. The third and most advanced stage of managing costs is to go for their sustained reduction, by challenging the norms/standards themselves.

After liberalisation, the two major factors which have direct bearing on corporate performance are quality and cost. The importance of managing costs has assumed prime focus particularly in the profit-making enterprises. Cost and management accountants now hold the key role in corporate decision making by their direct association with and active involvement in the decision making process. Cost control and reduction should be strengthened rightway. But cost leadership cannot be achieved overnight. There is a need for strategic long-term approach. In a global competitive environment, technology and brands give a temporary advantage. Product features and values are quickly observed and initiated by competitors. A most sustainable competitive advantage is a cost edge.

1.2 STRATEGIC COST MANAGEMENT

Cost management was an added bonus in the past. In the competitive environment, it has become a strategic priority for survival, growth and profitability. Thus, Strategic Cost Management (SCM) is cost analysis in a broader context, where the strategic elements become more explicit and formal. The strategic cost management involves usage of cost data to develop superior strategies to gain sustainable competitive advantage. In the past, the application of cost data in strategic planning has not received the attention it deserved. A holistic understanding of a firm's cost structure can go a long way in the search for sustainable competitive advantage. Thus, strategic cost management is the managerial use of cost information explicitly providing strategic perspectives.

1.2.1 Strategy

The term strategy is used in business to describe how an organisation is going to achieve its overall objectives. Most organisations have several alternatives for achieving its objectives. Strategy is concerned with deciding which alternative is to be adopted to accomplish the overall objectives of the organisation. Thus, a strategy is a unified, comprehensive, and integrated plan that relates to the strategic advantages of the firm to the challenges of the environment. It is designed to ensure that the basic objective of the enterprise are achieved through proper execution by the organisation.

Strategies are developed in order to achieve the objectives of an organisation. Strategy is also a future-oriented plan. It is an unified, comprehensive and integrated plan. It is unified because it unifies all the sections of the organisation together. It is comprehensive as it covers all the major aspects or areas of the organisation. An organisation needs to frame alternative strategies. The internal and the external environment affect the strategy formulation and its implementation. There is a need for proper allocation of resources for effective implementation of strategy. Strategy is a process which is universally applicable. It is also applicable to all functional areas. The development of a strategy can be with formal or rational emigrant or progressed, under a logical path. Strategy bridges the gap between ends and means.

Michael E. Porter has developed competitive strategy means deliberately choosing a different set of activities to deliver a unique mix of value. Porter argued that strategy is about competitive position about differentiating yourself in the eyes of the customer, about addition value through a mix of activities from those used by competitors. Strategy is a term that comes from Greek word *'strategia'* meaning 'generalship'. It also refers to the means by which policy is affected. Strategy is perspective, position, plan and pattern. Together, strategy and tactics bridge the gap between ends and means.

1.2.2 Strategic Management

Strategic Management is an ongoing process that evaluates and controls the business and the industry in which the company is involved. It assesses its competitors and sets goals and strategies to meet existing and potential competitors. Then it reassesses each strategy annually or quarterly to determine how it has been implemented and whether it has succeeded or needs replacement by a new strategy to meet changed circumstances.

Strategic management is a stream of decisions and actions which leads to the development of an effective strategy to help achieve corporate objectives. It is a systematic approach to a major and increasingly important responsibility of general management to position and relate the firm to its environment in a way which will assure its continued success.

A strategic management model has started process by defining the mission of the enterprise in the light of the profile, external environment and operating industry analysis. An individual firm needs to identify the activities they perform best and seeks ways to maximise their effect in order to gain maximum competitive advantage. The process of strategic management can be broadly divided into three phases as under:

(a) **Strategy Formulation:** In this process, emphasis is given on enterprise's mission, business goals and their relationship with external environment in which opportunities and threats exist. The mission states the philosophy and the purpose of the organisation. The objectives are the aims or ends which the organisation seeks to achieve. Thus, the mission and objectives must be clearly defined.

(b) **Strategy Implementation:** In this process, emphasis is given on leadership, organisation structure, organisational culture and their relationship with functional policies and resource allocation decisions. The strategy implementation involves the formulation of plans, programmes and projects. Strategy, by itself, does not lead to action. Various types of expansion plans need to be formulated. Plans result in different kinds of programmes. A programme is a broad plan which includes goals, policies, procedures and other aspects required to implement a plan. Programmes lead to the formulation of projects. A project is a specific programme for which the time schedule and costs are predetermined.

(c) **Strategy Evaluation:** In this process, managers try to assure that the strategic choice is properly implemented and is meeting the objectives of the enterprise. The strategy evaluation process involves the following elements:

(i) Setting of standards

(ii) Measurement of performance

(iii) Comparison of actual performance with standards

(iv) Finding out deviations

(v) Analysing deviations

(vi) Taking corrective measures.

1.2.3 Cost Management

Cost management identifies, collects, measures, classifies and reports information that is useful to managers and other internal users in cost ascertainment, planning, controlling and decision making. Cost management aims to produce and provide information to internal users and personnel working in the organisation.

Effective management of cost makes an organisation, more strong, more stable and helps in improving the potentials of a business. The organisation calls for a system that would monitor the full economic impact of the business, on resource acquisition and consumption. This provides supplying of information to the top management for exploring various alternatives by which cost-effectiveness can be improved. Cost management also helps in optimising resources which will improve overall efficiency of the organisation and help the firm to achieve its objectives.

It is useful to recall the elegant three step model for managing costs — cost information, control and reduction.

(i) **Cost Information:** There is no question of managing costs if the firm does not even know or take interest in costs. Every aspect of business must be subjected to an assessment of at least the actual costs, projects, materials, labour, energy, maintenance, overheads, brand building, selling and distribution and research and development, etc. The entire organisation must be informed with cost data relevant at each level function and location. The very awareness of cost may trigger some thinking and action. The management at all levels should encourage people to take interest in current cost information and make their own comparisons with the past costs and competitor's costs. The aim should be to encourage a cost-benefit orientation. Therefore, cost information should be disseminated not as a complaint or criticism but as a stimulus to innovation, integrity and improvisation at worker, supervisor and executive levels.

(ii) **Cost Control:** The management of the business can take the next step of introducing a cost control system and process in the organisation. Any control including cost control requires that there should be a norm or standard against which actuals can be compared. The variances are analysed and corrective actions are taken. The three C's of pricing need to be rank ordered as follows – competition, customer and cost. In a dynamic market, competition sets the price. From that after allowing a modest profit margin, one can arrive at the target cost. The product, processes, materials and other elements of cost will have to be within this target cost.

Another standard is provided by past performance peaks, due to favourable demand, power supply, raw materials availability or industrial peace. Workers can be motivated to at least recapture those peaks of outputs with corresponding lower cost standards. A further approach is in gathering intelligence on the cost structures of the most efficient existing and new competitors and benchmark our standards against the competitors. A conceptual method is to look at technical engineering and theoretical parameters wherever applicable and set the standards.

(iii) **Cost Reduction:** The most advanced stage of managing costs is to go for their sustained reduction by challenging the standards themselves. The recent concept of reengineering is on these lines. There is a need to create culture, a set of values and mindset in the organisation that all cost standards are not permanent, but temporary and that they must be subject to constant downward pressure. The managers have to take inter-firm comparisons and benchmarking global. There is a global market. No country, however, economically strong, such as the US and no block, however strong as the European community can protect its internal market.

There is also a need to reduce not only labour costs, but the bigger items like material and energy and the more avoidable items like interest and administrative overheads. Cost reduction should start at the project phase. Every new project of revamping, modernisation and onsite expansion should be subject to tighter standards. In greenfield project, international standards should be used for erection time, cost and quality and post-commisioning ramp up to full capacity. The modern businessmen should invest in design, development, research, value analysis, value engineering, training suggestion and incentive schemes to deepen cost reduction.

1.3 COST LEADERSHIP STRATEGY

In a global competitive environment, technology and brands give a temporary advantage. Product features and values are quickly observed and imitated by competitor. A most sustainable competitive advantage is a cost edge. Therefore, a company or a business organisation should try to be the cost leader of their industry. They should be the lowest cost producer business organisation. At least the business unit should be the lowest cost producer in same products or services, or territories or segments.

Every business unit should try to be among the cost leaders at least one-third of the lower cost producers in its respective industry. The unit should not use that cost advantage for fierce price cutting. It should be used, at least part of it, for a price advantage. The business unit can invest part of that cost advantage in tomorrow's technologies, materials and processes to build the foundation for the future, continuing cost leadership. The business unit can treat the vendor as an extended part of the home factory and help him with technology, systems and skills for cost leadership in his supplies. Similarly, the businessmen should build a strategic partnership with the dealer for superior cost-effective distribution and service.

Cost control and reduction should be strengthened by the corporates rigtway. But cost leadership cannot be achieved overnight. There is a need for a strategic long-term approach. Get the senior management team to brainstrom a shared vision for 2020. The vision should have two components – (a) Qualitative and (b) Quantitative. The qualitative components should cover the cost-effectiveness, value for money and cost leadership. Quantitative components should cover a demanding profit goal based on continuous cost reduction, innovation and higher productivity. The company should disseminate the draft vision to the divisions, Strategic Business Units (SBUs) and profit centres. There is a need for revisiting the vision and examine organisational vulnerabilities in achieving the cost and profit dimensions and raise sensitivity to strategic cost management issues. For this purpose, there is a need to take strategic vendors and dealers into confidence on the vision.

1.4 STRATEGIC BUSINESS PLANS

In multi-product or multi-geographical area companies, strategic business divisions are created to manage effectively each of the products or a group of products. Separate Strategic Business Units (SBUs) are created each focusing on specific products like toiletries, beverages, ice-creams, laundry products and cosmetics etc. A multi-product company like Hindustan Unilever may adopt the concept of SBU. The concept of SBU was developed by General Electric Company of USA to manage its multi-product business. Each SBU is managed independently as if it is a separate company by itself, with clearly defined products/markets. Each SBU formulates for itself a clearly defined strategy. However, the SBU strategy should be in line with the overall strategy of the organisation. Each SBU is allocated resources in the form of physical, human and financial depending upon its activities and contributions made by it to the organisation. Each SBU may compete with the other SBU of the same organisation.

The strategic business units should formulate detailed strategic business plans to help them achieve their growth and profit targets, with necessary thrust on cost reduction in the face of increasingly fierce competition. There is a need to empower the middle management to initiate a draft plan, in line with the divisional vision. The Divisional Management Committees have to set up a cross-functional team of one bright executive each from marketing, materials, manufacturing, finance and human resources and systems, as the planning task force. The finance member of the Planning Task Force should be preferably the division's Cost/Management Accountant. At the divisional level, the key finance task is cost management, whereas at corporate level, it is treasury management. The Divisional Management Committees should look at the strategies for cost reduction and cost leadership.

1.5 STRATEGIC COST MANAGEMENT PROGRAMME

The strategic cost management programme includes the following steps:

(a) **Focus:** Focus state starts with reviewing the different strategies of the company. Reviewing the strategies will lead to clear identification of performance gaps and it will help to bridge the gap by improving targets already set. Modifying the targets will lead to develop plan of action which will foster better internal communication within the organisation.

(b) **Planning and Training:** Planning plays a crucial role in implementing strategic cost management programme. To implement the planning, a manager should gather very efficient team members and train them accordingly. Setting up of project management structure will facilitate the implementation of strategic cost management by clearly identifying the day-to-day activities, steering guidance and offering ad hoc assistance.

(c) **Fact Finding:** This stage includes the tasks such as data gathering, conducting interview, developing benchmarks, and conducting customer surveys.

(d) **Analysis for Recommendations for Changes:** Analysis of activities plays a crucial role in ascertaining the cost of company. It can be done by various strategic cost management analytical tools, viz., cost driver analysis, activity based costing, selective business process reengineering, etc. An action plan for proposed change should address the following questions — what, who, when, and how aspects of the activities.

(e) **Implementation:** In implementation stage, the first task to be done is to define responsibilities and accountability of each individual and controlling, i.e., monitoring and corrective action should be taken at each stage of programme. And this is how the continuous improvement can be achieved.

1.6 IMPORTANCE OF STRATEGIC COST MANAGEMENT

In today's competitive environment, the most efficient companies view all their spending as an investment. These companies make smart spending decisions based on a strategic vision and their internal capabilities to deliver value from the investment. The companies have been under pressure to cut costs in the short term without really thinking about sustainable change and integration with the overall business strategy. In the current business environment of increased global competition, new markets, increasing regulations and changing demographics, companies should develop a multifaceted and renewable cost competence. It was observed by the experts that yesterday's tactical solutions, despite consuming considerable resources, have failed in many organisations to deliver the planned reduction of costs and have not resulted into competitive advantage. In case of many companies, the cost savings achieved in the short term, have leaked away and the cost base has returned to previous high levels but with the result of considerable damage to corporate structure, image, culture and morale. Therefore, it should be considered that the cost is a strategic issue.

There is a need to continuously strive to optimise the 'cost' in the context of the entire business model of the company. It also becomes necessary to change the business model itself to ensure that it remains competitive. Similarly, the execution of any choosen strategy has to be carefully managed to ensure the appropriate balance between revenue growth and cost. The companies that are taking the investment approach to managing cost are thriving in this new environment. Therefore, it has become necessary to link the cost management to strategies of the organisation. Strategic cost management is the provision and analysis of Cost and Management Accounting data about a business and its competitors for use in developing and monitoring the business strategy. The strategic cost management focuses on the cost reduction and continuous improvement and change. The traditional cost control systems mostly maintain status quo and the ways of performing the existing activities are not reviewed. Therefore, the strategic cost management goes a step ahead and uses several approaches adopted do not necessarily use the accounting technique. Thus, the basic aim of strategic cost management is to help the organisation to achieve the cost leadership and get the sustainable competitive advantage.

1.7 COST-BENEFIT ANALYSIS

Cost-benefit Analysis is a practical way of assessing the desirability of a project where it is important to take a long view. It implies the enumeration and evaluation of all the relevant costs and benefits. It covers the three important areas:

(i) Assessing the desirability of a project in the public

(ii) Identification of costs and benefits

(iii) Measurement of costs and benefits

Certain projects which appear very much profitable when their inputs and outputs are valued at actual prices are unattractive from the viewpoint of the national economy or public interest. While other apparently unprofitable projects have high economic returns. But the theory accepts that actual receipts and expenditures can be suitably adjusted so that the difference between them closely analogous to ordinary profit, may properly reflect the public gain.

(a) Cost: Accurate costs of production estimates and records are immensely used in project decision making. Costing provides a scientific base for several other management decisions. It is not merely a tool of control but also a device of management planning. Some important features of costing are very useful in project planning and decision making:

(i) Cost of production records provide ample information for planning, material, labour and factory cost.

(ii) Cost of production aids the management to fix the competitive prices.

(iii) Cost of production is useful in determining the level of production activities.

(iv) It also determines the minimum acceptable quality of product.

(v) Cost figures reveal the cost per unit of materials consumed and labour utilised.

(vi) A periodical review and analysis of the cost of production enables the management to identify the cause of inefficiency, wastages and losses.

(vii) The cost of production is dependent upon control over inventory receipts, issues and balance and flow of materials on the maintenance of records.

The costs may be classified as follows:

(i) **Direct Costs:** The costs incurred exclusively on the production of a commodity, on the execution of a job work or on performing a service are known as direct cost. For example, material costs, labour costs.

(ii) **Indirect Costs:** Indirect costs are those costs which are incurred on carrying the business as a whole. These costs are not incurred directly on a unit of production. For example, Factory Rent, Lighting, Stationery.

(iii) **Fixed Costs:** The costs which remain fixed irrespective of the volume of production are known as fixed costs. For example, Factory Manager's salary, Depreciation of machinery.

(iv) **Variable Costs:** Variable costs vary with the increase or decrease in production. For example, Material, Labour.

(v) **Marginal Cost:** The marginal cost is the cost of producing additional unit or units of production. It includes only variable costs like material and labour.

(vi) **Average Cost:** The average cost is calculated by dividing the total cost of production by the number of units produced. The analysis of average cost and marginal cost helps the management to determine the volume of production.

(vii) **Total Cost:** Total cost is the total of all costs incurred for carrying out production. It includes cost of material, labour and all overheads.

(viii) **Prime Cost:** The total of all direct material, labour and overheads is known as prime cost. It is a variable cost.

(ix) **Factory Cost:** Factory cost is the cost of production which includes prime cost and factory overheads.

(x) **Overhead Costs:** The indirect costs incurred by the factory are also known as overhead costs. It includes administrative and office overheads as well as selling and distribution overheads.

(b) Benefits: Project benefit monitoring and evaluation activities help considerably the enterprise to overcome its problems and accelerate the process of growth and development. Projects implemented by the enterprises are intended to eliminate the obstacles to create conditions which stimulate economic development. The banks and project executing agencies are careful to formulate, appraise and implement projects in a way that minimises risks and is cost-effective, results often differ from expectations because of the difficult and unforeseen conditions under which they are implemented. The projects which are intended to induce development as result of goods or services which are generated by the project and then used by beneficiaries to increase the effectiveness of these projects in generating benefit. These activities are generally incorporated into project preparation, appraisal implementation and follow-up activities.

Profitability analysis technique is also used in several organisations in order to assess the operational efficiency of a project and its profitability. It also seeks to correct the structural deficiencies and improve productivity and profits. Profit is the primary objective of an enterprise. The word profit implies a comparison of the operations of business between two specific dates, which are usually separated by an interval of one year. In order to optimise the resources of wealth on which national prosperity depends, the basic financial objective of an enterprise is to maximise, within socially acceptable limits, profits from the use of the funds employed. The maximisation of profit within a socially acceptable limit implies that a proper regard for public interest has been shown. Therefore, the crucial measure of the effective performance of a business is profit, which really is a measure of how well a business performs economically.

Cost-benefit analysis essentially involves the following:

(a) Identification of the economic costs and benefits.

(b) Valuation of economic costs and benefits.

(c) Comparison of costs and benefits.

In identifying the costs and benefits of a project, it is useful to start with a clear definition of the benefits expected from the project. A major benefit may be additional output of goods which are widely traded. The benefits may be measured in terms of cost savings or gains to the consumers. The project benefits may be measured in qualitative terms such as good quality of products or improvement in the quality of products. The benefits expected from a project will help define its costs. All costs incurred in realising the benefits should be taken into account, in the analysis, irrespective of whether they form a part of the financial cost of the project.

(c) Analysis: Economic analysis of projects should be based on incremental benefits and costs. It requires the comparison of the situation that would prevail without the project and the situation with the project. The project accounts should be based on streams of inputs and outputs and compounding flows of costs and benefits. The accounts may not reflect fully all resources required for realising the project benefits. Thus, a distinction should be made between the inclusion and exclusion in the cost-benefit analysis of certain types of inputs and outputs and the valuation of these inputs and outputs.

If a project is an integral part of a larger system, the expected benefits may not accrue if certain matching investments are not made in other parts of the system. Therefore, it is necessary to draw the boundaries of the project correctly so that all key investments are combined into a package. Then the total system costs necessary for realising the expected benefits should be estimated. In such cases, the entire system should be evaluated on the assumption that the complementary investments will have to be made. If the system is economically viable, the project can be considered as viable provided that it is also the least-cost alternative for achieving the desired results.

The costs and benefits should be valued according to their economic prices and not with their market prices. Thus, the costs and benefits should be valued in constant prices because the main objective of economic analysis is to assess the real contribution that a particular project is expected to make to the national economy. Any expected change in the general price level during the life of the project should be disregarded. But the anticipated changes in relative prices should be taken into consideration because relative price variations reflect changes in the claims on real resources of the country.

Financial and economic profitability will coincide if market prices are equal to the marginal social cost of production (the supply side) and the marginal social value (the demand price) of all inputs and outputs. Decision made on the basis of these prices ensure the most efficient allocation of resources. However, market prices do not always reflect social costs or social value because of a variety of market imperfections, taxes, subsidies, etc. For the purpose of cost-benefit analysis, discrepancies between market prices and social costs or value should be taken as given and policies that cause these discrepancies must be assumed as remaining effective. Economic analysis of projects requires estimates of the marginal social cost or value of the inputs used and the outputs produced by a project.

(d) Comparing Cost and Benefits: After identification and valuation of the costs and benefits of a project, there is a need for comparison of two streams in order to determine whether the project would result in an efficient use of resources from an economic point of view. A project must satisfy at least two conditions in order to be acceptable for investment. First, it must yield benefits in excess of costs over its life. Second, the benefits must be larger than the next best alternative projects. For comparing cost and benefits, the following measures are used in arriving at investment decisions.

(a) **Economic Internal Rate of Return (EIRR):** EIRR is the rate of discount at which the cost and benefit streams over the life of the project are equalised.

(b) **Cost-Benefit Ratio (CBR):** CBR compares the present values of the cost and benefit streams by discounting them at a rate equal to the opportunity cost of capital.

(c) **Net Present Value (NPV):** The NPV is the difference between the present value of benefit streams and present value of cost streams. In order to arrive at present values, a rate equal to the opportunity cost of capital is used.

(e) Social Cost-Benefit Analysis: A business enterprise is a social unit. It uses the resources of the society and produces goods and services for which the consumers are there in the society. Therefore, a business unit owes its very existence to the society. It is, therefore, necessary that a business unit should operate within the overall parameter determined by the society. However, profit making is one of the objectives of the business. Therefore, business units cannot be allowed to exist if its existence is detrimental to the interests of the society. Similarly, the society has also to see that such business activities should be undertaken for the benefit of the society. The basic philosophy of our mixed economy is that all sectors of the economy, public or private, small or big, should work for the overall good of the society. The social aspect has so far been ignored by the business. Therefore, it is being increasingly realised that commercial evaluation of industrial projects is not enough to justify circumstances of funds to a project, specially when it belongs to the public sector. Their evaluation should be done keeping in view the social costs and benefits associated with them.

(i) Social Costs

The term 'social costs' refers to all those harmful consequences and damages which the community as a whole sustains as a result of productive processes and for which private businessmen are not held responsible manifested. This definition is comprehensive enough to include even certain social opportunity costs, avoidable wastages and social inefficiencies of various kinds. Thus, the social cost-benefit analysis is a tool for evaluating the value of money particularly of public investments in many economies. It aids in making decisions with respect to the various aspects of a project and the design programmes of closely interrelated projects.

Social cost-benefit analysis is a practical way of assessing the desirability of projects, where it is important to take a long view. It implies the enumeration and evaluation of all the relevant cost and benefits. The essence of the theory of social cost-benefit analysis is that it does not accept that the actual receipts of a project adequately measure social benefits and actual expenditures measure social costs. The reason is that actual prices may be an inadequate indicator of economic benefits and costs. In India, the prices of necessary and essential goods are set low, despite their economic importance. Similarly, the prices of luxury or less essential goods are set little high, through the system of taxes and duties or subsidies. As a result, some projects which appear very profitable when their outputs and inputs are valued at actual prices are, in fact, unattractive from the viewpoint of national economy.

The objectives of social cost-benefit analysis is, in its widest sense, to secure and achieve the value of money in economic life by simply evaluating the costs and benefits of alternative economic choices and selecting an alternative which offers the largest net benefits over cost.

The social cost-benefit analysis involves the following steps:

(i) Estimate of costs and benefits which will accrue to the project implementing body.

(ii) Estimate of costs and benefits which will accrue to the individual members of society as consumer or supplier.

(iii) Estimate the cost and benefits which will accrue to the community.

(iv) Estimate of costs and benefits which will accrue to the National Exchequer.

(v) Discounting the costs and benefits which will accrue over a period of time to determine the feasibility of the project.

(ii) Technique of Social Cost-Benefit Analysis

The technique of social cost-benefit analysis involves the use of hypothetical rather than predicted actual prices while evaluating a project. The hypothetical prices (shadow) are used because these have better reflection of the real costs of inputs to society and the real benefits of the output to society than actual prices. The term 'shadow price' suggests that an analysis based on these prices is remote from reality and therefore academic and high brow. Though, the shadow prices are unreal in that they are not the current prices of goods in the market. But then no price, in a project analysis, can ever be an actual price as the analysis consider the future years of the project. A shadow price or an accounting price corresponds more closely to the realities of economic scarcity and needs.

The technique of social cost-benefit analysis also assumes that a country can buy and sell any quantity of a particular product at a given world price. Hence, all traded inputs and outputs are valued at their international prices which is the opportunity cost of a particular product to the country. Every input is treated as a foreign exchange outflow and every output is treated as a foreign exchange inflow. All non-tradable inputs are valued at accounting prices. Those costs are also broken up into tradable goods and other non-tradable goods.

(iii) Measurement of Social Cost Benefits

The United Nations Industrial Development Organisation (UNIDO) and the Centre for Organisation of Economic Cooperation and Development (COECD) have come with useful publications dealing with the problem of measuring social costs and social benefits. The following are the important criterias which can be used for measuring the social costs and benefits associated with the projects.

(a) **Employment Potential:** A project giving higher employment potential has to be selected over a project having a lower employment potential. Thus, the impact of the proposed project on the employment creation is an important consideration for selecting a project.

(b) **Capital-output Ratio:** This ratio measures the expected output in relation to the capital employed in the project. The desirability of a project can be judged on the basis of the return which the project is expected to give on capital employed in the project. Accordingly, a project giving a higher output per unit of capital employed is to be preferred over project giving a lower output.

(c) **Value added per unit of capital:** The term value added refers to the cost incurred by an organisation in converting materials into finished goods. The value added by a project can be ascertained by deducting the total value of bought-out inputs such as materials from the total value of production. The estimated value added by a project is considered in place of the total value of the output. The project having higher value added is to be ranked first and then other projects according to their ranks.

(d) **Savings in foreign exchange:** The projects can be ranked according to the net contribution the project is going to make to the foreign exchange reserves of the country. Thus, projects having greater potentiality in terms of foreign exchange benefits will have priority over other projects.

(iv) Sensitivity Analysis

Sensitivity analysis is a modelling procedure used in forecasting whereby changes are made in the estimates of the variables to establish whether any variation will critically affect the outcome of the forecast. It is a study to determine the responsiveness of the conclusions of an analysis to changes or errors in parameter values used in the analysis. It also seeks to test the responsiveness of outcomes from decision models to different input values and constraints as a basis for appraising the relative risk of alternative course of action.

The sensitivity analysis is the study of the key assumptions on which a management decision is based in order to predict outcomes of that decision if different assumptions are adopted. It is a technique that measures how the expected values in a decision model will be affected by the changes in the data. Sensitivity analysis is used in strategic decision making. It seeks to determine the range of variations in the co-efficient over which the solution will remain optimal. It is used in determination of risk factor in capital budgeting decisions. It helps to identify the most sensitive factor which may cause the error in estimation. It also provides the responsiveness of each factor on the project's Net Present Value or Internal Rate of Return. For example, a 10 % change in the selling price may cause 20% change in Net Present Value. The sensitivity analysis can be used for all other factors like material cost, labour cost, and variable costs. The most sensitive factor of all will be identified to evaluate the risk of that particular factor.

Sensitivity analysis involves the following steps:

(a) Identification of all those variables having influence on the Net Present Value or Internal Rate of Return of the project.

(b) Definition of the underlying quantitative relationship among the variables.

(c) Analysis of the impact of changes in each of the variables on the Net Present Value of the project.

The following procedure is used for making sensitivity analysis:

(i) List the key factors or parameters.

(ii) Attach the most likely values to each of the parameters and predict the most likely level of profit.

(iii) Calculate the effect of varying the values of all or selected few parameters.

(iv) List the outcomes of the alternative assumptions and make a subjective assessment of their likelihood.

(v) Draw the conclusions on any actions required which would make the achievement of the better outcomes more likely.

Sensitivity analysis helps to indicate the areas where improvements are likely to have the greatest impact on profits. It also facilitates the development of alternative or contingency plans, if the basic assumptions have to be changed.

The analysis of sensitivity offers the following advantages:

(i) It helps to improve managerial decision making.

(ii) It indicates which variables and assumptions are most critical.

(iii) It tells the management where to focus its analytical efforts.

(iv) It encourages the consideration of uncertainties and risks by manager at different levels.

(v) It identifies the specific areas to which managerial attention should be drawn even after the approval of a project and during its implementation.

(v) Limitations of Social Cost-benefit Analysis

The nature of social benefits and costs are such that there cannot be any standard method or technique applicable to all types of investment projects. Again, the problems of qualification and measurement of social costs and benefits are formidable. It is because many of these costs and benefits are intangible and their valuation in terms of money is bound to be subjective. However, a successful application of the techniques of analysis depends upon the accuracy and reliability of forecasts. However, the limitations of social cost-benefit analysis should not deter one from applying the techniques so far evolved. The element of subjectivity can be reduced by cross-checks. While the limitations should not be ignored, as it would be folly to disregard the gains of social evaluation of investments.

1.8 ILLUSTRATIONS

(1) Reliable Ltd. is currently under examination of a project which will yield the following returns over a period of time:

Year	*Gross Yield (₹)*
1	80,000
2	80,000
3	90,000
4	90,000
5	75,000

The cost of machinery to be installed works out to be ₹ 2,00,000. The machine is to be depreciated at 20% per annum on SLM basis. Scrap value at the end of 5th year is nil. Income tax rate is 30%. If the average cost of raising capital is 12%, would you recommend the acceptance of the project under the internal rate of return method?

Present value of money at the rate of interest is as under:

Year	@ 10%	@ 12%	@ 14%	@ 16%	@ 18%
1	0.909	0.893	0.877	0.862	0.847
2	0.826	0.797	0.769	0.743	0.718
3	0.751	0.712	0.675	0.641	0.609
4	0.683	0.636	0.592	0.552	0.516
5	0.621	0.567	0.519	0.476	0.437

Solution: Evaluation of the project under the Internal Rate of Return Method

(a) Calculation of Cash Flow after Tax

Year	Gross Yield	Depreciation	Net Yield	Tax	Net Cash	CFAT
1	80,000	40,000	40,000	12,000	28,000	68,000
2	80,000	40,000	40,000	12,000	28,000	68,000
3	90,000	40,000	50,000	15,000	35,000	75,000
4	90,000	40,000	50,000	15,000	35,000	75,000
5	75,000	40,000	35,000	10,500	24,500	64,500

(b) Calculation of IRR

The IRR can be calculated on the basis of trial and error method as follows:

It can be tested at 12% as follows:

Year	CFAT (₹)	DF @ 12%	PV (₹)	DF @ 18 %	PV (₹)
1	68,000	0.893	60,724	0.847	57,596
2	68,000	0.797	54,196	0.718	48,824
3	75,000	0.712	53,400	0.609	45,675
4	75,000	0.636	47,700	0.516	38,700
5	64,500	0.567	36,571	0.437	28,186
	Present Value of Cash Inflow		2,52,591		2,18,981
	– Present Value of Cash Outflow		2,00,000		2,00,000
	Net Present Value		**52,951**		**18,981**

Internal Rate of Return is the rate at which Net Present Value is zero. At 18% discounting factor, the Net Present Value is ₹ 18,981. Hence, the actual IRR is above 18%. Hence, the project can be accepted because it generates IRR which is higher than the cost of capital of 12%.

The actual IRR can be calculated by taking higher discounting factors as follows:

Year	*CFAT (₹)*	*DF @ 20%*	*PV (₹)*	*DF @ 22%*	*PV (₹)*
1	68,000	0.833	56,644	0.820	55,760
2	68,000	0.694	47,192	0.672	45,696
3	75,000	0.579	43,425	0.551	41,325
4	75,000	0.482	36,150	0.451	33,825
5	64,500	0.402	25,929	0.370	23,865
	PVCI		2,09,340	2,00,471	
	PVCO		2,00,000	2,00,000	
	NPV		**9,340**	**471**	

The Net Present Value at 22% discounting factor is near to zero, hence the actual IRR is 22%.

(2) A choice is to be made between two projects which require an equal investment of ₹ 5,00,000 and are expected to generate net cash flows as under:

End of Year	*Project 'A'*	*Project 'B'*
1	1,50,000	1,00,000
2	1,50,000	1,20,000
3	1,00,000	1,80,000
4	1,00,000	1,50,000
5	1,20,000	1,80,000
6	60,000	40,000

The cost of capital of the company is 10 per cent. The following are the present value factors @ 10% per annum.

Year	*PV Factors*
1	0.909
2	0.826
3	0.751
4	0.683
5	0.621
6	0.564

Which project should be chosen and why? Evaluate the project proposals using discounted cash flow method.

Solution:

Discounted Cash Flow Method

Year	*DF @ 10%*	*Project 'A'*		*Project 'B'*	
		CFAT	*PV*	*CFAT*	*PV*
1	0.909	1,50,000	1,36,350	1,00,000	90,900
2	0.826	1,50,000	1,23,900	1,20,000	99,120
3	0.751	1,00,000	75,100	1,80,000	1,35,180
4	0.683	1,00,000	68,300	1,50,000	1,02,450
5	0.621	1,20,000	74,520	1,80,000	1,11,780
6	0.564	60,000	33,840	40,000	22,560
	Present Value of Cash Inflows	5,12,010			5,61,990
	Present Value of Cash Outflows	5,00,000			5,00,000
	Net Present Value	**12,010**			**61,990**

Project B' should be chosen. Both the project require equal investment of ₹ 5,00,000. However, the net present value of Project 'B' is higher than the net project value of Project 'A'.

(3) X Ltd. is considering two projects. Project 'M' requires an investment of ₹ 22.5 lakhs and project 'N' requires an investment of ₹ 30 lakhs. Further details of these projects are given below:

Particulars	*M*	*N*
Economic Life *After Tax Annual Cash Flows* *Year*	*5 Years* *₹ lakhs*	*6 Years* *₹ lakhs*
1	5.00	6.00
2	7.50	8.00
3	10.00	10.00
4	9.00	12.00
5	8.50	10.50
6	-	9.50

The present value factor @ 12 per cent per annum are as follows:

Year	*PV Factor*
1	0.893
2	0.797
3	0.712
4	0.636
5	0.567
6	0.507

You are required to evaluate the two projects and recommend the project for implementation.

Solution:

(a) Calculation of Net Present Value

Year	*PV Factor*	*M*		*N*	
		CFAT	*PV*	*CFAT*	*PV*
1	0.893	5.0	4.465	6.0	5.358
2	0.797	7.5	5.977	8.0	6.376
3	0.712	10.0	7.120	10.0	7.120
4	0.636	9.0	5.724	12.0	7.632
5	0.567	8.5	5.954	10.50	5.953
6	0.507	-	-	9.50	6.084
Present Value of Cash Inflows			29.240		38.523
– Present Value of Cash Outflows			22.500		30.00
∴ Net Present Value			6.740		8.523

(b) Calculation of Profitability Index

Considering the NPV method, both the projects show positive NPV. As their investments and periods are different, the decision will be based on profitability index which is calculated as follows:

$$\text{Profitability Index} = \frac{\text{Present Value of Cash Inflows}}{\text{Present Value of Cash Outflows}}$$

$$\text{PI(M)} = \frac{29.240}{22.50} = 1.30$$

$$PI(N) = \frac{38.523}{30.00} = 1.28$$

As the profitability index of Project 'M' is higher, it is recommended for implementation.

(4) A company has to select one of the following two projects:

Particulars	*Project 'X' (₹ lakhs)*	*Project 'Y' (₹ lakhs)*
Cost	11	10
Cash Inflows:		
1st year	6	1
2nd year	2	1
3rd year	1	2
4th year	5	10

Using the internal rate of return method, suggest which project is preferable.

Note: The present value factor are as follows:

Year	*PV @ 10%*	*PV @ 12 %*	*PV @ 15%*
1	0.909	0.893	0.870
2	0.826	0.797	0.756
3	0.751	0.712	0.658
4	0.683	0.636	0.572

Solution:

(i) Calculation of NPV of project X

Year	*CF*	*PV @ 10%*	*PV @ 12%*	*PV @ 15%*
1	6	5.454	5.358	5.22
2	2	1.652	1.594	1.51
3	1	0.751	0.712	0.66
4	5	3.415	3.180	2.86
		11.272	**10.844**	**10.25**

The IRR is the rate at which the NPV is zero. The investment is ₹ 11 lakhs. Hence, the IRR is more than 10% and less than 12%. The actual IRR can be calculated by interpolation as follows:

$$IRR = 10 + \frac{11.272-11.00}{11.272-10.844} \times 2$$

$$= 10 + \frac{0.272}{0.428} \times 2$$

$= 10 + 1.3$

$= 11.3\%$

(ii) Calculation of NPV of Project 'Y'

Year	*CF*	*PV @ 10%*	*PV @ 12%*	*PV @ 15 %*
1	1	0.909	0.893	0.870
2	1	0.826	0.797	0.756
3	2	1.502	1.424	1.316
4	10	6.83	6.360	5.720
		10.067	**9.474**	**8.662**

The IRR is more than 10% but less than 12%. The actual IRR can be calculated by interpolation as follows:

$$\text{IRR} = 10 + \frac{0.067}{0.067+0.526} \times 2$$

$$= 10 + \frac{0.067}{0.593} \times 2$$

$= 10 + 0.23$

$= 10.23\%$

(iii) The internal rate return in case of Project 'X' is higher (11.3%) than the Project 'Y' (10.23%). Hence, Project 'X' is preferable.

(5) Prakash Industries Ltd. has prepared the following budgeted profitability statement for the year ended 31st March 2011.

		₹ Lakhs
Sales (25,000 units @ ₹ 40)		10.00
– **Variable Cost:**		
Materials	4.00	
Labour	3.00	7.00
Contribution		3.00
– Fixed Cost		2.00
Profit		**1.00**

Make the sensitivity analysis with the help of the following:

(a) Selling price is reduced by 10%.

(b) Sales units are reduced by 10% of the budgeted units of 25000.

(c) The labour cost increases by 30%.

(d) The material cost increases by 20%.

Solution:

Sensitivity Analysis

(₹ lakhs)

Particulars	*A*	*B*	*C*	*D*
Sales	9.00	9.00	10.00	10.00
– Variable Cost:				
Materials	4.00	3.60	4.00	4.80
Labour	3.00	2.70	3.90	3.00
Contribution	2.00	2.70	2.10	2.20
– Fixed Cost	2.00	2.00	2.00	2.00
Profit	-	**0.70**	**0.10**	**0.20**

Notes:

(a) Sales will be ₹ 9,00,000 if selling price is reduced by 10% = 25,000 × 36 = ₹ 9,00,000.

(b) Sales will be ₹ 9,00,000 if sales units are reduced by 10% = 40 × 22,500 = ₹ 9,00,000

(c) Labour cost will be ₹ 3.90 lakhs if it increases by 30% = 30% of ₹ 3 lakhs = ₹ 90,000.

(d) Material cost will be ₹ 4.80 lakhs if it increases by 20% = 20% of ₹ 4 lakhs = ₹ 80,000.

The sensitivity analysis shows that the profit will be ₹ 70,000 in case sales units are reduced by 10%. In other cases, profit will be lower than ₹ 70,000.

(6) From the following details of a project, calculate the sensitivity of the:

(a) Project cost

(b) Annual cash flow and

(c) Cost of capital

(d) Which variable is more sensitive?

Project cost ₹ 1200000

Annual cash flow ₹ 450000

Life of the project 4 years

Cost of capital 14%

The annuity factor at 14% for 4 years is 2.9137 and at 18% for 4 years is 2.6667.

Solution:

(i) Calculation of Net Present Value

Annual Cash Flow (45,000 × 2.9137)	₹ 13,11,165
– Project Cost	₹ 12,00,000
Net Present Value	₹ 1,11,165

(a) Sensitivity for project cost

If the project cost is increased by ₹ 1,11,165, the NPV will become zero.

$$\text{Sensitivity} = \frac{1{,}11{,}165}{12{,}00{,}000} \times 100 = 9.26\%$$

(b) Sensitivity for annual cash flow

If the present value of annual cash flow is lowered by ₹ 1,11,165, the NPV of the project will become zero. Hence, sensitivity for annual cash flow is

$$\text{Sensitivity} = \frac{1{,}11{,}165}{13{,}11{,}165} \times 100 = 8.48\%$$

(c) Sensitivity for Cost of Capital

Let 'X' be the annuity factor which gives a zero NPV, i.e., 'X' is the IRR.

$\therefore$ 4,50,000 X = ₹ 12,00,000

$$\therefore X = \frac{12{,}00{,}000}{4{,}50{,}000} = 2.6667$$

$$\therefore \text{Sensitivity} = \frac{18-14}{14} \times 100 = 29\%$$

(d) The cash inflow is more sensitive because only 8.48% of change in cash flow (reduction) will make the NPV of the project zero.

(7) The following details are available in respect of a project.

	₹ crores
Value of tradeable inputs at domestic prices	700
Value of non-tradeable inputs at domestic prices	180
Value of tradeable inputs at world prices	560
Sales realisation at domestic prices	1,000
Sales realisation at world prices	800

Calculate:

(a) Effective Rate of Protection (ERP) of the project and comment on the ERP.

(b) If the Exchange Rate of rupee per US dollar is ₹ 45, what is the Domestic Resource Cost of the project? ***(ICWA, Dec. 1996 Modified)***

Solution:

(a)

	At Domestic Price	*At World Price*
Sales realization (SP)	1000	800
Inputs costs		
Traded	700	560
Non-traded	180	180
Net value added	120	60

$$\text{ERP} = \frac{\text{Value added at Domestic prices} - \text{Value added at World prices}}{\text{Value added at World prices}}$$

$$= \frac{120-60}{60} \times 100$$

$$= 100\%$$

If the value added at domestic prices is same as the value added at world prices, ERP = 0. It means the project does not enjoy any protection. Hence, the project enjoys 100% protection against international competition.

$$\text{(b) DRC} = \frac{\text{Value added at Domestic Prices}}{\text{Value added at World Prices}} \times \text{Exchange Rate}$$

$$= \frac{120}{60} \times ₹45$$

= ₹ 90 crore

(8) A ferry service operated privately is presently being used to cross a river. The ferry operator charges ₹ 3 per person and his cost per person is ₹ 2. Throughout the year, 50,000 persons use the ferry service. The Government is considering construction of a bridge over the river. It is estimated that about 250000 persons would use the bridge after construction which is expected to cost ₹ 30 lakhs. Its annual maintenance would cost ₹ 10,000. It has an infinitely long life. Once the bridge is constructed, the ferry operator is expected to close down and sell the ferry boat for ₹ one lakh. Make the social cost-benefit analysis assuming that the monetary figures represent social values and the shadow price of investment is ₹ 1.

Solution: Social cost benefits of construction of a Bridge

(a) Costs:

Construction cost = 1 × 30 = ₹ 30 lakhs

Maintenance cost = 1 × 10,000 = ₹ 10,000 (Annual cost)

(b) Benefits:

Value of ferry boat released = ₹ 1,00,000

Saving in the cost of ferry operations = ₹ 1 lakh (5,00,000 × 2 – annual benefits)

Increase in consumer satisfaction = ₹ 3,00,000

The additional user's willingness to pay is the average willingness to pay assuming that demand schedule is linear.

$$= \frac{₹3+0}{2} = ₹\ 1.5$$

∴ The willingness to pay of the additional 2,00,000 persons = 2,00,000 × 1.5 = ₹ 3,00,000.

1.9 EXERCISES

(1) What is strategic cost management? What is its need and importance in these days?

(2) 'The most important strategic element for a firm are long-term growth and survival'. Explain the role of strategic cost management in achieving long-term growth and survival.

(3) What is sensitivity analysis? Explain why price sensitivity increases as a product moves from the introduction to maturity stages.

(4) What is social cost-benefit analysis? How are the investment projects in India evaluated from the social cost-benefit point of view?

(5) Write short notes on:

(a) Cost management

(b) Cost leadership strategy

(c) Strategic business plan

(d) Cost-benefit analysis

(e) Sensitivity analysis

(6) X Ltd. is considering a project with the following cash flows:

Particulars	*0*	*1*	2
Purchase of plant	7,000		
Running costs		2,000	2,500
Saving		6,000	7,000

The cost of capital is 8%. Measure the sensitivity of the project to changes in the levels of plant value, running costs, and savings (considering cash factor at a time) so that NPV becomes zero. Which factor is most sensitive to effect the acceptability of the project?

The PV factors at 8% discount are:

0	1.00
1	0.926
2	857

(**Answer:** Plant cost may be increased by 8%, running costs may be increased by 14% and savings may be reduced by 4.85%. Savings having the lowest sensitivity ratio gets affected most while accepting the project).

(7) In a capital rationing situation, Investment limit is ₹ 25 lakhs. Suggest the most desirable feasible combination on the basis of the following data:

Project	*Initial Outlay (₹ lakhs)*	*NPV (₹ lakhs)*
A	15.00	6.0
B	10.00	4.5
C	7.50	3.6
D	6.00	3.0

Projects B and C are mutually exclusive.

(**Answer:** A and B combination is a feasible combination giving rise to maximum value of ₹ 10.5 lakhs (NPV)).

(8) Oriental Pharma Ltd. is thinking of investing in a project costing of ₹ 10 lakhs. The life of the project is five years and the estimated salvage value of the project is zero. The company follows a straight line method of depreciation. The tax rate is 50%. The expected cash flows before tax are:

Years	1	2	3	4	5
Estimated cash flow (₹ lakh) (before tax):	2	3	3.5	4	4

You are required to determine:

(i) Payback period

(ii) Average rate of return

(iii) Internal rate of return

(iv) Net present value at 10% cost of capital

(v) Profitability index at 10% cost of capital

(**Answers:** Payback – 4 years, ARR – 26% NPV – ₹ 36,777, IRR – 8.645%, PI – 0.963).

(9) Ashok Enterprises is interested in assessing the cash flows associated with replacement of an old machine by a new machine. The old machine has a book value of ₹ 90,000 and it can be sold for ₹ 90,000. It has a remaining life of 5 years after which the salvage value is expected to be nil. It is being depreciated annually at the rate of 10% using written down value method. The new machine costs ₹ 4 lakhs. It is expected to fetch ₹ 2.5 lakhs after 5 years, when it will no longer be required. It will also be depreciated annually @ 10% using written down value method. The new machine is expected to save ₹ 1 lakh in the manufacturing costs. Investment in working capital would remain unaffected. The tax rate applicable to the firm is 50%. You are required to work out the incremental cash flows associated with the replacement of old machine and prepare a statement to be presented to the management for consideration.

(**Answer:** Operating cash flows = Incremental depreciation + Incremental profit after tax. Incremental depreciation = Depreciation of the new machine – Depreciation of the old machine. Incremental cash flows are higher than the investment).

(10) Z Ltd. is considering a project with the following cash flow:

Year	*Purchase of Plant* ₹	*Running Cost* ₹	*Savings* ₹
1	70,000	29,000	60,000
2	-	25,000	70,000

The cost of capital is 8%. Measure the sensitivity of the project to changes in the level of running cost, savings and planning cost. Which factor is the most sensitive?

The present values of ₹ 1 at 8% for year 1 and year 2 are ₹ 0.9259 and ₹ 0.8573 respectively.

(**Answer:** Sensitivity to plant cost = 8%, Running cost = 14% and savings = 5%. Thus, savings is most sensitive).

(11) Government is planning to discontinue the passenger boat service between West end and East end across the River 'Bhima', which was used by the villagers. It is estimated that the annual cost of boat operations are ₹ 7.4 lakhs including ₹ 40,000 towards depreciation. The boat could be sold for ₹ 2,00,000 to the other agency. The service is used throughout the year with 600 single journeys each day. The single fare is ₹ 3 per passenger. The service is losing money and deficit is met out of tax revenue.

If the line is closed, it is estimated that 500 journeys will be made by private buses at the same fare and 100 journeys will not be made at all. The bus fares exactly meet the bus operator's extra costs. Bus journey takes 30 minutes longer than the boat journey. The average value of passenger's time is ₹ 2 per hour. Estimate the social cost and benefits associated with the proposal.

(**Hints:** Social costs, i.e., cost of additional journey = ₹ 500 × 0.5 × 2 × 365 = ₹ 1,82,500, Social benefits = Savings in operating costs by closing down the line ₹ 7,00,000 + Resale value of boat = ₹ 20,00,000).

❑ ❑ ❑

Chapter

2

Different Aspects of Strategic Cost Management

STRUCTURE:

2.1 Introduction

2.2 Value Analysis and Value Engineering

2.3 Wastage Control

2.4 Disposal Management

2.5 Business Process Reengineering

2.6 Total Quality Management

2.7 Total Productive Maintenance

2.8 Energy Audit

2.9 Control of Total Distribution Cost and Supply Cost

2.10 Cost Reduction

2.11 Product Life Cycle Costing

2.12 Exercises

2.1 INTRODUCTION

Companies are engaged in decision making that affects their long-run competitive position and profitability. Strategic planning and decision making require a much broader set of cost information than that is provided by product costs. Obtaining a competitive advantage is the goal of strategic cost management. Different strategies create different bundles of activities. Cost information about customers, suppliers and different product designs is needed to support strategic management objectives. The set of information should include information about the firm's environment and internal workings. It should be prospective and should provide insights about future periods and activities. The objective of strategic cost management is to reduce costs while strengthening a firm's strategic position. Knowledge of organisational and operational activities and their associated cost drivers is fundamental to strategic cost analysis. Knowledge of the firm's value chain and the industrial value chain is also critical. Value chain analysis relies on identifying and exploiting internal and external linkages. Life cycle cost management is related to strategic cost and analysis. Life cycle cost management requires an understanding of the three types of life cycle viewpoint: the marketing viewpoint, production viewpoint and the consumable life viewpoint. Target costing plays an essential role in life cycle cost management by providing a methodology for reducing costs in the design stage by considering and exploiting both customer and supplier linkages.

2.2 VALUE ANALYSIS AND VALUE ENGINEERING

Value analysis is a systematic interdisciplinary examination of factors affecting the cost of a product or service in order to derive means of achieving the specific purpose most economically at the required standard of quality and reliability. It may be considered as a method of ensuring worth, whereby the value of each product or service is analysed, part by part with the objective of achieving the required function with reduced cost. Thus, value analysis is a planned scientific approach to cost reduction. It reviews the material consumption of a product and production design so that modification or improvement can be made which do not reduce the value of the product to the customer. In value analysis, the following aspects of value are considered:

(i) Cost value, i.e., its cost of sale.

(ii) Exchange value, i.e., its market value.

(iii) Use value, i.e., it attempts to provide the same use value at the lowest cost.

(iv) Esteem value, i.e., the prestige the customer attaches to the product.

Value analysis is a tool of cost reduction and aims at cost reduction from the point of view of value. A cost reduction may be used for improving the use and esteem value of products thereby attracting more customers with a less than proportionate increase in cost. Value analysis makes a close study of a product to provide higher satisfaction to customers in respect of use value and esteem value. It also ensures quality production with the latest methods of production with minimum possible cost. It also ensures higher productivity by continuous process of searching for improvement in all spheres. It helps in infusing a spirit of cooperation and raising the morale of employees.

Value analysis is formal system developed after World War II, when there was shortage of materials and the manufacturers were forced to look for cheaper methods of production. It was observed that cheaper methods of production could be achieved without any loss in quality or value. This has developed the value analysis, the systematic investigation of every source of cost and technique of production with the aim of getting rid of all unnecessary costs.

Value analysis includes the investigation of specifications, design, planning, buying, manufacture, testing, sales and distribution. The main areas of value analysis are product design, components, material costs and production overheads. The origin of value analysis was in the engineering industry but its principles and applications spread much wider. Value analysis can be applied to service or aspects of office work to management information systems.

The relation between value, cost and function can be expressed as:

$$\text{Value} = \frac{\text{Function}}{\text{Cost}}$$

The value can be improved by:

(i) Improving the function

(ii) Reducing the cost

(iii) Improving function and reducing cost

(iv) Improving functions at a higher rate with slight increase in cost.

Value Added

Value added is the difference between the sales values and the purchased cost of materials and services. The aim of the company is towards improving added value rather than profit. By increasing added value, more wealth can be created by raising productivity in the use of inputs. Value will be added when an activity results in an addition to a product or service which the ultimate consumer considers to be valuable and which is therefore something for which they are willing to pay. The profit is equal to sales minus total cost. When variable cost is deducted from sales, we get contribution and if fixed cost is deducted from contribution we get profit. Similarly, when material cost is deducted from sales, we get value added which is equal to labour cost, all other overheads and profit. A company makes its profit by working on the material and in converting it by increasing its sales value.

Value added concept can be used in the following cases:

(i) Divisional performance measurement

(ii) Indirect tax levy

(iii) Incentive schemes

Illustration 2.1: Anand Ltd. manufactures two products X and Y with same type of labour. The unit sale price and costs are as follows:

Particulars	X (₹)		Y (₹)	
Selling price		2,000		1,200
Direct material	1,200		480	
Direct labour	200		200	
Variable overhead	100	1,500	100	780
Contribution		500		420
Fixed overhead		300		220
Profit		**200**		**200**

You are required to find out:

(a) Which product appears to be more profitable based on profit to sales ratio and profit-volume ratio.

(b) The added value.

(c) Comment on the profitability based on contribution to added value ratio.

Solution:

(a) (i) Calculation of Profit to Sales Ratio

$$\frac{\text{Profit}}{\text{Sales}} \times 100$$

$$X = \frac{200}{2000} \times 100 = 10\%$$

$$Y = \frac{200}{1200} \times 100 = 16.67\%$$

(ii) Profit-volume Ratio (P/V Ratio)

$$\text{P/ V Ratio} = \frac{\text{Contribution}}{\text{Sales}} \times 100$$

$$\therefore X = \frac{500}{2000} \times 100$$

$$= 25\%$$

$$Y = \frac{420}{1200} \times 100 = 35\%$$

As profit from both the products is same. Product 'Y' appears to be more profitable because profit/sales and P/V Ratios are higher.

(b) Calculation of Value added (₹)

	X	Y
Selling Price	2,000	1,200
Less: Material Cost	1,200	480
Value Added	800	720

Contribution to Value Added Ratio

$$= \frac{\text{Contribution}}{\text{Value added}} \times 100$$

$$X = \frac{500}{800} \times 100$$

$$= 62.5\%$$

$$Y = \frac{420}{720} \times 100$$

$$= 58.3\%$$

(c) It can be observed that contribution from Product X is higher and the added value is also higher. Since the contribution to value added ratio of Product 'X' is higher, Product 'X' is more profitable than Product 'Y'.

Value Chain Analysis

The value chain approach was developed by Michael Porter in the 1980s in his book *"Competitive Advantage: Creating and Sustaining Superior Performance"*. The concept of value added, in the form of the value chain, can be utilised to develop an organisation's sustainable competitive advantage in the business arena of the 21st century. All organisations consist of activities that link together to develop the value of the business and together these activities form the organisation's value chain. These activities are purchasing, manufacturing, distribution and marketing. The value chain framework can be used as a powerful analysis tool for the strategic planning of an organisation. Thus, the aim of the value chain framework is to maximise value creation while minimising costs.

The following are the main business functions of the value chain:

(i) Research and Development

(ii) Designing product, services or process

(iii) Production

(iv) Marketing and sales

(v) Distribution

(vi) Customer service

Value chain analysis is identifying and exploiting internal and external linkages with the objective of strengthening a firm's strategic position. The exploitation of linkages relies on analysing how costs and other non-financial factors vary as different bundles of activities are considered. Managing organisational and operational cost drivers to create long-term cost reduction outcomes is an important input in value chains analysis, when cost leadership is emphasised.

Value chain analysis is a powerful tool for managers to identify the key activities within the firm which form the value chain for that organisation and have a potential of a sustainable competitive advantage for a company. Competitive advantage of an organisation lies in its ability to perform crucial activities along the value chain better than its competitors. The value chain framework is an interdependent system or network of activities connected by linkages. When the system is managed carefully, the linkages can be a vital source of competitive advantage. The value chain analysis essentially entails the linkage of two areas. Firstly, the value chain links the value of the organisation's activities with its main functional parts. Then the assessment of the contribution of each part in the overall added value of the business is made. In order to conduct the value chain analysis, the company is split into primary and supportive activities. Primary activities are those that are related with production while supportive activities are those that provide the background necessary for the effectiveness and efficiency of the firm. Value chain analysis is a three step process:

(i) **Activity Analysis:** To identify the activities undertaken to deliver product or service.

(ii) **Value Analysis:** For each activity, you think through what you would do to add the greatest value for your customer.

(iii) **Evaluation and Planning:** You have to evaluate whether it is worth making changes and then plan for action.

2.2 VALUE ENGINEERING

Value engineering is the application of identical techniques to new products so as to design and develop new products of a given value at minimum possible cost. Value engineering is defined as "a systematic analysis and evaluation of the techniques and functions in the various spheres of an organisation with a view to explore channels of performance improvement so that the value in a particular product can be improved."

The term value engineering and value analysis are often used interchangeably as both of them have many identical steps in their working procedures. However, the main difference arises to area of applications. The value analysis can be applied to any kind of cost but value engineering can be applied to direct material, labour and costs. Value engineering is normally used in the design and development stages of a product. However, value analysis can be applied to products already in the market. The need for value arises when the sales are getting reduced. Thus, costs subjected to value analysis may require the application of value engineering. It is developed and implemented widely in industry as a cost-saving tool.

Value engineering helps to provide a systematised method of establishing a high value design. It can be applied to anything that is under construction, designing development subjected to its philosophy but at the optimum time. Anything that is designed for low-cost manufacture at the outset will always show an overall cost advantage over a remodelled item to reduce cost at some point in the programme. It is obvious for some projects putting the value engineering concepts to practice in their designs. However, it is indeed a rare case as it is time-consuming for the people of different disciplines who have to extract time out of their routine task and share their experiences to speculate, analyse and recommend. It demands well organised, centrally controlled and directed function. Value engineering should not be treated as a mere vital but should be carefully dealt as its effect comes from the fresh approach that the team managers bring to the task. The institutional approach on the value engineering (bloom) philosophy might slay its bloom rather should be encouraged through an essential element of creativity. It can be best tackled on a project-by-project basis with a value engineer and a team unequivocally assembled for the job. The implementation programme may prolong till the finalisation once the objectives have been matched with the design works as specified.

2.3 WASTAGE CONTROL

Waste is the portion of basic raw materials lost in processing having no recoverable value. It is the discarded substances having no value. It is that part of material which is either lost, shrinks or evaporate in the manufacturing process. It is invisible or a residual which is visible but having measureable recovery value. Sometimes, waste disposal entails additional expense. For example, gases, dust, smoke and unsalable residues. Benzene evaporating in dry cleaning process or paint dissipating during drying determination of perishable materials are also waste. The effect of waste is to increase the unit cost of production since the total cost is spread over a smaller number of good products.

Scrap is the incidental residue from certain types of manufacture usually of small amount and low value recoverable without further processing. It is defined as discarded material from manufacturing operations that has measurable but relatively minor recovery value. For example, outlined metal from a stamping operation, shavings, filing, boring, turming, sawdust and short lengths from wood work. They are usually disposed off without further treatment. Scrap may be reused in the production process in place of raw material.

Defectives are the portion of production which can be rectified and turned out as good units in the application of additional material, labour and other services. Defective products may be the result of substandard materials, bad supervision, bad planning, poor workmanship, inadequate equipments and careless inspection. The defectives are those units which do not meet with dimensional or quality standards and are reworked for rectification of defects by application of material, labour and processing and salvaged to the point of either standard product or substandard product to be sold as 'seconds'.

If the defect is such that even after rework or reconditioning it cannot be sold as seconds, then it becomes scrap, or as an extreme case, may be waste.

Spoilage refers to production that does not meet with dimensional or quality standards in such a way that it cannot be rectified economically and is junked and sold for a disposal value. It consists of goods damaged beyond the rectification in course of manufacturing process and is disposed off without reprocessing. Spoilage cost is the difference between costs accumulated to point of rejection less disposal or salvage value. Spoilage occurs due to samé defects in operation or materials which may or may not be inherent in the manufacturing process or operation. The manner of disposal of spoiled work depends on the nature and extent of spoilage.

In order to keep a control on waste, a periodical report should be prepared by each department indicating nature of waste, quantity of waste generated, value and percentage comparison between normal and actual waste. Report should be reviewed by the departmental head for further corrective action.

Scrap control starts from the designing product process. Efforts should be made to maximise utilisation of material and minimum wastage of material in the processing. A standard allowance for the scrap should be fixed and actuals should be compared against it. A periodical report indicating type of scrap, nature of product, good production units, scrap units, actual and normal output, percentage of scrap to good units and standard allowance and value of scraps should be prepared from the data collected at the shop level and placed before the departmental head for review and remarks.

Effective control should be exercised on the physical units of defectives as well as on the cost of salvaging. The best way is to fix standard or norms for defectives and rework and rectification costs and compare actual against them.

When the work on inspection is found to be spoiled, the inspector makes out a spoilage report in the proper format. The actual spoilage is compared with the standard or normal spoilage and steps are taken to remove any abnormal spoilage. The planning department takes immediate steps to replace the parts scrapped.

The accounting treatment is different for different kinds of waste. Good units should absorb the cost of waste. However, if any value is realised from the sale of waste, the process account concerned may be credited. Where the value of scrap is negligible, absorb the cost and the realised amount from sale of scrap may be treated as other income. However, when the value of scrap is significant and identifiable with job or process, the cost can be transferred to scrap account and the realisation from sales may be credited to job or process account. The difference may be transferred to the Costing Profit and Loss account. When the value is significant but scraps are not identified with particular job or process, the net realisation after deducting selling cost is transferred to either overheads or material cost recovery.

Illustration 2.2: A Roller Mill produced 400 tonnes of M.S. Bars spending ₹ 3,60,000 towards material and ₹ 1,20,000 towards rolling charges. 10 per cent of the output was found defective which was sold at 10% less than the market price. The sales realisation should give the company an overall profit of 12.5% on cost. The scrap arising in the process fetched a realisation of ₹ 30,000. Find out the selling price per tonne of both the categories of bars.

Solution:

Computation of Selling Price of Bars

Particulars	₹
Cost of materials	3,60,000
Less: Scrap realized	30,000
	3,30,000
Rolling charges	1,20,000
Total cost	4,50,000
Add: Profit (12.5%)	56,250
Sales value	5,06,250

Effective output $(360 + \frac{9}{10} \times 40)$ = 396 tonnes

Selling price per tonne of good output $= \frac{5,06,250}{396}$

= ₹ 278.41

Selling price of defective bars (per tonne) $= 278.41 \times \frac{90}{100}$

= ₹ 250.57

Illustration 2.3: In the month of June 2012, 6,000 kg of raw material A costing ₹ 15 per kg were processed through unit no. 3 for manufacture of solvent X. The total operating cost of unit no.3 for the month was ₹ 1,20,000. Out of the output, 10% was unusable and was disposed off at ₹ 2.5 per kg. Prepare an account for the month's operation unit no. 3 assuming that spoilage was:

(i) Part of the normal production

(ii) An abnormal loss due to poor quality material.

Solution:

(i) Where spoilage is part of normal production process:

Raw material cost (6,000 kg @ ₹ 15)	₹ 90,000
Less: Scrap value (600 kg @ ₹ 2.5)	1,500
	88,500

Add: Operating cost during the month	1,20,000
Total	2,08,500

∴ Cost of normal production of ₹ 5,400 kg of solvent X = ₹ 2,08,500

$$\therefore \text{Cost per kg} = \frac{2,08,500}{5,400} = ₹\ 38.61$$

(ii) Where spoilage is an abnormal loss due to poor quality material:

Raw material cost = 6,000 kg @ ₹ 15	= ₹	90,000
Operating cost incurred	= ₹	1,20,000
Total		2,10,000

Production during the month = 6,000 kg

$$\therefore \text{Cost per kg of solvent X} = \frac{₹\ 21,000}{6,000} = ₹ 35$$

∴ Cost of abnormal spoilage = ₹ 21,000 – ₹ 1,500 = ₹ 19,500

∴ Amount to be debited to Profit and Loss account = ₹ 19,500

2.4 DISPOSAL MANAGEMENT

Waste is a discarded substance having no value. It is that part of material which is either lost, shrinks or evaporate in the manufacturing process and hence invisible or a residue which is visible but having measurable recovery value. Sometimes, waste disposal entails additional expense. Scrap is also a discarded material from manufacturing operations that has measurable value but reasonably minor recovery value. These are usually disposed off without further treatment. They may be reintroduced into the production process in place of raw material such as scraps in metallurgical industries. Defective products are those which do not meet with dimensional or quality standards and are reworked for rectification of defects by application of material, labour and or processing and salvaged to the point of either standard product or substandard product, to be sold as seconds. If the defect is such that even after rework or reconditioning it cannot be sold as seconds then it becomes scrap or as an extreme case, may be waste. Spoilage refers to production that does not meet with dimensional or quality standards in such a way that it cannot be rectified economically and is junked and sold for a disposal value. Net spoilage cost is the difference between the cost accumulated up to the point of rejection less disposal or salvage value.

Pricing decisions must consider the relative marketability of inventory. Due to damage or obsolescence or lack of demand, inventory may not be saleable through normal marketing channels or under normal operating conditions. In such cases, incremental analysis is appropriate for decision making as all prior costs of producing or acquiring inventory are sunk costs and therefore, irrelevant to the decisions.

Illustration 2.4: 'C' Ltd. has on hand 5,000 units of a product that cannot be sold through regular sales. These were produced at a total cost of ₹ 1,50,000 and would normally have been sold for ₹ 40 per unit. The following alternatives are being considered:

(a) Sell the item as scrap for ₹ 2 per unit.

(b) Repackage at a cost of ₹ 20,000 and sell then at ₹ 8 per unit.

(c) Dispose them off at the city dump at removal cost of ₹ 500.

Which alternative should be accepted?

Solution:

Decision Analysis

Particulars	*(i) Sell as Scrap (₹)*	*(ii) Repackage and Sell (₹)*	*(iii) Disposal (₹)*
Sales	10,000	40,000	-
Less: Costs			
Repackage cost	-	20,000	-
Removal cost	-	-	500
Contribution	10,000	20,000	-500

As alternative II provides maximum profit, it should be accepted.

Illustration 2.5: The Premier Chemicals Ltd. manufactures two Chemical solvents A and B in fixed proportions of 1 : 2 respectively. During the month 60,000 liters were produced and common processing costs of ₹ 240000 were incurred. A and B solvents could be sold in their present form for ₹ 6 and ₹ 8 per liter respectively. However, solvent A can be sold as A-plus for ₹ 8 per liter by adding an extra ingredient costing ₹ 1.50 per liter. Solvent B can be sold as super-B for ₹ 12 per liter if it is reprocessed at an additional cost for ₹ 4 per liter plus an additional ₹ 40,000 per month for hiring a special filtering machine with a capacity of 40,000 liters per month. Should the solvents be sold at the split off point or be further processed?

Solution:

Decision Analysis

Particulars	*Solvents*	
	A	*B*
Incremental Revenue	₹ 40,000	₹ 1,60,000
Less: Incremental cost		
Manufacturing cost	30,000	1,60,000
Less: Hiring costs	-	40,000
Contribution	10,000	– 40,000

Solvent A should be processed further and Solvent B should be sold at the split-off point.

2.5 BUSINESS PROCESS REENGINEERING

Business process reengineering has emerged as a powerful tool to overcome the hurdles in business organisation. It focuses on rethinking and redesigning in the day-to-day working processes. It is about reorienting the business process from prospective customer's thinking in process and ensuring that activities are adding value. Business process reengineering means starting all over, starting from scratch. It starts from the top management and with a corporate vision. It includes targeting customers and trying to improve systems and procedures to achieve this. It results into increasing the clock speed of the organisation. It includes drilling down the thinking process for each vital element of the organisation like personnel structure, design, drawings, accounting practices, material finance and management information system and find out the constraints or bottlenecks in the process. It avoids unnecessary work, duplication of work, demolish absolute methods and systems if required by the management.

A business process is a group of logically related tasks performed to achieve the goals of an organisation. A process is a structured and measured set of tasks designed to produce a specified output for a particular market. It implies a strong emphasis on the way in which work is done within an organisation. Processes may be defined on the basis of entities, objects or activities. Business processes are a set of activities that transform a set of inputs into a set of output in the firm of goods or services, for another person or process, using people and tools. The common business in the organisation are order processing, billing, purchasing, receiving credit appraisal and performance appraisal. The Business Processes are redesigned for the critical analysis and radical redesign of existing processes to achieve improvements in performance.

Definition: Carr and K. David defined Business Process Reengineering as, "the technique that concentrates on the process to bring about radical change in the organisation facilitating dramatic improvement in performance in core business processes which are critical for competitive advantage."

Hammer and Champy have also defined Business Process Reengineering as, "the fundamental rethinking and radical design of business processes to achieve dramatic improvements in critical contemporary measures of performance such as cost, quality, service and speed."

R. Radhakrishnan and S. Balakrishnan have defined business process reengineering as "Starting all over again". It does not mean timkering with what already exists or matching incremental changes that leave basic structures intact. It means abandoning long established procedures and looking a fresh at the work required to create a company's product or service and to deliver value to the customer.

These definitions contain four keywords: Fundamental, Radical, Dramatic and Processes. Reengineering first determines what a company must do and then how to do it. These are the fundamental questions which forces people to look at the tacit rule and assumptions that underline the way they conduct their businesses. Radical design means getting to the root of things. It includes disregarding all existing structures and procedures and investing completely new ways of doing the work. Dramatic means achieving quantum leaps in performance. Dramatic improvement demands replacing the old with something new. Reengineering should be brought in only when a need exists for heavy correction. Process is a collection of activities that take one or more kinds of input and create an output that is of value to the customer.

According to Peter Drucker, the activities identified by experts are necessary for success in performing BPR. The methods commonly accepted by most of the experts are at the core of successful BPR. In addition, optional activities proposed by various management consulting firms who have had success in assisting their clients with BPR are also included. These methods, procedures and tasks are identified to help organisations to divide how they should perform BPR to meet the unique needs of their industry, people and culture.

The Need for BPR

In the global market, organisations must change their priorities from a traditionally popular focus on planning, control and managed growth to emphasise speed, innovation, flexibility, quality, service and cost. Reengineering is the only solution to change the organisation. To be a truly world-class organisation, the company needs to work as a team and all the functional areas of the business need to be properly integrated with each understanding the importance of cross-functional process. As the basis of competition changes from cost and quality to flexibility and responsiveness, the value of process management is now being recognised. The role that process management can play in creating sustainable competitive advantage was termed as Business Process Reengineering. The proper aim of reengineering in today's environment is to facilitate the match between market opportunities and corporate capabilities and ensuring growth. Both TQM and Reengineering approaches share certain principles and adopt a process perspective, so that it is possible to make some general propositions on managing change that will enable a company to reinvent its competitive advantage. It is the value of adding process that enables long-term success for an organisation. The achievement of these ends requires radical bottom-up redesign input and affective, unwavering top-down leadership.

Benefits of BPR

Business Process Reengineering has been accepted in industry as a strategic initiative for managing change and the efforts for directing change are steered in multiple directions such as structure, people, management and system. It has been used by many companies for the pursuit of organisational efficiency through automation, labour saving, streamlining of system and procedures and management reforms through business, market, technology and organisational development. The major benefits of BPR are as follows:

(a) 70 per cent decrease in cycle time

(b) 40 per cent reduction in costs

(c) 40 per cent increase in customer satisfaction, quality and revenue

(d) 25 per cent growth in market share.

Thus, Business Process Reengineering has been considered as a multidimensional problem solving approach emphasising very significant improvements in organisational performance in terms of multiple parameters such as quality, cost, delivery and service level to gain competitive advantage.

Although reengineering is very important for business organisations, it is complex to implement. A total systems is needed to redesign the existing business processes by focusing upon competition, customers and change. However, leading business organisations are becoming more and more assertive in using this technology to support innovative business process rather than refining prevalent ways of doing the work.

General Principles of BPR

The general principles of Business Process Reengineering emerged during 1990s are as follows:

1. To focus on end customers and generate greater value for customers.
2. To focus on harnessing more of the potential of people and applying into those activities which identify and deliver value to customers.
3. To encourage learning and development by building creative working environments.
4. To remove non-value added activities, undertake parallel activities and speed up response.
5. To think and execute as much activity as possible horizontally, on flows and processes through the organisation.
6. To concentrate on output rather than input and link performance measures and rewards concentrating to customer-related outputs.
7. To have networking related to people and activities.
8. To give priority to the delivery of value rather than the maintenance of management control.
9. To move discretion and authority closer to the customer and re-allocate responsibilities between the organisation, its suppliers and customers.
10. To encourage involvement and participation of the people in the process.
11. To ensure that people are equipped, motivated and empowered to do their work.
12. To build learning, renewal and short feedback loops into business process.

BPR Implementation

The following are the common steps to be taken for BPR implementation:

(a) **Beginning organisational change:** It includes assessing the current state of the organisations, then explain the need for change. There is a need to explain the desired change and communicate the change to the people involved in the process.

(b) **Building the reengineering organisation:** It includes creating infrastructure to support reengineering efforts.

(c) **Identify BPR opportunities:** It is helpful to begin thinking about potential change levels which way lead to dramatic changes in the organisational process.

(d) **Understanding existing process:** Modelling the current process is an important part of this step. It helps to migrate from old process to a new one. Then it is necessary to estimate the current costs, robustness and functional value of each technology and information systems currently used.

(e) **Reengineering process:** In this process, actual reengineering starts. It will provide insight as to how technology can be applied in new and innovative ways. The reengineering team will have brainstorming sessions.

(f) **Blueprint of new business system:** Blueprint is a detailed plan required to build something in accordance with the designer's intentions. It contains models of redesigned organisational structure, detailed technology specifications, and new management system.

(g) **Performing transformations:** It includes a plan for migrating to the new process. Migration strategy includes a full cut over the new process entirely a phased approach, a pilot project or creating an entirely new business unit. Successful transformation depends on consciously managing behavioural as well as structural change, with both sensitivity to employee attitudes and perceptions and a tough-minded concern for results.

BPR and ERP

Enterprise Resource Planning is the latest high-end solution that Information Technology has lent to business application. The ERP solutions seek to streamline and integrate operation processes and information flows in the company to synergise the resources of an organisation namely, men material, money and machine through information. ERP systems come as standardised software packages from firms like SAP, Baan, Oracle, Peoplesoft and J.D. Edwards allowing customer to buy these standard requirements rather than having to develop complex software solutions. ERP systems are genetic rather "semi-finished" products with database tables and variable parameters that can be customised, configured or integrated with additional third party software that supports certain key areas within an organisation. ERP systems are used to optimise a company's day-to-day business whereby optimisation can be seen as the process of reducing the space of potential problems and enhancement of the business by utilising the integration between business units. Thus, ERP system is a software that automates finance and human resources departments and helps manufacturers handle jobs such as order processing and production scheduling. The implementation of an ERP system forces the business to do process reengineering. The term ERP is a new kind of manufacturing systems that has Material Resource Planning (MRP), finance and human resources fully integrated on a single database. Thus, ERP systems are packaged software solutions that integrate data across an organisation and impose standardised procedures on the input, use and dissemination that are considered the best practices in the industry. Business Process Reengineering is a prerequisite for going ahead with a powerful planning tool. An in-depth BPR study has to be done before taking up ERP. Business process reengineering brings out deficiencies in the existing system and attempts to maximise productivity through restructuring and reorganising the human resources as well as divisions and departments in the organisation.

The principle followed for BPR may be defined as the USA principle. It means understand, simplify and automate principle. This involves understanding the existing practices, simplifying the process and automating the process. Various tools used for this principle are given below:

(a) Understand, simplify and Automate

(b) Diagramming and eliminating

(c) Story building and combining ERP

(d) Brainstorming and rearranging

Once the BPR is complete, the next task is to evaluate and select suitable package for implementation. Evaluation of the right ERP package is considered a more crucial step. It is difficult to draw the line between changing business processes to suit the system or retaining business processes and paying the cost, in money and time, to change the system. As time and cost squeeze the implementation, the usual path is not to modify the system but to change the way people work.

2.6 TOTAL QUALITY MANAGEMENT

Total Quality Management is the integration of all functions and processes within an organisation in order to achieve continuous improvement of the quality of goods and services. It is a management approach of an organisation centred on quality based on the participation of all its members and aiming at long-term success through customer satisfaction and benefits to all members of the organisation and to the society. Total quality management is one of the quality-oriented approaches that many organisations adopt. It is generally acknowledged that manufacturing companies need to be quality-oriented in conducting their business to survive the business in the world. TQM is an integrated management philosophy and a set practices that emphasise top management commitment, customer focus, supplier relationship, benchmarking, quality-oriented training, employee focus, zero-defects, process improvement and quality measurement.

Total Quality Management can be defined as "a management philosophy that seeks to improve the quality of products and services by improving work processes in response to feedback from employees and customers."

ISO defines TQM as "a management approach of an organisation, centered on quality, based on the participation of all its members and aiming at long-term success through customer satisfaction and benefits to all members of the organisation and to society."

TQM comprises four process steps as under:

1. **Kaizen:** It focuses on continuous process improvement to make processes visible, repeatable and measurable.

2. **Atarmae Hinshitsu:** It focuses on intangible effects and processes and ways to optimise and reduce their effects.

3. **Kansei:** It means examining the way user applies the product beyond the immediate product.

4. **Miryokuteki Hinshitsu:** It broadens management concern beyond the immediate product.

TQM requires that the company maintains the quality standard in all aspects of its business. This requires ensuring that things are done right the first time and that defects and waste are eliminated from operations. It is a management strategy aimed at embedding awareness of quality in all organisational process. It has been widely used in manufacturing, education, government and service industries as well as NASA space and science programmes.

W. Edwards Deming is the pioneer in igniting the quality revolution in Japan in 1946. It was then taken to United States in 1980s. Armand V. Feigenbam was developing a similar set of principles at General Electric in the United States. The American Society for Quality pointed out that the term Total Quality Management was first used by the US Naval Air System Command to describe its Japanese style management approach to quality improvement.

The characteristics of TQM are as follows:

1. TQM is customer-oriented.
2. It requires a long-term commitment for continuous improvement of all processes.
3. The success of TQM demands the leadership of top management and continuous involvement.
4. The responsibility for establishment and improvement of systems lies with the management of an organisation.
5. It is a strategy for continuously improving performance at all levels and in all areas of responsibility.

Thus, TQM is a process for managing quality. It is a continuous way of life. It is a philosophy of perpetual improvement in every thing we do.

Total = Quality involves everyone and all activities in the organisation.

Quality = Conformance to requirements (meeting customer requirements).

Management = Quality can and must be managed.

Potential Benefits of TQM

The advantages of TQM are given below:

1. TQM helps to focus clearly on the needs of the market.
2. TQM facilitates to aspire for a top quality performer in every sphere of activity.
3. It channelises the procedures necessary to achieve a quality performance.

4. It helps to examine critically and continuously all processes to remove non-productive activities and waste.
5. It gears organisations to fully understand the competition and develop an effective combating strategy.
6. It helps to develop good procedures for communication and acknowledging good work.
7. It helps to review the process needed to develop the strategy of never-ending improvement. Quality improvement efforts cannot be restricted to any time period.

The ten steps to TQM are as follows:

1. Pursue new strategic thinking.
2. Know your customers.
3. Set true customer requirements.
4. Concentrate on prevention, not correction.
5. Reduce chronic waste.
6. Pursue a continuous improvement strategy.
7. Use structured methodology for process improvement.
8. Reduce variation.
9. Use a balanced approach.
10. Apply to all functions.

The concept of TQM is based on a number of ideas. It is a start to finish process that integrates interrelated functions at all levels. It is a systems approach that considers every integration between the various elements of the organisation. The term TQM emphasises various key issues. The cost of quality as the measure of non-quality and a measure of how the quality process is progressing. A cultural change that appreciates the primary need to meet customer requirements, implements a management philosophy that acknowledges this emphasis, encourages employee involvement and embraces the ethics of continuous improvement. The enabling mechanism of change includes training and education, communication, recognition, management behaviour, teamwork and customer satisfaction programmes. TQM can be implemented by defining the mission, identifying the output and the customer, negotiating customer requirements, developing a supplier specification that details customer objective and determining the activities required to fill those objectives. Management behaviour includes setting role model, use of quality process and tools, encouraging communication, sponsoring feedback activities and fostering and providing environment.

Principles of TQM

The principles of TQM are as follows:

1. Quality can and must be managed.
2. Everyone has a customer and is a supplier.
3. Process, not people are the problem.
4. Every employee is responsible for quality.
5. Problems must be prevented, not just fixed.
6. Quality must be measured.
7. Quality improvement must be continuous.
8. The quality standard should be defect free.
9. Goals are based on requirements, not negotiated.
10. Life cycle cost, not front-end costs.
11. Management must be involved and take lead.

TQM has been accepted by both services and manufacturing organisations globally as a systematic management approach to meet the competitive challenges. It redefines the quality with emphasis on top management commitment and customer satisfaction. The benefits of TQM are numerous and are increasingly realised by organisations. It provides a linkage between productivity and quality. The application of TQM tools increases a company's efficiency. The focus of TQM is on involvement of everyone in organisation in continuous improvement, commitment to satisfy customers, participation through teamwork, commitment and leadership of top management.

2.7 TOTAL PRODUCTIVE MAINTENANCE

The main function of the maintenance department is to keep the plant and machinery in good and running condition without affecting the normal flow of production. Costs of regular and routine maintenance or preventive maintenance costs should be collected under standard order numbers as part of production overhead. Repairs and maintenance department is treated as a service cost centre and all costs collected under this service cost centre are apportioned to other cost centres on the basis of machines hours, value of machines, hours worked and services rendered. The costs of major repairs and overheads which increase the life of the asset are capitalised and written off with the asset as depreciation.

Where it is necessary to dismantle the existing installation and re-erect the plant at a different location, the expenditure involved is charged to overhead. When an asset is prematurely dismantled on being absolute or redundant, the cost of dismantling should be added to the asset dismantled and set off against any salvage or compensation money or sales proceed received. The final gain or loss on realisation should be transferred to the profit and loss account, unless any gain is transferred to the capital reserve. The cost incurred for fixing new plant is generally capitalised and written off with the asset as depreciation. The cost of moving and refixing existing plant does not generally add to the value of the asset and therefore may be treated as an item of production overhead. In some cases, expenses are incurred in preparing a site for the installation of new plant and the plan is abandoned before the plant is installed. Such expenditure neither adds to the value of the asset nor it is a normal cost of production and as such it is charged directly to profit and loss account.

The cost of small tools differs in different organisations. In some organisations, tools purchased are capitalised and depreciation is charged as production overhead. There is a difficulty in ascertaining the life of small tools and this method is not much popular and therefore small tools are revalued at the end of the year and the difference is charged to factory overhead. Alternatively, cost of small tools is charged to all departments on the basis of actual issues. The alternative method is the book or the purchase price of small tools to a separate standing order and distribute to other departments on some suitable basis and finally absorbed by the products.

Mechanised tabulation expenses, if the mechanised tabulation department renders services to all divisions of the firm such as manufacturing, administration, selling and distribution, the expenses are apportioned to these divisions on a suitable basis, such as, number of cards punched for each division, tabulation hours etc., where such expenses can be identified to a particular department. These are charged directly to that department. When companies allocate support department costs only to the producing departments, then use the direct method of allocation. The direct method is the simplest and most straightforward way to allocate support department costs. Variable service costs are allocated directly to producing departments in proportion to each department's usage of the service. Fixed costs are also allocated directly to the producing departments but in proportion to the producing department's normal or practical capacity.

The power may be purchased or generated in the factory. The cost of purchased power is apportioned to different cost centres on the basis of meter reading and where no meters are provided the power cost is apportioned on the basis of horse power of machines, horse power multiplied by hours run, rated capacity or such other technical assessment. The power generated in the factory is treated as separate service cost centre and all expenses are collected in a power house cost sheet. The total costs of power house cost centre is apportioned to other cost centres on the basis of consumption of power. The maintenance costs caused by power department belongs to power department. Some of the costs caused by power are hidden in the maintenance department because maintenance costs would be lower if the power department does not exist. As a result, a production department that is a heavy user of power and an average or below average user of maintenance may then receive under the direct method, a cost allocation that is understated.

Illustration 2.6: Avanti Ltd. produces machine parts on a job order basis. Most business is obtained through bidding. Most firms competing with Avanti bid full cost plus a 20 per cent mark-up. Recently, with the expectation of gaining more sales, Avanti reduced its mark-up from 25 per cent to 20 per cent. The company operates two service departments and two production departments. The budgeted costs and the normal activity levels for each department are given below:

Particulars (₹)	*Production Depts.*		*Service Depts.*	
	A	*B*	*C*	*D*
Overhead cost	1,00,000	50,000	1,00,000	2,00,000
No. of Employees	30	30	8	7
Maintenance Hours	6,400	1,600	2,000	200
Machine Hours	10,000	1,000	-	-
Labour Hours	1,000	10,000	-	-

The direct costs of Department C are allocated on the basis of employees. Those of Department D are allocated on the basis of maintenance hours. Departmental overhead rates are used to assign cost to products. Department A uses machine hours and Department B uses labour hours.

The company is preparing to bid on a job that requires threee machine hours per unit produced in Department A and no time in Department B. The expected cost of materials are ₹ 50 and labour ₹ 17.

You are required to allocate the service costs to producing departments using: (a) Direct method, (b) Sequential method and (c) Reciprocal method and find out the bid under each method. Which method would you recommend and why?

Solution:

(a) Direct method

(₹)

Particulars	*Producing depts.*		*Servicing depts.*	
	A	*B*	*C*	*D*
Direct costs	1,00,000	50,000	1,00,000	2,00,000
Department 'C'	50,000	50,000	–1,00,000	—
Department 'D'	1,60,000	40,000	—	–2,00,000
Total	3,10,000	1,40,000	—	—

Note:

(i) Employee ratio is equal.

(ii) Ratio of maintenance hours is 4 : 1.

Overhead rate of Dept. 'A' = 3,10,000/ 10,000 = ₹ 31 per machine hour

(b) Sequential Method

(₹)

Particulars	*Producing Depts.*		*Servicing Depts.*	
	A	*B*	*C*	*D*
Direct costs	1,00,000	50,000	1,00,000	2,00,000
Department 'D'	1,28,000	32,000	40,000	–2,00,000
Department 'C'	70,000	70,000	–1,40,000	-
Total	2,98,000	1,52,000	—	—

Note:

Ratio of maintenance hours = 32 : 8 : 10

Ratio of employees is equal.

Dept. A — overhead rate = 2,98,000/10,000 = ₹ 29 : 80

(c) Reciprocal Method

(₹)

Particulars	*Producing depts.*		*Servicing depts.*	
	A	*B*	*C*	*D*
Direct costs	1,00,000	50,000	1,00,000	2,00,000
Department D	13,7563	34,391	42,988	– 2,14,942
Department C	64,023	64,023	– 1,42,988	14,942
Total	3,01,586	1,48,414	—	—

Allocation Ratios

Particulars	*Proportion of output used by*			
	A	*B*	*C*	*D*
C	–	0.1045	0.44775	0.44775
D	0.200	–	0.6400	0.1600

C = 1,00,000 + 0.2000 D

D = 2,00,000 + 0.1045 C

C = 1,00,000 + 0.2 (2,00,000 + 0.1405 C)

C = ₹ 1,00,000 + 40,000 + 0.029C

∴ 0.9791 C = ₹ 1, 40,000

C = ₹ 1,42,988

D = ₹ 2,00,000 + 0.1045 (₹ 1,42,988)

D = ₹ 2,14,942

Dept. + Overhead Rate = ₹ 3,01,586/10,000

= ₹ 30.16 per machine hour

(d) Calculations of Bids ₹

Particulars	*Method*		
	Direct	*Sequential*	*Reciprocal*
Material	50	50	50
Labour	17	17	17
Prime cost	67	67	67
Overheads (3 × 31)	93	89.40	90.48
Total Cost	160	156.40	157.48
Profit (20%)	32	31.28	31.50
Bid Price	192	187.68	188.98

Sequential Method can be recommended because the cost is lower.

2.8 ENERGY AUDIT

Energy has been universally recognised as one of the most important inputs for economic growth and human development. There is a strong relationship between economic development and energy consumption. On one hand, growth of an economy, with its global competitiveness hinges on the availability of cost-effective and environmentally benign energy sources and on the other hand the level of economic development has been observed to be reliant on the energy demand. The energy intensity of India is over twice that of the developed economies. The indicator of energy GDP elasticity, that is, the growth rate of energy to the growth rate of GDP captures both the structure of the economy as well as the efficiency.

The energy sector in India has been receiving high priority in the planning process. The total outlay on energy in the 10th five year plan (2000-07) was projected tobe 4.03 trillion rupees at 2001-02 prices which was just 26.7% of the total outlay. In 2003, India ranked sixth in the world in total energy consumption and needed to accelerate the development of the sector to meet its growth aspirations. The country though rich in coal and abundantly endowed with renewable energy in the form of solar, wind, hydro and bio-energy has very small hydrocarbon reserves, i.e., 0.4 per cent of the world's reserves, world standard, India's current level of energy consumption is very low. For the year 2004-05, the total annual energy consumption for India was estimated at 572 mtoe (Million tonnes oil equivalent) and the per capita consumption at 531 kgoe (kilograms oil equivalent). The per capita TPES consumption (kgoe) of the world is 1767.

Renewable energy provides millions of people with access to electricity and improving their living conditions and reducing poverty. It is estimated that the wind energy about 2% of the total solar energy reaching the earth, which is almost 2 billion tonnes of oil equivalent a year or 200 times that is consumed by all the world economies. However, only a small fraction of the potential has been tapped although India is one of the world leaders in installed wind power generation with a capacity of over 10,000 MW. India currently ranks as the world's 11th biggest energy producer accounting for about 2.4% of the world's total annual energy production. Again, India is the world's 6th largest energy consumer accounting for about 3.3% of the world's total energy consumption. Although India is the 3rd largest producer of hard coal after China and the US, it also imports around 1.4 million barrels of oil per day for 60% of its total needs.

70% of the coal produced every year in India has been used for thermal generation. Fossil fuels for long have been the initial sources of energy even in India. However, consistent use of fossil fuels has led to large-scale problems. The greenhouse effect caused by the emission of greenhouse gases as a result of burning up these fossil fuels has long been documented as major source of trouble for environmental safety. The industrial sector in India is a major energy consumer accounting for nearly 50% of energy produced. The Indian industry is highly energy intensive one and its energy-GDP efficiency is around 1.5 far higher than the developed nations. Indian industries have been regarded as a role model across the world when it comes to social responsibility. Energy saving is today in top in the list of social responsibility of every individual. Energy saving measures also help in curtailing pollution that is one of the major factors contributing to global warming.

The IEA defines energy supply to be 'secure' if it is adequate, affordable and reliable. Consumers expect the lights to always come on at the flick of a switch, their buildings to be maintained at a comfortable temperature all year round and to be able to purchase vehicle fuel or public transport tickets whenever they wish to travel. Electricity, heat and mobility are usually considered to be basic necessities of life and therefore should be affordable to all at any time. Indian Renewable Energy Development Agency, established in 1987, promotes renewable energy and energy conservation projects. It is administered by the Ministry of Renewable Energy. Renewable sources account for about 60,000 MW out of India's capacity of about 80,000 MW, but the government believes that the country can raise output of renewable energy to 80,000 MW in a little over a decade.

Sunborne energy and Indo solar are the leading manufacturers of solar power and photovoltaic cells respectively, solar power is affordable and used widespread across India. India will have the world's first market for trading in energy savings. Under the National Action Plan on Ultimate Change, the Power Ministry has prepared the blueprint for trading in energy by industrial plants that save energy beyond the targets set for them. The government will set mandatory targets to be achieved by each large industrial unit and plant in energy intensive sectors. The government has been further strengthening its energy security which will automatically bring co-benefits of reduction in the global warming causing emissions. PAT, i.e., Perform, Achieve and Trade scheme. Energy reduction targets would be set in terms of the specific energy consumption for each plant individually to ensure that there are no blanket benchmarks that create an uneven turf for different sizes and type of players. The industry will be given three years to achieve them. Those units that surpass their targets will be provided 'Energy certificates" which will be tradable on the existing power exchanges in the country. The companies which will fail the targets set for them will have to buy these certificates under an open market mechanism if the failed companies do not meet their targets either by achieving energy savings or by buying the energy certificates would be penalised by the government under the Energy Conservation Act. Under the plan, BEE will accredit private agencies to audit the actual energy consumed by the industrial units and retain the power to carry out random checks.

The following are the suggestions and policy implementation of the energy security:

(1) Conventional lights are one of the major awareness whereby a huge amount of electric can be saved and carbon emission caused due to this can be subsequently avoided.

(2) Government should take an initiative stand and set an example by replacing all the conventional streetlights by LED lights and use these lights in the government offices too.

(3) There are tremendous opportunities for energy conservation through enhanced grid efficiency and improved industrial productivity facilitated by better utilisation of scarce energy resources.

(4) It is necessary to raise awareness of the financial benefits of energy efficiency. The purchase price of a electric motor is just 1% of what the owner spends on energy to run the equipment over its lifetime.

(5) Create incentives for business and local authorities to save energy. The government should make energy efficiency a criterion of every project they fund, treaty they negotiate, research agreement they support school or hospital they build, others will follow where government leads.

(6) Incentives for promoting renewable should be linked to outcomes and not just outlays. Power regulators should create alternative incentives structures such as mandated feed in laws or differential tariffs or specifying renewable portfolio percentage in total supply.

(7) The Lucifer company products are having certain special features for which it is recommended for continuous use of these products.

Energy Audit — Check List

The indicative list of areas to be covered in the Performance Appraisal Report as per the companies (Cost Audit Report) Rules 2011 are as follows:

(1) **Power:**

(a) Improve power factor by installing capacitor to reduce KVA demand changes and also line losses within plant.

(b) Improvement of power factor in the range of 0.96 to unity.

(c) Avoid repeated rewinding of motors.

(d) Replace underloaded/overloaded motor with proper size motors and replace the motor with energy efficiency motors.

(e) Optimise the tariff structure with utility supplier.

(f) Shift loads to oft-peak times.

(g) Minimise maximum demand by tripping loads through a demand controller.

(h) Relocate transformers close to main loads.

(i) Export power to grid if you have any surplus in your captive generation.

(2) DG Set:

(a) Maintain diesel engines regularly.

(b) Measure fuel consumption per KWH of electricity generated regularly.

(c) Use waste heat to generate steam, hot water/power as absorption chiller or preheat process of utility feeds.

(d) Clean air filters regularly.

(3) Illumination:

(a) Use an electronic ballest in place of conventional choke.

(b) Use CFL lamp in place of GLS lamp.

(c) Clean the lamps and fixtures regularly.

(d) Use 36W tubelight instead of 40W tubelight.

(e) Use of sodium vapour lamps for any lighting in place of mercury vapour lamps.

(4) Fuel:

(a) Cost-benefit analysis of various types of oil.

(b) Furnace oil, LSHS oil, HS oil, LD oil etc. should be evaluated from time to time for using as fuel for boiler and DG set.

(c) Quality and size of coal should be tested regularly.

(d) Substitute coal by PET coke or lignite or bagasse to reduce the effective cost of steam/power.

(5) Boiler for Steam:

(a) Use only treated water in Boiler.

(b) Stop steam leakage.

(c) Maintain steam pipe installation.

(d) Inspect heaters for proper oil temperature.

(e) Reduce hot water wastage to drain.

(f) Use waste steam for water heating.

(g) Cleaning of tubes should be carried out periodically.

(6) **Water:** Use water harvesting system — consider the installation of a thermal solar system for warm water for use in canteen.

(7) **Air-conditioning:** Consider reducing ceiling heights, use of double doors, automatic doors, air curtains, double glazed windows, polyester sun films etc. reduces heat imgress and air-conditioning load of buildings.

(8) **Cooling Towers:** Replacement of inefficient aluminum or fabricated steel fans by moulded FRP fans with acrofoil designs. Install automatic on-off switching of cooling tower fans.

(9) **Compressed Air:**

(a) Change the oil filter regularly.

(b) Stop use of compressed air for floor/machines cleaning.

(c) Check for compressed air leakage.

(10) **Furnace:** Recover and utilise waste heat from furnace fine gas for preheating of combustion air.

(a) Control express air in furnaces.

(b) Produce heat losses through furnace openings.

(c) Proper design of leads of melting furnace and training of operators to close lids.

(d) Match the load to the furnace capacity.

(11) **Computers:** Turn off your computers when not in use, screen savers save computer screens and not energy setting computers, monitors and coplers to use sleep mode when not in use helps cut energy cost by approx. 40%.

2.9 CONTROL OF TOTAL DISTRIBUTION COST AND SUPPLY COST

Selling overhead is that part of the total overhead which is incurred for seeking to create and stimulate demand for screening orders. Distribution overheads is that part of total overhead which is incurred in sequence of operations which begins with making the packed product available for despatch and ends with making the reconditioned empty package. Selling overhead is incurred for the purpose of promoting sales and retaining customers. Selling expenses should be necessarily incurred but their nature and extent depend largely upon economic factors and the business policy of the organisation. Expenditure on advertisement depends on the types, extent and duration of advertisement which in turn are dependent upon the advertisement policy of the organisation. The

nature and amount of which are closely related to the basic needs of production. Selling overhead may be increased or reduced as a matter of policy. Selling overheads are therefore more in nature of policy costs.

Selling and distribution overhead has no direct relationship with production cost since selling costs may vary widely depending upon the channel of distribution adopted, sales promotion policy, availability of finance and extent of competition. One or more of these consideration set the limit to selling expenditure. Advertisement expenditure may be limited to the finance available, salesman's commission and salaries may be limited to the benefits given by competitors or sales programme for a period.

The selling and distribution costs have increased to a great extent without having any direct relation to the selling affinity. In order to judge the effectiveness, classification and analysis of selling and distribution expenses should be made by channels of distribution, departments, territories, salesmen, order period of lines of products and customers. Continuous efforts should be made for the preparation and use of budgets and standards for selling and distribution overheads in order to control costs by delegating responsibility. Comparative statements of actual results and budgets set should be submitted to management each month or quarter. In whatever way selling and distribution costs are analysed, costs should be allocated to departments, territories and products. Cost which cannot be allocated are apportioned to them on some suitable basis. One can get the desired result by utilising the same procedure of allocation, apportionment and absorption.

Selling and distribution costs are allocated to sales service department and sales territories. Costs which cannot be allocated are apportioned to such departments by selecting some suitable basis such as population, coverage, net sales, sales quota and floor space. The total selling and distribution costs of sales and service departments are apportioned to sales territories or some equitable basis. The selling and distribution costs of each territory are then compared against the sales of each territory and ultimately a comparative territorial profit and loss statement can be presented to management.

Illustration 2.7: Bata Ltd. maintains three salesmen, X, Y, and Z in territory 'A'. The following information is obtained for the month of March 2012.

	(₹)
Salesmen's salary	25000
Commission	4000
Travelling Expenses	6000
Stationery	2000
Telephone	3000
Territory Expenses	20,000
Net sales	2,00,000
Cost of sales	60% of sales

From the following additional information, prepare a sales performance statement.

Salesman	*Sales*	*Salary*	*Commission*	*Travelling*	*Stationery*	*Telephone*
X	80,000	11,500	2,000	4,000	1,000	1,500
Y	70,000	7,000	1,000	1,500	500	500
Z	50,000	6,500	1,000	500	500	1000
Total	**2,00,000**	**25,000**	**4,000**	**6,000**	**2,000**	**3,000**

Solution:

Selling and Distribution Overhead Summary

Items	*Total*	*X (₹)*	*Y (₹)*	*Z (₹)*
Salary	25,000	11,500	7,000	6,500
Commission	4,000	2,000	1,000	1,000
Travelling	6,000	4,000	1,500	500
Stationery	2,000	1,000	500	500
Telephone	3,000	1,500	500	1,000
Direct cost	40,000	20,000	10,500	9,500
Territorial Overhead on the basis of net sales	20,000	8,000	7,000	5,000
Total S & D Costs	**60,000**	**28,000**	**17,500**	**14,500**

Illustration 2.8: Z Ltd. produces a single product in three sizes, A, B and C. Prepare a statement showing the selling and distribution expenses apportioned over these three sizes on the basis indicated and expenses the total appropriated to each sizes.

The expenses and basis of apportionment are given below:

Expenses	*(₹)*	*Basis of Apportionment*
Salaries (sales)	1,00,000	Direct charge
Commission (sales)	60,000	Sales turnover
Expenses (sales office)	20,000	Number of orders
Advertising (specific)	2,20,000	Direct charge
Advertising (general)	50,000	Sales turnover
Packing Expenses	30,000	Size of product
Delivery Expenses	40,000	Size of product
Warehouse Expenses	10,000	Size of product
Credit Collection Expenses	12,000	Number of orders
Total	**5,42,000**	

Data relating to the three sizes are:

	Total (₹)	*Size A* (₹)	*Size B* (₹)	*Size C* (₹)
No. of Salesmen	10	4	5	1
No. of Orders	1,600	700	800	100
% of Specific Advertising	100	30	40	30
No. of Units Sold	8,240	3,440	3,200	1,600
Sales Turnover	2,00,000	5,80,000	8,00,000	6,20,000
Capacity in cubic metre per unit	-	5	8	17

Solution:

Comparative Statement of Costs

Item of Exp.	*Basis*	*Total* (₹)	*Size A* (₹)	*Size B* (₹)	*Size C* (₹)
Salesmen's Salaries	No. of salesman	1,00,000	40,000	50,000	10,000
Sales Commission	3% of turnover	60,000	17,400	24,000	18,600
Sales Expenses	No. of orders	20,000	9,000	10,000	1,000
Specific Advt.	3 : 4 : 3	2,20,000	66,000	88,000	66,000
General Advt.	2.5% of turnover	50,000	14,500	20,000	15,500
Packing	Cubic capacity	30,000	7,360	10,970	11,670
Delivery expenses	Cubic capacity	40,000	9,800	14,640	15,560
Warehouse expenses	Cubic capacity	10,000	2,450	3,660	3,890
Credit collection expenses	No. of orders	12,000	5,250	6,000	750
	Total S & D Expenses	**5,4,2000**	**1,71,760**	**2,27,270**	**1,42,470**

2.10 COST REDUCTION

The amount of profit in any organisation can be maximised by either increasing the amount of sales or reducing costs. However, in the global market, it may be very difficult to increase the sales price of the products. In fact, an increase in sales price may have an adverse impact on the total volume of sales, which in turn will lead to lower profits. Therefore, cost reduction techniques occupy a prominent position in any organisation to maximise its profits.

Cost reduction is a planned positive approach to reducing expenditure. It refers to the real and permanent reduction in the unit cost of the goods manufactured or services rendered without impairing their suitability for the use of originally intended. This reduction in per unit cost of production may be effected either by reduction in unit cost of production or by increasing productivity. The reduction in unit cost of production is usually brought by elimination of wasteful and non-essential elements in the design of products and from techniques and practices carried out in connection therewith. Any reduction in costs due to windfalls, changes in government policy like reduction in taxes or duties due to price agreements do not come into the area of cost reduction as these are not real and permanent reductions in costs due to planned efforts. Any reduction in costs by increased productivity accompanied by deterioration of quality shall not be covered by the term cost reduction. However, both the above aspects are very closely interlinked and generally act together. It is possible only when the teamwork and cooperation forms the basic features of any planned approach to cost reduction.

Cost reduction is a continuous and planned process of analysing all the factors affecting the costs in an organisation. It is a corrective function, which can operate along with efficient cost control system. In other words, there is always a scope for cost reduction even under controlled conditions. It assumes the existence of concealed potential savings in the standards or norms unchanged and therefore aims at improving them by bringing out more savings. However, it is not concerned with maintenance of performance according to standards.

With squeezing margins due to increasing competition, the managements are paying more attention to cost reduction as a way of preserving or improving profitability. The cost reduction to be effective must be real and permanent. Similarly, cost reduction approach should embrace all the functions and divisions of a business as any isolation in approach where any individual department is singled out for reprimand prompts a demotivating awareness that other departments are not being asked to cut costs and this may not only affect the team spirit but also may have serious effects on the level of service provided to other non-reprimanded departments. Thus, cost reduction to be successful requires the cooperation at all levels of the organisation so that a combined action is taken with the common aim of benefit to the business. The organisation for initiation of cost reduction programme may vary depending upon its size, the nature of business, the availability of information and the individual requirements. The effective course may be to formulate a committee with representatives from all sections of the business. The committee has to draw up a programme for cost reduction and decide the area of potential savings and allot the assignments the executives their responsibilities. It has also to fix the priorities amongst the various areas for cost reduction and review the actual performance from time to time.

Cost Reduction Programme

A cost reduction programme consists of the important steps. All the responsibility centres, where costs are incurred should be listed and grouped together according to the departmental responsibility. Each such group should be subject to value analysis scheme to ensure that optimum performance is given by each department. The various areas for cost reduction should be evaluated. Suitable cost reduction techniques should be applied to all such areas to effect real and permanent reduction in unit cost of goods manufactured or services rendered.

Any technique employed for cost reduction should be appropriate to the organisation or activity under consideration. Its introduction and implementation should be preplanned effectively on a participative basis. Its progress should be monitored regularly. Its scope should range across the entire spectrum of an organisation's operations.

Areas Covered by Cost Reduction

The following are the critical areas for application of various cost reduction programme.

(i) **Design:** It should include the critical analysis of all products within the product range of the organisation. Application of value analysis method at the designing stage would go long way in maximising the profits.

(ii) **Organisation:** Organisation can be improved by defining each function and responsibility. There should be well-defined channels of communication. Delegation of authority should be encouraged to ensure quick and effective decision making. Cooperation and close relationship between the various executives should be encouraged. Encouragement in the form of incentives should be offered to the employees.

(iii) **Production Planning and Control:** It covers planning inventory control, materials handling and usage, inspection, repairs and maintenance, minimisation of wastages and reducing idle time. An efficient cost reduction plan should aim at reducing per unit cost on these counts.

(iv) **Factory Layout and Equipments:** An effective arrangement of plant, machinery, equipments is a fundamental requirement. The successful layout should make optimal use of space, flexibility, control, work satisfaction and productivity.

(v) **Utility Services:** Effective cost reduction can be possible with supply of power, water, steam, transport and ventilation. There should be proper system for preventive and curative maintenance.

(vi) **Marketing:** There can be considerable scope for comprehensive reorganisation of existing methods of marketing and substantial reduction in costs. Rearrangement of territories, efficient and economical channels of distribution, market research, alternative media, optimum utilisation of salesmen's working time are some of the areas to be studied.

(vii) **Finance:** Investment in right machinery and equipments, at the right time can yield significant cost advantages. The methods of funding capital should be cost-effective. The funds should be secured at economical cost and employed economically so as to give maximum returns.

Cost Reduction Techniques

The various techniques used for achieving cost reduction are as follows:

1. Value analysis
2. Budgetary control
3. Quality control
4. Market research
5. Economic batch quantity
6. Cost-benefit analysis
7. Contribution analysis
8. ABC analysis
9. PERT analysis
10. Mechanisation

Illustration 2.9: 'K' Ltd. is at present working at 90% of its capacity, producing 13,500 units per annum. It operates flexible budgetary control system. The following figures are obtained from its budget.

Activity level	90%	100%
Units	13,500	15,000
Cost elements		
Sales	1,500,000	16,00,000
Fixed cost	3,00,000	3,00,000
Semi-fixed costs	98,000	1,00,000
Variable expenses	1,42,000	1,50,000

Labour and material cost per unit are constant under present condition. Profit margin is 10 per cent. You are required to determine the differential cost of producing 1,500 units. What price would you recommend for exporting these 1,500 units, considering the fact that overseas prices are much lower than the domestic prices?

Solution:

(a) Calculation of Labour and Material Cost

Sales at 90% capacity	13,500 units
Sales value at 90% capacity	15,00,000
Less: Profit (10% on sales)	1,50,000
Cost of goods sold	1350000

Less: variable expenses	1,42,000	
Semi-variable expenses	98,000	
Fixed expenses	3,00,000	5,40,000
Labour and material cost		8,10,000

$$\therefore \text{Material and labour cost at 100\% capacity} = \frac{8,10,000}{90\%} = ₹\ 9,00,000$$

(b) Flexible Budget

Activity Level	*90%*	*100%*	*Differential*
Sales — units	13,500	15,000	1,500
Cost Elements			
Material Labour	8,10,000	9,00,000	90,000
Variable Expenses	142000	1,50,000	8,000
Semi-fixed Expenses	98,000	1,00,000	2,000
Fixed Expenses	3,00,000	3,00,000	-
Total Cost	**13,50,000**	**14,50,000**	**1,00,000**

(c) The export price should be quoted not lower than ₹ 60.67 (i.e., $\frac{1,00,000}{15,000}$) per unit, assuming that export price will have no effect on domestic market.

Illustration 2.10: A company produces and sells 1,000 units of product per month at ₹ 20 each. Marginal cost per unit is ₹ 12 and fixed cost per month is ₹ 3,000. It is proposed to reduce price by 20%. Find the additional sales required to earn the same amount of profit.

Solution:

(a) Calculation of Present Profit

Sales 1,000 units @ ₹ 20	= ₹ 20,000
Less: Marginal cost (1,000 × 12)	= ₹ 12,000
Contribution	8,000
Less: Fixed cost	3,000
∴ Profit	5,000

(b) Calculation of Sales Required to Earn Profit ₹ 5,000

Contribution = Fixed Cost + Profit

Revised selling price = 20 – 4 = ₹ 16

∴ Contribution per unit = 16 – 12 = ₹ 4

∴ No. of units required to sell $= \frac{8,000}{4}$

= 2,000 units

2.11 PRODUCT LIFE CYCLE COSTING

Strategic cost management emphasises the importance of an external focus and the need to recognise and exploit both internal and external linkages. Life cycle cost management is a related approach that builds a conceptual framework which facilitates management's ability to exploit internal and external linkages. Product life cycle is simply the time a product exists from competition to abandonment. Product life cycle refers to a product class as a whole.

Life cycle costing can be defined as "the accumulation of costs for activities that occur over the entire life cycle of a product from inception to abandonment by the manufacturer and the customer." Life cycle begins with the identification of new consumer needs and the invention of a new product and is often followed by patent protection and further development to make it saleable. It is followed by rapid expansion in its sales as the product gains market acceptance. The competition enter the market with imitation and rival products and distinctness of the new product starts diminishing. The speed of degeneration differs from product to product. The innovation of a new product and its degeneration into a common product is known as life cycle of a product.

Life cycle analysis provides a framework for managing the cost and performance of a product over the duration of its life. Life cycle is important to cost control because of the interdependencies of activities in different time periods. The output of the design activities has a significant impact on the cost and performance of subsequent activities. Cost systems primarily focus on the cost of physical production without accumulating costs over the entire design, maintenance, market and support cycle of a product. Resources committed to the development of products and the manufacturing process represent a sizeable investment of capital. The benefits accrue over many years and under conventional accounting are not directly identified with the product being developed. They are treated instead as a period expense and allocated to all products. Companies which use life cycle models for planning and budgeting new products do not integrate these models into cost systems. It is important to provide feedback on planning effectiveness and the impact of design, decisions on operational and support costs. Period reporting hinder management's understanding of product-line profitability and the potential cost impact of long-term decisions such as engineering design changes. Life cycle costing and reporting provide management with a better picture of product profitability and help manage to gauge their planning activities.

The characteristics of product life cycle are as follows:

1. The products have finite life and pass through the cycle of development, introduction, growth, maturity, decline and deletion at varying speeds.
2. Product cost, revenue and profit patterns tend to follow predictable courses through the product life cycle.
3. Profit per unit varies as products move through their life cycles.
4. Each phase of product life cycle poses different threats and opportunities that give rise to different strategic actions.
5. Product requires different functional emphasis in each phase.

Life cycle costing provides a long-term perspective to product or service cost. It considers the entire life cycle of the product or service. It also provides a more complete perspective of product cost or profitability. Life cycle of a product can be divided into seven stages as follows:

1. **Analysis:** It is the assessment of the idea and effects of the investment.
2. **Startup:** It is the dedication of the manufacturing facilities and practical assessment of the effects of the investment.
3. **Entry in the Market:** In this stage, the product is actually introduced in the market.
4. **Growth:** The product is produced and sold more and more so as to achieve desired growth.
5. **Maturity:** The growth of the product reaches at the highest level and further growth is not possible.
6. **Decline:** As the growth is stopped, the product demand declines in the market.
7. **Withdrawal:** As the decline is deep, the company withdraws the product from the market.

There are a number of important points associated with life cycle costing as an approach of cost management successfully. There is a need to invest more in pre-manufacturing assets and in people skills to increase the probability of low cost, higher quality and innovation. The companies should use more resources in the early phases of a product life cycle. Target costing is the key to establish cost goals for a product. Performance evaluation and compensation systems should reinforce a whole life cycle cost perspective. All sources of organisational resistance to product life cycle cost management should be dealt with in implementing a culture of cost-consciousness and continuous improvement. A cost analyst with excellent knowledge and experience can compensate for various database difficulties. Thus, the management has to play a very important role in making product life cycle costing efforts worthwhile. The risk management is the essence of life cycle costing.

2.12 EXERCISES

1. Explain the concept of Total Quality Management.
2. What is Business Process Reengineering?
3. Explain the concept of life cycle costing.
4. Distinguish between Value Analysis and Value Engineering.
5. What is cost reduction? How is it different from cost control?
6. Write short notes on:
   (a) Waste Control
   (b) Disposal Management
   (c) Energy Audit
   (d) Business Process Reengineering
   (e) Product Life Cycle Costing.
7. X Ltd. expects to earn added value of ₹ 4,00,000 in 2012. It expects a value added/labour cost ratio 2 : 1. The labour costs were ₹ 2,00,000 but actual added value earned in 2012 was is ₹ 4,80,000. Bonus is paid: (a) at 50% of any surplus added value earned and (b) 50% of saving on the amount of labour cost. You are required to calculate the bonus amount.

   (**Ans:** (a) 50% of 80,000 = ₹ 40,000 (b) 50% of ₹ 40,000 = ₹ 20,000)
8. Calculate the raw material cost of 100 yards of cloth made in jute mill. The cotton contains 45% of wrap yarn and 55% of weft yarn and weight 10.02 per yard. Wastage of yarn is 2% and 5% of weft. Both the yarns are spun from jute fibre at ₹ 1.25 for warp and ₹ 108 for weft per quintal, after treating with a mixture of oil at 50 paise per kg and water such a way that warp contains 5% oil and weft contains 7% of oil loss of fibre upto spinning is 5% warp and 10% weft. All percentages except the yarn content in cloth are input based.

   (**Ans:** ₹ 17.47 for warp + ₹ 20.33 for weft)
9. A power plant has just sufficient capacity to supply power to two consuming departments A and B, when both are working at full capacities consuming 15,000 units and 10,000 units respectively. But actually departments A and B consumed 12,000 units and 4,000 units in December, 2011. Explain the methods of allocating power plant expenses stating the best methods. The power plant expenses of ₹ 6,600 consist of a fixed expense of ₹ 5,000 and variable expenses of ₹ 1,600.

   (**Ans:** Dept. A – ₹ 4,200, Dept. B – ₹ 2,400. The basis for fixed expenses is full normal capacity and for variable expenses actual consumption)

10. Bata Ltd. maintains three salesmen, X, Y and Z in territory 1. The following information is obtained for the month of March 2012.

Salary of salesmen	₹ 2,500
Commission	400
Travelling expenses	600
Stationery	200
Telephone	300
Territorial expenses	2,000
Net sales	20,000
Cost of sales	60% of sales

From the following additional information, prepare a sales performance statement showing distribution of selling and distribution overheads among the three salesmen:

Salesmen	*Sales* ₹	*Salary* ₹	*Commission* ₹	*Travelling Expenses* ₹	*Stationery* ₹	*Telephone* ₹
X	8,000	1,150	200	400	100	150
Y	7,000	700	100	150	50	50
Z	5,000	650	100	50	50	100
Total	**20,000**	**2,500**	**400**	**600**	**200**	**300**

(**Ans.:** X – ₹ 2,800, Y – ₹ 1,750, and Z – ₹ 1,450.)

Chapter

3

Activity Based Costing

STRUCTURE:

3.1 Introduction

3.2 Activity Based Costing

3.3 Identifying Activities

3.4 Development of ABC

3.5 Activity Based Costing Procedure

3.6 Benefits of Activity Based Costing

3.7 Implementation of Activity Based Costing System

3.8 Activity Based Costing in Service Sector

3.9 Activity Based Management

3.10 Limitations of Activity Based Costing

3.11 Illustrations

3.12 Target Costing

3.13 Exercises

3.1 INTRODUCTION

Activity Based Costing (ABC) is a new practice or intermediate change in the process of attribution of costs to jobs or processes. Earlier, costs were first collected for production departments and service departments separately and then the costs of production departments were absorbed by the jobs or processes. In the context of Activity Based Costing, the costs are collected according to the activities carried out in the organisation such as materials ordering, materials handling, inspection, machine setups, customer support services, etc. The jobs and processes for which cost collection is being attempted are loaded with costs of these activities rationally. This method assigns costs to activities based on their use of activities. Thus, ABC is an information system that provides costs and non-financial information about activities and cost objects to help identify improvement areas and plot safe courses of solution to the problems. Traditionally, costing systems use volume-related measures such as direct labour hours or machine hours to allocate overheads to the products. However, many organisational resources exist for activities that are unrelated to physical volume. Today, volume-related activities consist of support activities such as materials handling, material procurement, performing setups, production scheduling and inspection activities. Overheads costs were small and inappropriate overhead allocation were not significant. However, information processing costs are higher it was difficult to justify more sophisticated overhead allocation methods. Nowadays, companies produce wide range of products and services, and direct labour represents only a small percentage of total costs. The global competition has made decision errors due to poor cost information more probable and more costly. These changes have contributed to introduction of Activity Based Costing.

3.2 ACTIVITY BASED COSTING

Activity Based Costing is a method of measuring the cost and performance of activities and cost objects.

ABC is an information system that provides cost and non-financial information about activities and cost objects to help identify improvement areas and plot safe courses of solutions to the problems.

Activity based costing assigns the cost of activities to individual product based on their relative consumption of the individual activities. Determining the cost of an activity is critical for this approach to product costing.

With Activity based costing, multiple activities are identified in the production process that are associated with costs.

Activity based costing system provides improvement in performance of activities with cost as the focus. At the top management level, it helps to determine product-wise, customer-wise and dealer-wise profitability. At an operational level, ABC helps identify improvement activities. Activity based costing is a system that focuses on activities, as the activities cause costs and products create demand for activities. ABC system is based on the understanding that:

(a) Identifying major activities that take place in an organisation.

(b) Creating a cost pool or cost centre for each activity.

(c) Determine cost driver for each major activity.

(d) Assigning cost of activities to products based on product's consumption or demand for activities.

ABC emphasises the need to obtain a better understanding of the behaviour of overhead costs and it seeks to ascertain causes of costs and their relation with the products or services. ABC also recognises, that in the long run, most of the costs are not fixed and seeks to understand the forces that cause overhead costs to change over time. Thus, a link is made between activities and products by assigning costs to products based on individual product's consumption or demand for each activity.

3.3 IDENTIFYING ACTIVITIES

The first step in the ABC is to choose the activities that result in incurring of overhead costs. This has to be done systematically and involves examining physical plans of the workplace and payroll listings. These activities do not necessarily coincide with existing departments but rather represent a group of transactions that support the production process. Typical activities used in ABC are designing, ordering, scheduling, materials handling, inventory control and quality control. The activities should be at a reasonable level of aggregation. To break down activities into actions and tasks is usually too detailed for products costing. Such actions and tasks are normally combined into large purpose-oriented activities. For example, activities may be listed as follows:

- Production schedule charges
- Customer liaison
- Purchasing
- Production process setup
- Quality control
- Materials handling
- Maintenance

Final choice of activities will be judgemental in any organisation. At the time of introduction of ABC activity, cost pools ran into hundreds. It is felt that 20 to 30 cost pools have become common. The choice is between information details and cost of setting up and operating the system. An activity, such as quality control can be subdivided into appraisal activity and prevention activity. The benefit of this would be more detailed profits of cost reported to management and a possible increase in the homogeneity of the costs in each activity cost pool.

3.4 DEVELOPMENT OF ACTIVITY BASED COSTING SYSTEM

The following factors are responsible for the development of activity based costing system in India.

(i) Growing overhead costs due to increasingly automated production.

(ii) Decreasing costs of information processing because of continual improvements and increasing application of information technology.

(iii) Increasing market competition which necessiated more accurate product costs.

(iv) Increasing product diversity to secure economies of scope and increased market share.

(v) Failure of traditional costing to capture cause and effect relationship.

(vi) Failure of traditional costing to highlight interrelationship among activities in different departments.

(vii) Growing dissatisfaction among the working executives regarding traditional costing which is based on averages and estimates.

(viii) Traditional costing systems are driven by the need to value stocks rather than to provide meaningful product cost.

(ix) Direct labour has reduced as a percentage of total costs for majority of manufacturing companies.

(x) Overhead functions such as product design, quality control, customer service, production planning and sales order processing are as important to customer as physical processes on the shop floor.

3.5 ACTIVITY BASED COSTING PROCESS

The following steps are used to apply costs to products under an ABC system.

(a) Identifying Activities: The first step is to choose the activities that result in incurring of overhead costs. These activities do not necessarily coincide with existing departments but rather represent a group of transactions that support the production process. Typical activities are designing, ordering, scheduling, materials handling, inventory control etc. Each of these activities is composed of transactions that result in costs. More than one cost pool can be established for each activity. A cost pool is an account to record the costs of an activity with a specific cost driver.

(b) Trace Costs to Activities: Once the activities have been chosen, costs must be traced to the cost pools for different activities. To facilitate this tracing, cost drivers are chosen to act as vehicles for distributing costs. These costs drivers are also called as resource drivers. A predetermined rate is estimated for each resource driver. Consumption of the resource driver in combination with the predetermined rate determines the distribution of the resource costs to the activities.

(c) Determine Cost Drivers for Activities: The term cost driver has been used to describe the events on forces, that are significant determinants of the cost of activities. If production scheduling cost is generated by the number of production runs, that each production generates, then number of setups would represent the cost driver for production scheduling. A cost driver is a variable, that determines the work volume or workload of a particular activity. It provides the justification for amount of resources consumed by an activity and hence its cost. It will be a significant measure of activity cost variation due to the casual relationship between resources and cost. Cost drivers are also known as activity drivers. Activity drivers represent the event that cause costs within an activity. For example, activity drivers for the purchasing activity will include negotiations with vendors, ordering materials, scheduling their arrivals and inspection. Each of these activity drivers represents costly procedures that are performed in the purchasing activity. An activity driver is chosen for each cost pool. If two cost pools are used for the same cost driver, then the cost pools could be combined for product costing purposes.

(d) Cost Driver Analysis: All the activities have cost drivers. These cost drivers can be volume-related or non-volume-related. There is a tendency to identify greater number of cost drivers than can be used for cost accumulation or activity elimination. A cost driver should be easy to understand directly related to activity being performed and appropriate to performance measurement. Costs have been traditionally accumulated into one or two cost pools or fixed factory overhead and one or two cost drivers have been used to assign costs to products. The use of single cost pools and single drivers may produce illogical products or services costs for internal management use in complex production environment. The accounting system should recognise that costs are created and incurred at the different levels as follows:

(i) Unit level cost

(ii) Batch level cost

(iii) Product or process level costs

(iv) Facility level costs

(v) Organisation level costs.

(e) Applying Costs to Products: The application of costs to various products is calculated by multiplying the application rate times with the usage of the activity driver in manufacturing a product or providing a service. It is tracing the cost of the activities to products according to product's demand. It is done by using the cost driver as measure of demand. A product demand for the activities is measured by the number of transactions it generates for the cost driver. The best way to complete the final step is to apply cost driver rate to individual products. If a cost driver rate is to be practical, the variable chosen must be measurable in a way which permits its identification with individual products.

The following is the representative list showing how activity drivers are listed for specific types of costs:

Cost Type	*Related Activity Drivers*
Marketing and Sales	Number of customer service contracts
	Number of orders processed
	Number of sales contracts

Manufacturing	Direct labour hours
	Field support visits
	Jobs scheduled
	Machine hours
	Machine setups
	Purchase orders
Quality Control	Number of inspections
	Number of supplier reviews
Administration	Hours charged
	Number of contracts
Facility	Amount of space utilisation
Human Resources	Employee head count
Engineering	Hours charged to design
	Hours charged to process planning
	Hours charged to tool design
Accounting	Number of billings
	Number of cash receipts
	Number of cheque payments
	Number of ledger accounts

3.6 BENEFITS OF ACTIVITY BASED COSTING

The following are the benefits of activity based costing:

1. It helps to determine the cost of each activity.
2. It helps to determine the return on investment to be expected for each investment option.
3. It helps to identify area to reduce costs.
4. It helps to identify non-value-added costs.
5. It helps to make right choice of products to be sold.
6. It provides reliable data for decision making as to make or buy.
7. It effectively appraises a distribution channel cost.
8. It helps to measure inter-divisional performance.
9. It also helps to collect benchmark costs.
10. It also helps to determine the costs of product and charge the right price.

11. It helps to identify most profitable customers.
12. It helps to understand the impact of new technology on all elements of performance.

3.7 IMPLEMENTATION OF ACTIVITY BASED COSTING SYSTEM

The following steps should be taken to implement the activity based costing system in an organisation:

(i) To obtain support of the top management.
(ii) To prepare project schedule and budget.
(iii) To assemble the ABC Team.
(iv) To provide training to the member of the team.
(v) To gather information, data and accounts.
(vi) To conduct modelling and analysis.
(vii) To select and acquire the package of software.
(viii) To create a software linkage.
(ix) To test the software in order to check whether the system works effectively.
(x) To design reports.
(xi) To design policies and procedures.
(xii) To implement the ABC system.
(xiii) To make follow up on the installation.

3.8 ACTIVITY BASED COSTING IN SERVICE SECTOR

The ABC approach can also be applicable to service sector. The design of ABC system for service organisations involves basically the same systems. The work carried out by the staff and equipments should be arranged into various activities. This can be achieved by a combination of interview and self-analysis by staff and management involved. The output measured may provide the cost driver which can be used to associate the cost with a cost object. This will mean end services will have the cost of activities traced to them. Each activity's output should be traceable to the source of the demand for it. If the object is to cost a service provided to external customer, then tracing the output directly to this object will best meet the aim. However, it should be realised that direct link of this type may not always exist. One activity is providing the service for another service rather than for end service. In such a situation, cross-activity changing system may have to be instituted in order to obtain a cost system which reflect how resources are actually being used.

3.9 ACTIVITY BASED MANAGEMENT

The Activity Based Cost Management is a discipline that focuses on the management activities such as the route to improving the value received by the customer and the profit achieved by providing this value. This discipline also includes cost driver analysis, activity analysis and performance measurement. Activity based management draws on activity based costing as its major source of information. ABC supplies the information and ABM uses this information in various analysis designed to yield continuous improvements.

For continuous improvement, activity based management attempts to use cost driver analysis. The factors that cause activities to be performed need to be identified in order to manage activity costs. Cost driver analysis identifies these causal factors. For example, a cost driver analysis study may determine that slow processing of customer invoices results largely from lack of training of the customer invoice associates. Activity analysis identifies the activities of an organisation and the activity centres that should be used in an ABC system. Activity analysis also identifies value-added and non-value-added activities. The degree to which activities are grouped together into activity centres depends on the costs and benefits of the alternatives. The number of activity centres is likely to change over time as organisational needs for activity information evolve.

The performance analysis involves the identification of appropriate measures to report the performance of activity centres or other organisational units consistent with each unit's goals and objectives. Performance analysis aims to identify the best ways to measure the performance of factors that are important to organisations in order to stimulate continuous improvement in the organisation. Thus, activity based management is a discipline that focuses on efficient and effective management of activities as the route to improve the value received by customers and profits received by providing this value. This discipline of focusing on activities is being effectively used in cost reduction, business process reengineering, benchmarking and performance measurement. ABM brings about a change in viewing at the objective by incorporation of financial perspective, innovation and learning perspective.

3.10 LIMITATIONS OF ACTIVITY BASED COSTING

Activity based costing is based on historical costs. For planning and decision-making, relevant costs are generally used as compared to historical costs. ABC does not make difference between fixed costs and variable costs. For many short-run decisions, it is important to identify variable costs. ABC is only as accurate as the quality of the cost drivers. The distribution and application of costs becomes an arbitrary allocation process when the cost drivers are not associated with the factors that are causing costs. ABC tends to be more expensive than the traditional methods of applying costs to different products. An environmental change must be created for implementation of ABC system. It requires overcoming a variety of individual, organisational and environmental barriers. ABC system does not conform to Generally Accepted Accounting Principles. ABC suggests that some non-product costs be allocated to products whereas certain traditionally designed product cost may not be allocated to products. Finally, ABC system does not promote Total Quality Management and continous improvement. It does not make company a long-term global competitor.

Illustration 3.1: Maruti Ltd. produces three products A, B and C for which the standard costs and quantities per unit are given below:

Product	*A*	*B*	*C*
Quantity produced	10,000	20,000	30,000
Direct material (p.u.) ₹	50	40	30
Direct labour (p.u.) ₹	30	40	50
Labour Hours (p.u.)	3	4	5
Machine Hours (p.u.)	4	4	7
No. of purchase requisitions	1,200	1,800	2,000
No. of setups	240	260	300

The production overheads of the departments are as follows:

Department 1 = ₹ 11,00,000

Department 2 = ₹ 15,00,000

Department 1 is labour-intensive and Department 2 is machine-intensive.

Total Labour Hours in Dept. 1 = 1,83,333 hours

Total Labour Hours in Dept. 2 = 5,00,000 hours

Production overhead split by activity are as follows:

Receiving/Inspecting	₹ 14,00,000
Production Scheduling/Machine Setup	₹ 12,00,000
Total	₹ 26,00,000
Number of batches received/inspected	₹ 5,000
Number of batches for scheduling and setup	₹ 800

Your are required to prepare product cost statement under: (a) Traditional absorption costing system and (b) Activity based costing system.

Solution:

(a) Production Cost Statement (Absorption Costing) (₹)

Product	*A*	*B*	*C*
Direct Material	50	40	30
Direct Labour	30	40	50
Overheads			
Dept. 1 (H × R)	18	24	30
Dept. 2 (H × R)	12	12	21
Total Cost per unit	**110**	**116**	**131**

Absorption Rates are determined as under:

Dept. 1 = ₹ 11,00,000/1,83,333 hours = ₹ 6 per hour

Dept. 2 = ₹ 15,00,000/5,00,000 hours = ₹ 3 per hour

(b) Production Cost under ABC Costing System

Product	*Production cost per unit (₹)*		
	A	*B*	*C*
Direct materials	50	40	30
Direct labour	30	40	50
Overheads:			
Receiving	34	25	19
Production scheduling	36	20	15
Total cost	**150**	**125**	**114**

Absorption Rates are determined as under:

Receiving/Inspecting = ₹ 14,00,000/5,000 = ₹ 280 per requisition

Production scheduling and machine setup = ₹ 12,00,000/800 = ₹ 1,500 per setup

Overheads are allocated as under:

Product	*Requisitions × Cost per requisition/unit*	*Per unit (₹)*
A	(1,200 × 280 ÷ 10,000)	34
B	(1,800 × 280 ÷ 20,000)	25
C	(2,000 × 280 ÷ 30,000)	19
	Setups × Rate ÷ Units	
A	(240 × 1500 ÷ 10,000)	36
B	(260 × 1,500 ÷ 20,000)	20
C	(300 × 1,500 ÷ 30,000)	15

The production cost per unit is different under the different methods of absorption.

Illustration 3.2: Adarsh Motors produces electric motors. The company makes a standard electric-starter motor for a major auto manufacturer and also produces electric motor that are specifically ordered. The company has four essential activities — designing, ordering, machining and marketing, Adarsh Motors incurs the following costs during the particular month:

Particulars	Standard Motors (₹)		Special Order Motors (₹)
Direct materials	30 lakhs		10 lakhs
Direct labour	10 lakhs		2 lakhs
Overheads:			
Indirect labour		35 lakhs	
Depreciation — Building		2 lakhs	
Depreciation — Machine		10 lakhs	
Maintenance		3 lakhs	
Utilities		10 lakhs	
Total		**60 lakhs**	

Traditional cost accounting applies the overhead costs based on single measure of activity. With ABC, activities are chosen and the overhead costs are distributed to cost tools within these activities through resource drivers. The company performs the following activities: designing, ordering, machining and marketing. Each activity has one cost pool. The overhead costs are distributed to the cost pools of the activities using the following resource drivers:

Overheads	*Driver*
Indirect Labour	Labour hours
Depreciation — Building	Area of Building
Depreciation — Machinery	Machine time
Maintenance	Area of Building
Utilities	Amps used

The usage of the resource drivers by activity are as follows:

Particulars	*Designing*	*Ordering*	*Machining*	*Marketing*	*Total*
Labour Hours	1.00	0.20	1.00	1.30	3.50
Sq. ft. area	50,000	30,000	1,00,000	20,000	2,00,000
Machine time	0	0	10,00,000	0	10,00,000
Amps	**2,00,000**	**1,00,000**	**16,00,000**	**1,00,000**	**20,00,000**

The cost driver used for each product are given below:

Cost Driver Usage	*Standard Motors*	*Special Order Motors*
Design Charges	2,250	10,000
No. of Orders	1,500	5,000
Machine Time → Hours	100	52.5
No. of Contracts	2000	5,000

Prepare a Product Cost Statement using: (a) Traditional absorption costing and (b) Activity based costing.

Solution:

(a) Product Cost Statement (Traditional) (₹. lakhs)

Particulars	*Standard Motors*	*Special Order Motors*
Direct materials	30	10
Direct labour	10	2
Overheads	50	10
Total	**90**	**22**

Overheads can be absorbed on direct labour

$$\therefore \frac{\text{Overheads}}{\text{Direct Labour}} \times 100$$

$$= \frac{60}{12} \times 100 = 500\%$$

Overheads for Standard Motors = 500% of 10 lakhs

= ₹ 50 lakhs

Overheads for Special Order Motors = 500% of Direct labour of ₹ 2

= ₹ 10 lakhs

(b) Production Cost using ABC

Particulars	*Standard Motors (₹ lakhs)*	*Special Order Motors (₹ lakhs)*
Direct Labour	30	10
Direct Materials	10	2
Overheads	27	33
Total	**67**	**45**

Working:

(i) Calculation of Resource Driver Application

Overheads	*Driver*	*Cost ₹*	*Usage*	*Rate*
Indirect labour	Hours	35 L	3.5 L	₹ 10 per Hour
Depreciation — B	Area	2 L	2 L	₹ 1 per Sq. ft.
Depreciation — M	Time	10 L	50,000	₹ 20 per Hour
Maintenance	Area	3 L	2 L	₹ 1.5 per Sq. ft.
Utilities	Amps	10 L	20 L	₹ 0.50 per Amp

(ii) Allocation of Overhead Costs (₹ lakhs)

Particulars	*Designing*	*Ordering*	*Machining*	*Marketing*	*Total*
Indirect labour	10	2	10	13	35
Depreciation — B	0.50	0.30	1	0.20	2
Depreciation — M	-	-	10	-	10
Maintenance	0.75	0.45	1.50	0.30	3
Utilities	1.0	0.50	8.0	0.50	10
Total	**12.25**	**3.25**	**30.50**	**14.0**	**60**

(iii) Allocation of Overheads to the Products

Activity	*Basis*	*Std. Motors (₹ lakhs)*	*Special Order Motors (₹ lakhs)*
Designing	Charges	2.25	10.00
Ordering	Orders	0.75	2.50
Machining	Hours	20.00	10.50
Marketing	Contacts	4.00	10.00
Total		**27.00**	**33.00**

(iv) Application Rates

$$\text{Designing} = \frac{12{,}25{,}000}{12{,}250} = ₹\ 100 \text{ per charge}$$

$$\text{Ordering} = \frac{3{,}25{,}000}{6{,}500} = ₹\ 50 \text{ per order}$$

$$\text{Machining} = \frac{3{,}05{,}000}{152.5} = ₹\ 2{,}000 \text{ per hour}$$

$$\text{Marketing} = \frac{14,00,000}{7,000} = ₹\ 200 \text{ per contract}$$

Illustration 3.3: Ideal Ltd. produces a large number of products including X and Y. X is a complex produce of which 1,000 units are made and sold in each period. Y is a simple product of which 25,000 units are made and sold in each period. Product X requires one direct labour hour to produce while Product Y requires 0.6 hours to produce. The company employs 12 support staff and a direct labour force that works 4,00,000 hours per period. Overhead costs are ₹ 5,00,000 per period.

The support staff are engaged in three activities as follows:

Number of Staff	*Activities*	*Consignments*
6	Receiving components	25,000
3	Receiving raw materials	10,000
3	Disbursing	5,000 runs

Product X requires 200 component consignments, 50 raw material consignments and 10 production runs per period. Product Y requires 100 component consignments, 8 raw material consignments and 5 production runs per period.

You are required to prepare:

(a) a statement of overhead cost on the basis of traditional system of overhead absorption using direct labour hours and

(b) to identify appropriate cost drivers and calculate overhead cost of X and Y using an Activity Based Costing system.

Solution:

(a) Traditional Method

$$\text{Overhead Absorption Rate} = \frac{\text{Overhead}}{\text{Direct labour hours}}$$

$$= ₹\ \frac{5,00,000}{400,000}$$

$$= ₹\ 1.25 \text{ per hour}$$

Overhead of products:

X = 1 × 1.25 = ₹ 1.25 per unit

Y = 0.6 × 1.25 = ₹ 0.75 per unit

(b) Activity Based Costing

The appropriate cost drives will be:

— Receiving components,

— Receiving raw materials,

— Disbursing kits.

Related overhead costs to these drivers using the number of indirect staff engaged in each activity will be as follows:

(i) Receiving Components = $\frac{2,50,000}{25,000}$ = ₹ 10 per receipt

(ii) Receiving Raw Materials = $\frac{12,500}{10,000}$ = ₹ 12.50 per receipt

(iii) Disbursing Kits = $\frac{1,25,000}{5,000}$ = ₹ 25 per issue

∴ The Overhead Cost of Product (₹)

	Total	*Per unit*
X = (200 × 10 + 50 × 12.50 + 10 × 25)	2,875	2.87
Y = (100 × 10 + 8 × 12.50 + 5 × 25)	1,225	0.05

Illustration 3.4: Philips Ltd. is noted for its full line of quality lamps. The company operates one of its plant in Loni, Pune. The plant produces two types of lamps — classical and modern. The President of the company recently decided to change from a unit based traditional costing system to an activity based costing system. Before making the change countrywide, the President wanted to assess the effect on the product costs of Loni plant. This plant was chosen because it produces only two types of lamps. To assess the effect of the change, the following data have been gathered:

Lamp	*Quantity*	*Prime Costs*	*Machine Hours*	*Material Moves*	*Setups*
Classical	4,00,000	8,00,000	1,00,000	2,00,000	100
Modern	1,00,000	1,50,000	25,000	1,00,000	50
Total cost		**9,50,000**	***5,00,000**	**8,50,000**	**6,50,000**

* Cost of Operating Production Equipments

Under the current system, the cost of operating equipment materials handling and setups are assigned to the lamps on the basis of machine hours. Lamps are produced and moved in batches. You are required to compute:

(a) the unit cost of each lamp using the current unit based approach.

(b) the unit cost of each lamp using an activity based costing approach.

Solution:

(a) Current Unit Based Approach

Total overhead = 5 L + 8.5 L + 6.5 L = 20 L

$$\text{The plantwide rate} = \frac{20,00,000}{1,25,000}$$

$$= ₹\ 16 \text{ per machine hour}$$

The overhead is assigned as follows:

Classical Lamps = 16 × 1,00,000 = ₹ 16,00,000

Modern Lamps = 16 × 25,000 = ₹ 4,00,000

The unit costs for the two products are as follows:

Classical Lamps = ₹ 8 L + 16 L ÷ 4 L = ₹ 6

Modern Lamps = ₹ 1,50,000 + 4,00,000 ÷ 1,00,000 = ₹ 5.50

(b) Activity Based Costing

Calculation of rates for each pool

$$\text{Machining Pool} = \frac{5,00,000}{1,25,000} = ₹\ 4$$

Batch Pool = Materials Handling	₹ 8,50,000
Setups	₹ 6,50,000
Total	₹ 15,00,000
No. of setups	150

$$\therefore \text{Rate per setup} = \frac{1,50,000}{150} = ₹\ 10,000$$

Allocation of overheads:

Classical Lamps = 4 × 1,00,000 = 4,00,000

+ 10,000 × 100 = 10,00,000

14,00,000

Modern Lamps $= 4 \times 25{,}000 \quad = 1{,}00{,}000$

$+ 10{,}000 \times 50 \quad = 5{,}00{,}000$

6,00,000

Calculations of Unit Costs

Particulars	*Classical (₹)*	*Modern (₹)*
Prime cost	8,00,000	1,50,000
Overhead cost	14,00,000	6,00,000
Total	**22,00,000**	**7,50,000**
Unit produced	4,00,000	1,00,000
Cost of per unit	5.50	7.50

Illustration 3.5: A company produces three products, the standard costs of which are given below:

	A (₹)	*B (₹)*	*C (₹)*
Direct Material	50	40	30
Direct Labour	30	40	50
Production Overhead	30	40	50
	110	**120**	**130**
Units produced	10,000	20,000	30,000

The company wishes to introduce ABC system and has identified two major cost pools for production overhead and their association cost drivers. Information on these activities are given below:

Activity Cost Pool	**Cost Driver**	**Cost (₹)**
Receiving/Inspecting	Purchase Requisitions	₹ 14,00,000
Production Scheduling	No. of batches	₹ 12,00,000

Further relevant information on the three products are given below:

	A	**B**	**C**
No. of Purchase Requisitions	1,200	1,800	2,000
No. of Setups	240	260	300

You are required to calculate the activity based production cost of these products.

Solution:

Activity Based Costing (₹)

Particulars	*A*	*B*	*C*
Direct Materials	50	40	30
Direct Labour	30	40	50
Production Overheads:			
(a) Receiving Inspections and Quality Assurance	33.60	25.20	18.66
(b) Production Scheduling/Machine Setups	36.00	19.50	15.00
Total	**149.60**	**124.70**	**113.66**

Workings:

Overheads

Product A = $\frac{280 \times 1{,}200}{10{,}000}$ = ₹ 33.60 $\quad \frac{280 \times 1{,}800}{20{,}000}$ = ₹ 25.20 $\quad \frac{280 \times 2{,}000}{30{,}000}$ = ₹ 18.66

Product B = $\frac{1{,}500 \times 240}{10{,}000}$ = ₹ 36 $\quad \frac{1{,}500 \times 260}{20{,}000}$ = ₹ 19.50 $\quad \frac{1{,}500 \times 300}{30{,}000}$ = ₹ 15

Illustration 3.6: Modern Ltd. produces four products A, B, C and D using the same plant and proceses. The following information relates to a production period:

Product	*Volume*	*Material Cost p.u. (₹)*	*Direct Labour p.u. (₹)*	*Machine Time p.u. hours (₹)*	*Labour Cost per unit (₹)*
A	500	5	0.5	0.25	3
B	5,000	5	0.5	0.25	3
C	600	16	2.0	1.00	12
D	7,000	17	1.5	1.50	9

Total production overhead recorded by the cost accounting system is analysed under the following headings:

Factory overhead applicable to machine-oriented activity is ₹ 37,424 Setup costs are ₹ 4,355. The cost of ordering materials is ₹ 1,920. Handling materials ₹ 7,580. Administration for spare parts ₹ 8,600. These overhead costs are absorbed by products or a machine hour rate of ₹ 4.80 per hour, giving an overhead cost per product of:

A = ₹ 1.20, B = ₹ 1.20, C = ₹ 4.80 and D = ₹ 7.20.

However, investigation into production overhead activities for the period reveals the following details:

Products	*No. of Setups*	*No. of Material orders*	*No. of Times Material was Handled*	*No. of Spare Parts*
A	1	1	2	2
B	6	4	10	5
C	2	1	3	1
D	8	4	12	4

You are required to compute an overhead cost per product using activity based costing.

Solution:

(i) Calculation of Cost per unit under A & B

Product	*A(₹)*	*B(₹)*	*C(₹)*	*D(₹)*
Activities:	-	-	-	-
Setups	256	1,536	512	2,048
Orders	192	768	192	768
Handling	562	2,810	843	3,372
Spare parts	1,434	3,585	717	2,868
Machine time	375	3,750	1,800	31,500
Total	**2,819**	**12,449**	**4,064**	**40,556**
No. of units	500	5,000	600	7,000
Cost per unit	5.64	2.49	6.77	5.79

Working:

(i) Cost per setup $= \dfrac{4{,}335}{1+6+2+8} = \dfrac{4{,}335}{17} =$ ₹ 256

(ii) Cost per order $= \dfrac{1{,}920}{1+4+1+4} = \dfrac{1{,}920}{10} =$ ₹ 192

(iii) Cost per handling materials $= \dfrac{7{,}580}{2+10+3+12} = \dfrac{7{,}580}{27} =$ ₹ 281

(iv) Cost per spare part $= \dfrac{8{,}600}{2+5+1+4} = \dfrac{8{,}600}{12} =$ ₹ 717

(v) Cost per machine hour $= \dfrac{37{,}424}{12{,}475} =$ ₹ 3 per hour

(vi) Setup cost = A = 1 × 256 = ₹ 256

B = 6 × 256 = ₹ 1,536

C = 2 × 256 = ₹ 512

D = 8 × 256 = ₹ 2,048

Illustration 3.7: Ganesh Hospital has three materials-related activities: ordering materials, inspecting and counting incoming shipments and moving the materials to the hospital pharmacy or stores. Cost and driver data for these three secondary activities related to materials are given below:

Activity	*Cost ₹*	*Driver*	*Activity rates ₹*
Purchasing materials	1,00,000	Purchase orders	20
Inspection and counting	60,000	Hours	10
Moving materials	50,000	Number of moves	6

The bill of activities provides the following information concerning consumption of the secondary activities of Amoxicillin:

Number of purchase orders	100
Inspection hours	20
Number of moves	100

Find out the secondary activity cost per bill assuming that 1,000 bottles of Amoxicillin, each contains 10 tablets.

Solution:

Secondary Activity Cost (₹)

Purchasing Materials	100 × 20	2,000
Inspecting and counting	20 × 10	200
Moving materials	100 × 6	600
Total	—	**2,800**

$$\therefore \text{Cost per bill} = \frac{2,800}{10,000} = ₹\ 0.28$$

Illustration 3.8: Himalaya Publishing House prepares two versions of books. One is paperback and the other is hand-sewn and leather bound. Management is considering publishing only the higher quality books. The firm assigns its ₹ 50,000 of overhead to the two types of books. The overhead is composed of ₹ 20,000 of utilities and ₹ 30,000 of quality control inspector's salaries. Additional data are given below:

Particulars	*Paperback* (₹)	*Leather Bound* (₹)
Revenues	1,60,000	1,40,000
Direct Materials	80,000	40,000
Direct Labour	45,000	20,000
Production Units	50,000	35,000
Machine Hours	4,250	750
Inspections	250	1,250

You are required to:

(a) Compute the overhead costs that should be allocated to each type of book using cost drivers appropriate for each type of overhead cost.

(b) The firm has used machine hours to allocate overhead in the past.

(c) Should the firm stop producing the paperback book?

Solution:

(a) Overhead Allocation as per ABC System

Particulars	*Paperback*	*Leather Bound*	*Total*
Machine hours	4,250	750	5,000
Rate per hour	4	4	4
Unit cost	17,000	3,000	20,000
Number of Inspections	250	1,250	1,500
Rate per Inspection	20	20	20
Cost	5,000	25,000	30,000
Total traceable overhead	**22,000**	**28,000**	**50,000**

Machine Hour Rate = 20,000/5,000 = 4 per Machine hour

Rate per Inspection = 30,000/1,500 = ₹ 20 per inspection

Statement of Income using ABC System

Particulars	*Paperback*	*Leather Bound*
Revenues	1,60,000	1,40,000
Less: Costs		
Materials	80,000	40,000
Labour	45,000	20,000
Overheads	22,000	28,000
	1,47,000	88,000
Profit	**13,000**	**52,000**

(b) Overhead Allocation as per Traditional Method

		(₹)
Machine Hour Rate = 50,000/5,000	=	10
Overhead of Paperback = 10 × 4,250	=	42,500
Overhead of Leather Bound = 10 × 750	=	7,500
Total		50,000

Statement of Income using Traditional Method

Particulars	*Paperback* (₹)	*Leather Bound* (₹)
Revenue	1,60,000	1,40,000
Less: Costs		
Materials	80,000	40,000
Labour	45,000	20,000
Overheads	42,500	7,500
	1,67,500	67,500
Profit	–7,500	72,500

Using Activity based costing system, both the books are profitable, while using traditional absorption costing, paperback book generates loss of ₹ 7,500. Hence, the management should continue producing paperback books but it should use ABC for allocation of overhead costs.

Illustration 3.9: Tips Ltd. assembles two products from bought out in components A and B. The details of manufacture are as follows:

Particulars	*A*	*B*
Output in units	1,000	1,500
Component numbers	80	40
Component cost (₹)	45	36
Number of Production runs	200	50
Machine Hours per 100 units	2.6	5.3
Items packed in cartoons of	10 units	50 units
Overhead Costs:		
Compound purchasing and handling	₹ 14,000	
Production control	₹ 18,000	
Machine setup costs	₹ 25,000	
Machine running costs	₹ 64,000	
Packing	₹ 30,000	

You are required to calculate:

(a) The overhead recovery rates using ABC method.

(b) Cost of production of the two components.

Solution:

(a) Calculation of overhead recovery rates

(i) Component Purchasing and Handling $= \frac{\text{Purchase cost}}{\text{Component numbers}}$

$$= \frac{14{,}000}{(1000 \times 80 + 1{,}500 \times 40)}$$

$$= \frac{14{,}000}{80{,}000 + 60{,}000} = \frac{14{,}000}{1{,}40{,}000} = ₹\ 0.10$$

(ii) Production control costs $= \frac{\text{Production control overhead}}{\text{Number of production runs}}$

$$= \frac{18{,}000}{200 + 50}$$

= ₹ 72 per production run

(iii) Machine setup cost $= \frac{\text{Machine setup cost}}{\text{No. of production runs}}$

$$= \frac{25{,}000}{200 + 50}$$

$$= \frac{25{,}000}{250}$$

= ₹ 100 per production run

(iv) Machine running costs $= \dfrac{\text{Machine running costs}}{\text{Machine hours}}$

$$= \frac{64{,}000}{(2.6 \times 100 + 5.3 \times 150)}$$

$$= \frac{64{,}000}{1{,}055} = ₹\ 60.66$$

(v) Packing cost $= \dfrac{\text{Packing cost}}{\text{No. of cartoons packed}}$

$$= \frac{₹\ 30{,}000}{100 + 30}$$

$$= \frac{30{,}000}{130} = ₹\ 231$$

(b) Statement of cost of production

Particulars	*A*	*B*
Direct materials	45	36
Purchasing and handling	8	4
Production control	14.4	2.40
Machine setup	20.0	3.33
Machine running	1.58	3.21
Packing	23.10	4.62
Total	**112.08**	**53.56**

Working:

1. **Purchasing and Handling:**

   A – 80 components @ ₹ 0.10 = ₹ 8

   B – 40 components @ ₹ 0.10 = ₹ 4

2. **Production Control:**

   Number of units made in one production run

$$= \frac{\text{Total output}}{\text{No. of production runs}}$$

$$A = \frac{1{,}000}{200} = 5$$

$$B = \frac{1{,}500}{50} = 30$$

$$\therefore \text{Cost per item} = A = \frac{72}{5} = ₹\ 14.4$$

$$B = \frac{72}{30} = ₹\ 2.40$$

3. Machine setups:

Number of units made in one production run

A 5 units, B – 30 units

Cost per item:

$$A = \frac{100}{5} = ₹\ 20$$

$$B = \frac{100}{30} = ₹\ 3.33$$

4. Machine Running Cost per Item:

$$A = \frac{2.6}{100} \times 60.66 = ₹\ 1.58$$

$$B = \frac{5.3}{100} \times 60.66 = ₹\ 3.21$$

5. Packing Cost:

A = 231 ÷ 10 = ₹ 23.10

B = 231 ÷ 50 = ₹ 4.62

Illustration 3.10: Shree Ltd. manufactures two products A and B. The Product A is a low-volume item and its sales are only 5,000 units per annum. The Product B is a high-volume item and its sales are 20,000 units per annum. Both products require two direct labour hours for completion. The company works 50,000 direct labour hours each year as given below:

Product A – 5,000 units @ 2 hours each	= 10,000 hours
Product B – 20,000 units @ 2 hours each	= 40,000 hours
Total	50,000 hours

Detailed costs for materials and labour for each product (per unit) are given below:

	A	B
Direct Materials (₹)	25	15
Direct Labour (at ₹ per hour)	10	10

The company's total manufacturing overhead costs are ₹ 75,000 per annum.

The company has analysed its operations and has determined that five activities act as cost drivers in the incurrence of overhead costs. Data relating to the five activities are given below:

		Number of events or transactions		
Activity	*Traceable costs* (₹)	*Total*	*Product A*	*Product B*
Machine Setups	2,30,000	5,000	3,000	2,000
Quality Inspection	1,60,000	8,000	5,000	3,000
Production Orders	81,000	600	200	400
Machine Hours Worked	3,14,000	40,000	12,000	28,000
Material Receipts	90,000	750	150	600
Total	**8,75,000**			

You are required to compute per unit cost for each product using:

(a) Direct Labour Hour Rate method for absorption of overhead costs.

(b) Activity Based Costing Technique for absorption of overhead costs.

Solution:

(a) Computation of Product Cost using Direct Labour Hour Rate Method

$$\text{D.L.H.R.} = \frac{\text{Manufacturing overhead costs}}{\text{Direct labour hours}}$$

$$= \frac{8,75,000}{50,000}$$

= ₹ 17.50 per hour

Total Manufacturing Costs

	Product	
	A (₹)	*B (₹)*
Direct Materials	25	15
Direct Labour	10	10
Manufacturing Overheads	35	35
Total	**70**	**60**

(b) Computation of Product Cost using ABC Method

(i) Overhead Rates by Activity

Activity	*Traceable Cost*	*Number of Transactions*	*Rate per Transaction*
Machine Setups	2,30,000	5,000	46 per setup
Quality Inspections	1,60,000	8,000	20 per inspection
Production Orders	81,000	600	135 per order
Machine Hours Worked	3,14,000	40,000	7.85 per hour
Material Receipts	90,000	750	120 per Receipt

(ii) Overhead Cost per Unit of Product

Particulars	*Product A*		*Product B*	
	Event	₹	*Event*	₹
Machine Setups	3,000	1,38,000	2,000	92,000
Quality Inspections	5,000	1,00,000	3,000	60,000
Production Orders	200	27,000	400	54,000
Machine Hours Worked	12,000	94,200	28,000	2,19,800
Material Receipts	150	18,000	600	72,000
Total Overhead Costs		3,77,200		4,97,800
No. of Units Produced		5000		20,000
Overhead Cost per unit		75.44		24.89

(iii) Computation of Total Cost of Products

	A	*B*
Direct Materials	25	15
Direct Labour	10	10
Manufacturing Overheads	75.44	24.89
Total	**110.44**	**49.89**

3.12 TARGET COSTING

Target costing is a device to continuously control costs and manage profits over a product's life cycle. It is a part of comprehensive strategic profit planning and management system. When a decision to enter a new market is being considered, the prices of the competitors of their products are an important factor in making this decision. Target cost is the estimated long-term cost of the product which enables a company to enter or to remain successfully in the competitive market. The target cost concept has an external market focus as its starting point. Under target costing, in the product concept stage, selling price and required profit are set after consideration of the medium term profit plans, which links the operational to the long-term strategic plans.

Target cost is, "a market based cost that is calculated using a sales price necessary to capture a predetermined market share." In competitive industries, a unit sales price would be established independent of the initial product cost. If the target cost is below the initial forecast of product cost, the company drives the unit cost down over a designed period to compete.

Target Cost = Sales Price (for the target market share) – Desired Profit

Japanese cost management is known to be guided by the concept of target cost. Management decides, before the product is designed, what a product should cost, based on marketing (rather than manufacturing) factors. The target costing philosophy leads to a market-driven approach to accounting. Target costs are conceptually different from standard costs. Standard costs are predetermined costs calibrated from an internal analysis by industrial engineers. Target costs are based on external analysis of markets and competitors. Several Japanese firms are known to compute two separate variances, one comparing actual costs with target cost and another comparing actual costs with standard costs.

Under Target Costing, in the product concept stage, selling price and required profit are set after consideration of the medium term profit plans, which links the operational to the long-term strategic plans. Since market price in most cases has to be accepted by a producer for a competitive product, target cost is reduced to the residual or allowable sum.

In fact, target costing leads to total cost control as about 90% of costs are determined at the product's design stage. If it is thought that the product cannot generate the required profit, it will not be produced as such and aspects of the product would be redesigned until the target is met. Value engineering and value analysis may be used to identify innovative and cost-effective product features in the planning and concept stages. Throughout the product's life, target costing continues to be used to control costs. Thus, all costs including both variable and fixed costs/overheads are expected to reduce on a regular basis. Target Profit is a commitment agreed to by all the people in a firm who have any part to play in achieving it. The only evidence on the use of Target costing at the moment comes from Japan but in time the idea will doubtless spread in the same way the JIT system became popular.

While introducing a new product, a company can test the market to determine the price it can charge in order to be competitive with products of similar function and quality already in the market. A target cost is the maximum manufactured cost for a product. It is arrived at by subtracting its expected market price from the required margin on sales.

Target costing is a market-driven design methodology. It estimates the cost for a product and then designs the product to meet the cost. It is used to encourage the various departments involved in design and production to find less expensive ways of achieving similar or better product features and quality.

Target costing is a cost management tool which reduces a product's cost over its entire life cycle. Target costing includes actions management takes to establish reasonable target costs, develop methods for achieving those targets and develop means by which to test the cost-effectiveness of different cost-cutting scenarios.

3.12.1 Planning Phase

Under target costing, a product's design begins at the opposite end. The company has to establish a price at which the product can be competitive and then assign a team to develop cost scenario and search for ways to design and manufacture the product to meet the cost constraints. The following steps should be taken in order to establish a reasonable target cost.

(a) Market research should be done to determine several factors. The products of competitors should be analysed with regard to price, quality, service and support, delivery and technology. After a preliminary test of competitor's product, it is necessary to establish the features consumers value in this type of product and the important features that are lacking.

(b) After preliminary testing, a company should be able to pinpoint a market niche it believes is undersupplied and in which it believes it might have some competitive advantage. Thereafter, a company can set a target cost close to competitor's products of similar functions and value. The target cost is bound to change in the development and design stages. However, the new target costs should only be allowed to decrease, unless the company can provide added features that add value to the product.

3.12.2 Development Phase

The company should find the ways to attain the target cost. First, in-depth study of the most competitive product on the market should be conducted. This study will show materials used and features provided and it will give an indication of the manufacturing process needed to complete the product. Once a better understanding of the design has been achieved, the company can target the costs against this best design. But its competition will probably be engaged in similar analysis and will further improve its product towards best design. It is necessary while performing competitive cost analysis and trying to establish the competitor's cost structure that adequate attention be paid to the competitive advantages of the competitor, such as technology, location and vertical integration.

The company should develop estimates for the internal cost structure of its own products. This should be done most effectively by analysing internal costs of similar products already being produced by the company. Focusing on cost drivers can help reduce waste, improve quality, minimise non-value-added activities and identify ineffective product design. The use of multiple drivers leads both to a better understanding of the inputs and resources required to produce products and a better cost analysis through more detailed cost information.

The product development team should be able to generate cost estimates under different scenarios. The designers, manufacturers, marketers and engineers of the team should conduct a session on brainstorming to generate ideas on how to substantially reduce costs or add features to the product without increasing target costs. In the brainstorming session, the best ideas are integrated into the development of the product.

3.12.3 Production Phase

In this stage, target costing becomes a tool for reducing costs of existing products. The design, manufacturing and engineering groups should develop the optional cost-effective process at the beginning of production. The search for better less expensive products should continue in the framework of continuous improvement. The ABC technique can be useful as a tool for target costing of existing products. Target costing at the activity level makes opportunities for cost reduction highly visible. Target costing is also strongly linked to consumer requirements and tries to identify the features that the consumers want. Target costing also provides incentives to move towards less expensive means as well as production techniques that provide a more even flow of goods. Just-in-time provides an environment where there is better monitoring of costs and product quality as well as access to ideas for continuous improvement and better production strategies.

3.12.4 Benefits of Target Costing

The following are the benefits of target costing:

(i) Target costing helps to reduce the development cycle of a product. Cost can be targeted at the time when the product is designed.

(ii) The process of target costing provides detailed information on the costs involved in producing a new product as well as a better way of testing different cost scenarios through the use of Activity based costing.

(iii) Target costing is also used to forecast future costs and to provide motivation to meet future cost goals.

(iv) Target costing is used to control costs before the company even incurs any production costs which save a great deal of time and money.

(v) The internal costing model using Activity Based Costing can provide an excellent understanding of the dynamics of production costs and can help to eliminate waste, reduce non-value-added activities, improve quality, simplify the process and attack the root causes of costs.

(vi) Target costing also helps to increase the profitability of a new product through promoting cost reduction while improving the quality.

There are, however, certain limitations of target costing. It is difficult to use with complex products that require many sub-assemblies such as automobiles. Tracking costs becomes too complicated and tedious and cost analysis must be performed at various levels.

3.13 EXERCISES

1. Explain the concept of Activity Based Costing.
2. What are the purposes of Activity Based Costing?
3. How are the overheads allocated to products or services under ABC system?
4. Explain the difference between Activity Based Costing and Conventional Costing.
5. What is Cost Driver Analysis? Indicate the Activity Drivers in respect of the following:
   (a) Accounting costs
   (b) Manufacturing cost
   (c) Human Resource costs
   (d) Marketing and Sales costs
6. Explain the concept of cost allocation, cost apportionment and absorption. Explain briefly the alternative approach of activity based costing in order to ascertain total product costs.
7. "Attributing direct costs and absorbing overhead costs to the product/service through an activity based costing approach will result in a better understanding of the true cost of the final output." Explain.
8. What is target costing? What are its benefits?
9. Write short notes on:
   (a) Cost Drivers
   (b) Activity Cost Pool
   (c) Value-added Activities
   (d) Activity Based Management
   (e) Target Cost
10. Arvind Ltd. produces two products A and B. Both are produced on the same equipment and use similar processes. The product differ by volume. Product A is high-volume product and Product B is low-volume product. The details of product inputs and cost activities are as follows:

	Product A	*Product B*
Machine Hours per unit	2	2
Direct Labour Hours per unit	4	4
Annual Output (units)	1,000	10,000
Total Machine Hours	2,000	20,000

Total Direct Labour Hours	4,000	40,000
Number of Purchase Orders	80	160
Number of Setups	40	60

The cost centre costs are ₹ 4,40,000 but have been further analysed as follows:

	₹
Volume related	1,10,000
Purchasing related	1,20,000
Setup related	2,10,000

You are required to calculate product costs under (a) traditional costing system and (b) ABC system.

(**Ans.** Product A = ₹ 40, ₹ 134, Product B = ₹ 40, ₹ 30.60)

11. Timken Ltd. makes three products using the same production methods and equipments for each. The details of the three products are given below:

Product	***Hours per unit***		***Materials per unit (₹)***	***Volume units***
	Labour Hours	***Machine Hours***		
X	0.5	1.5	20	750
Y	1.5	1.0	12	1250
Z	1.0	3.0	25	7000

Direct labour costs ₹ 6 per hour and production overheads are absorbed on a machine labour hour basis. The cost for the period is ₹ 28 per machine hour. The further analysis shows that the total of production overheads can be divided as follows:

	%
Cost relating to setups	35
Cost relating to machinery	20
Cost relating to materials handing	15
Cost relating to inspection	30
Total production overhead	100

The following activity volumes are associated with the product line for the periods as a whole. Total activities for the period:

Product	***No. of setups***	***No. of movements of materials***	***No. of inspections***
X	75	12	150
Y	115	21	180
Z	480	87	670
	670	**120**	**1000**

You are required to calculate the cost per unit for each product using: (a) conventional method and (b) ABC method.

(**Ans.** X = ₹ 65, ₹ 118, Y = ₹ 49, ₹ 100, and Z = ₹ 115, ₹ 100)

12. Ravi Ltd. provides you with the following data:

Standard Rate – ₹ 10 per direct labour hour

Standard Allowance – 2 direct labour hour per unit

Actual spent ₹ 22,000

Actual direct labour hours 2,400

The data related to ABC system are as under:

Standard Cost Driver Rates:	₹ 100 per setup
	₹ 5 per inspection
	₹ 4 per materials move
Actual Cost Driver:	110 setups
	1,050 inspections
	1,200 material moves
Actual Spent:	₹ 11,500 on setup
	₹ 5,800 on quality control
	₹ 4,700 on materials handling

You are required to calculate overhead variance based on (a) conventional costing system and (b) ABC system.

(**Ans.** Setup related variance	₹ 500(A)
Quality control related variance	₹ 550(A)
Materials handling related variance	₹ 100 (F)

13. Trupti Ltd. has the following activities and associated cost behaviours:

Activities	**Cost Behaviour**
Labour	₹ 10 per direct labour hour
Setups	Variable ₹ 100 per setup
	Fixed ₹ 30,000 per setup
	Step = 10 setups

Receiving Step – fixed ₹ 40,000 per step ₹

Step = 2,000 hours

Activities with step cost behaviour are being fully utilised by existing products. Any new product demands will increase resource spending on these activities. Two designs are being considered for a new product – Design I and II. The following information is provided about each design (1000 units of the product will be produced).

Cost Driver	*Design I*	*Design II*
Direct Labour Hours	3,000	2,000
Number of Setups	10	20
Receiving Hours	2,000	4,000

The company has recently developed a cost equation for manufacturing @ 175 using direct labour hours as the driver. The equation has $R^2 = 0.60$ and is given below:

Y = ₹ 1,50,000 + ₹ 20X.

You are required to compute the cost of each design using Activity based costing.

(**Ans.** ₹ 1,62,000)

14. ABC Ltd. manufactures four products A, B, C and D using the same plant and processes. The following information relates to a particular period:

Product	*Volwume*	*Material Cost per unit (₹)*	*Direct Labour Per unit*	*Machine Time per unit*	*Labour Cost per unit*
A	500	5	0.5 Hours	0.25 Hours	3
B	5,000	5	0.5 Hours	0.25 Hours	3
C	600	16	2.0 Hours	1.00 Hours	12
D	7,000	17	1.5 Hours	1.50 Hours	09

Total production overhead recorded by the cost accounting system is analysed under the following headings:

Factory overhead applicable to machine-oriented activity is ₹ 37,424 Setup costs are ₹ 4,355. The cost of ordering materials is ₹ 1,920. Handling materials is ₹ 7,580.

Administration for spare parts is ₹ 8,600. These overhead costs are absorbed by products on a machine hour rate of ₹ 4.80 per hour giving an overhead cost per product of:

A = ₹ 1.20, B = ₹ 1.20, C = ₹ 4.80, D = ₹ 7.20

However, investigation into the production overhead activities for the period reveals the following totals:

Product	*No. of Setups*	*No. of Materials Orders*	*No. of Items Material was Handled*	*No. of Spare Parts*
A	1	1	2	2
B	6	4	10	5
C	2	1	3	1
D	8	4	12	4

You are required to compute cost per unit using activity based costing tracing overheads to production units by means of cost driver.

15. The nursing supervisor of cardiology unit of Goodhealth Hospitals, Mumbai, disclosed the following information:

Activity	*Supervisors*	*Nurses*
Supervising Nurses	100%	0%
Treating Patients	0	25
Providing Hygienic Care	0	20
Responding to Requests	0	40
Monitoring Patients	0	15

The time spent an each activity is the driver used to assign the labour costs to the activity. If the time spent is 100 per cent, then labour is exclusive to the activity and direct tracing is the cost assignment method. On the other hand, the nursing resource is shared by several activities and driver tracing used for the cost assignment. Assume the general ledger reveals that the supervisor's salary is ₹ 50,000 and that the salaries of the nurses is ₹ 3,00,000. The assignment of resource costs to activities requires that the resource costs is unbundled and reassigned. The unbundled concept for nursing care activities in the cardiology unit are given below:

Cardiology Unit

Chart of Accounts View	(₹)	*ABC View*	(₹)
Supervision	50,000	Supervising Nurses	52,280
Suppliers	40,600	Treating Patients	90,000
Uniforms	8,200	Providing Hygienic Care	76,600
Salaries	3,00,000	Responding to Requests	1,33,200
Computer	1,200	Monitoring Patients	1,27,920
Monitor	80,000		
	4,80,000		**4,80,000**

From the work distribution matrix, the four primary activities using nursing resources are in the proportion of 25%, 20%, 40% and 15% respectively.

The bill of activities of cardiology unit for a particular period is as follows:

Activity	*Activity Driver*	*Normal*	*Intermediate*	*Intensive*	*Total*
Production (Output)	Patient Days	10,000	5,000	3,000	–
Treating Patient	Treatments	5,000	10,000	15,000	30,000
Providing Hygienic Care	Hygienic Hours	5,000	25,000	8,500	16,000
Responding to Requests	Requests	30,000	40,000	10,000	80,000
Monitoring Patients	Monitoring Hours	20,000	60,000	1,20,000	2,00,000

You are required to calculate nursing cost per Patient Day.

(**Ans.** Normal = ₹ 11.59, Intermediate = ₹ 33.20, Intensive = ₹ 66.25)

❑ ❑ ❑

Chapter

Value Chain Analysis and Long-term Cost Management

STRUCTURE:

4.1 Introduction

4.2 Value Analysis

4.3 Value Chain Analysis

4.4 Exploiting Internal Linkages

4.5 Exploiting Supplier Linkages

4.6 Exploiting Customer Linkages

4.7 Value Chain Framework

4.8 Organisational Activities and Cost Drivers

4.9 Operational Activities and Cost Drivers

4.10 Value Chain Analysis and Traditional Cost Management

4.11 The Role of Management Accountant

4.12 Long-term Cost Management

4.13 Exercises

4.1 INTRODUCTION

Strategic cost management involves usage of cost data to develop superior strategies to gain sustainable competitive advantage. The process of strategic cost management encompasses value chain analysis and quality costing. Value chain is the linked set of value-creating activities from the supply of the basic raw material to the ultimate end-use product delivered into the final customer's hands. No individual firm is likely to span the entire value chain. Each firm should be understood in the context of the overall value chain of value-creating activities. The value chain analysis requires an external focus in which the focus is internal to the firm. Value chain analysis is identifying and exploiting internal and external linkages with the objective of strengthening a firm's strategic position. The exploitation of linkages relies on analysing how costs and other non-financial factors vary as different bundles of activities are considered. Again managing organisational and operational cost drivers to create long-term cost reduction outcomes is an important input in the value chain analysis; when the cost leadership is emphasised. The objective is to control cost drivers better than competitors.

4.2 VALUE ANALYSIS

Value analysis is a systematic interdisciplinary examination of factors affecting the cost of a product or service in order to derive means of achieving the specific purpose most economically at the required standard of quality and reliability.

Value analysis is a planned, scientific approach to cost reduction which reviews the material consumption of a product and production design, so that modification or improvement can be made which do not reduce the value of the product to the customer.

Value analysis is a formal system used when shortages of materials forced manufacturers to look for cheaper methods of production. Thus, value analysis embraces the investigation of specifications, design, planning, buying, manufacture, testing, sales and distribution of goods. The important areas for the value analysis includes product design, components, materials and production methods.

The relation between value, cost and function can be expressed as follows:

$$\text{Value} = \frac{\text{Function}}{\text{Cost}}$$

Value analysis may be considered as a method of ensuring worth whereby the value of each product is analysed part by part with the objective of achieving the required function with reduced cost. Therefore, value analysis is a planned, scientific approach to cost reduction which reviews the material consumption of a product and production design etc. so that improvement can be made.

Value of a product can be improved by the following ways:

(i) Improving the function, cost remains the same

(ii) Reducing the cost, function remains the same

(iii) Improving function and reducing costs

(iv) Improving the function at a higher rate with a small increase in cost.

In a pharmaceutical company, medicines in glass bottles were so long exported in wooden cases. A value analysis study was carried out on these packing cases and the result was a recommendation that corrugated fibre board cases were to be used. The idea was implemented and the new fibre board containers were a complete success. Cost saving on these cases alone were 52% and further saving took place towards export freight charges and storage space. Handling containers in the factory was also easier because of the reduced weight of containers.

4.3 VALUE CHAIN ANALYSIS

Value Chain Analysis is identifying and exploiting internal and external linkages with the objective of strengthening a firm's strategic position. The exploitation of linkages relies on analysing how costs and other non-financial factors vary as different bundles of activities are considered. Modern organisations change their structure and processes as and when needed to meet new challenges and take advantage of new opportunities. This includes new approaches to differentiation. Moreover, managing organisational and operational cost drivers to create long-term cost reduction outcomes is an important input in value chain analysis when cost leadership is emphasised. The objective of value chain analysis is to control cost drivers better than competitors, thus creating a competitive advantage.

Value chain is the lined set of value-creating activities from the supply of the basic raw material to the ultimate end-use product delivered into the final consumer's hands. No individual firm is likely to span the entire value chain. Each firm should be understood in the context of the overall value chain of value-creating activities. Michael Porter has already pointed out that a business unit can develop competitive advantage based on cost or on product differentiation or on both.

The primary focus of the low cost strategy is to achieve through economics of scale of production, learning curve effect, tight cost control, cost minimisation in R & D, service sales force or administration.

The differentiation strategy consists in differentiating the product by creating something perceived as unique. Product differentiation can be achieved through brand loyalty, superior customer service, dealer network, product design and features. Whether a firm can develop and sustain differentiation depends on how well the firm manages its value chain relative to the value chain of its competitors. Value chain analysis is essential to determine exactly wherein the chain customer value can be enhanced or costs are lowered.

A firm is only a part of the larger set of activities in the value delivery system. Thus, no single firm spans the entire value chain in which it operates. The value chain concept highlights four areas which can improve profits. These areas are as follows:

(i) Linkages with suppliers

(ii) Linkage with customers

(iii) Process linkages with value chain of a business unit

(iv) Linkages across business unit value chain within the firm.

4.4 EXPLOITING INTERNAL LINKAGES

Sound strategic cost management mandates the consideration of internal value chain in which a firm participates. Activities before and after production should be identified and their linkages should be recognised and exploited. Exploiting internal linkages means that relationship between activities are assessed and used to reduce costs and increase value. The internal value chain activities of an organisation are shown in the following Exhibit.

Exhibit 4.1: Internal Value Chain Activities of Organisation

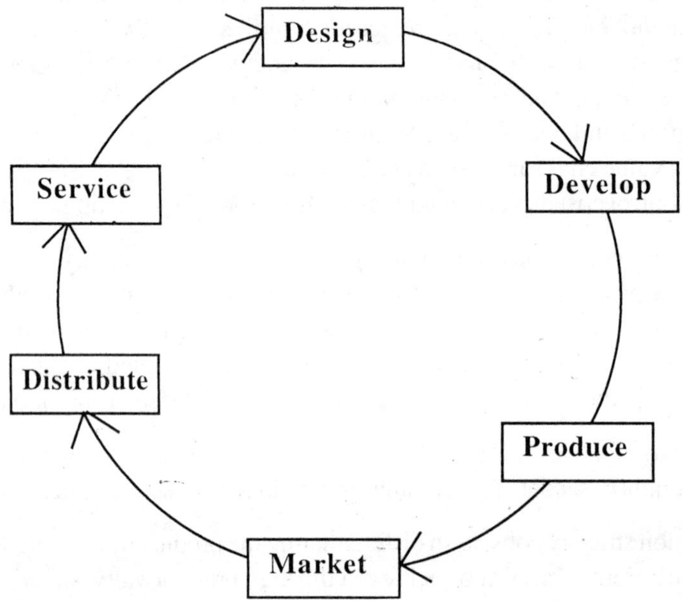

As shown in the above Exhibit, product design and development activities occur before production and are linked to production activities. The way the product is designed affects the costs of production. Knowledge of cost drivers is required to know how the production costs are affected. Thus, knowing the cost drivers of activities is crucial for understanding and exploiting linkages. If design engineers know that the number of parts is a cost driver for various production activities, then designing the product so that it has fewer parts would reduce the cost of production. For example, material usage, direct labour usage, assembly, inspection, materials handling and purchasing where costs could be affected by number of parts. Japanese manufacturers between 1977 and 1984, decreased the number of parts in VCRs by 50 per cent, enabling them to reduce prices nearly about 70%.

The design activity is also linked to the service activity in the firm's value chain. There is less likelihood of product failure by producing a product with fewer parts and thus, less cost associated with warranty agreements as an important customer service. Moreover, the cost of repairing products under warranty should also decrease because fewer parts usually means simple repair procedures.

Illustration 4.1: Sun Pharma Ltd. produces a variety of high-tech medical products. One of the products has 20 parts. Design engineers have been told that the number of parts is a significant cost driver and that reducing the number of parts will reduce the demand for various activities downstream in the value chain. Based on this point, design engineering has produced a new configuration for the products that requires only eight parts. Management wants to know the cost reduction produced by the new design. They also plan on reducing the price per unit by the per unit savings. Currently 10,000 units of products are produced. The effect of the new design on the demand for four activities is given below:

Activities	*Activity Driver*	*Activity Capacity*	*Current Activity Demand*	*Expected Activity Demand*
Material usage	No. of parts	2,00,000	2,00,000	80,000
Assembling parts	Direct labour hours	10,000	10,000	5,000
Purchasing parts	No. of orders	15,000	12,500	6,500
Warranty repair	No. of defective products	1,000	800	500

The following additional activity cost data are provided:

(i) Material usage – ₹ 3 per part used but no fixed activity cost.

(ii) Assembly – ₹ 12 per direct labour hour but no fixed activity cost.

(iii) Purchasing – Three clerks each earning ₹ 30,000 per annum and each clerk is capable of processing 5,000 purchase orders. Variable activity costs are ₹ 0.50 per purchase order processed for forms and postage.

(iv) Warranty – Two repair agents, each paid a salary of ₹ 28,000 per annum and each repair agent is capable of repairing 500 units per year. Variable activity costs are ₹ 20 per product repaired.

Using the information and cost data, you are required to calculate the potential savings produced by the new design.

Solution:

Calculation of Potential Savings:

Material Usage [3 × (2,00,000 – 80,000)]	₹ 3,60,000
Labour Usage [12 × (10,000 – 5,000)]	₹ 60,000
Purchasing [30,000 + 0.50 (12,500 – 6,500)]	₹ 33,000
Warranty Repairs [28,000 + 20 (800 – 500)]	₹ 34,000
Total	₹ 4,87,000
Units Produced	₹ 10,000

$$\text{Savings per unit} = \frac{4,87,000}{10,000} = ₹\ 48.70$$

Cost behaviour of individual activities is vital for assessing the impact of the new design. Knowing the cost of the different design strategies is made possible by assessing the linkages of activities and the effects of changes in demand for the activities. The resource usage model plays a key role in this analysis. The activity based costing model and knowledge of activity cost behaviour are powerful and integral components of Strategic Cost Management.

4.5 EXPLOITING SUPPLIER LINKAGES

Each firm has its own value chain in the organisation. Each firm also belongs to a broader value chain, i.e., the industrial value chain. For example, the value chain for the petroleum industry is shown in the following way:

Exhibit. 4.2: Value Chain for the Petroleum Industry

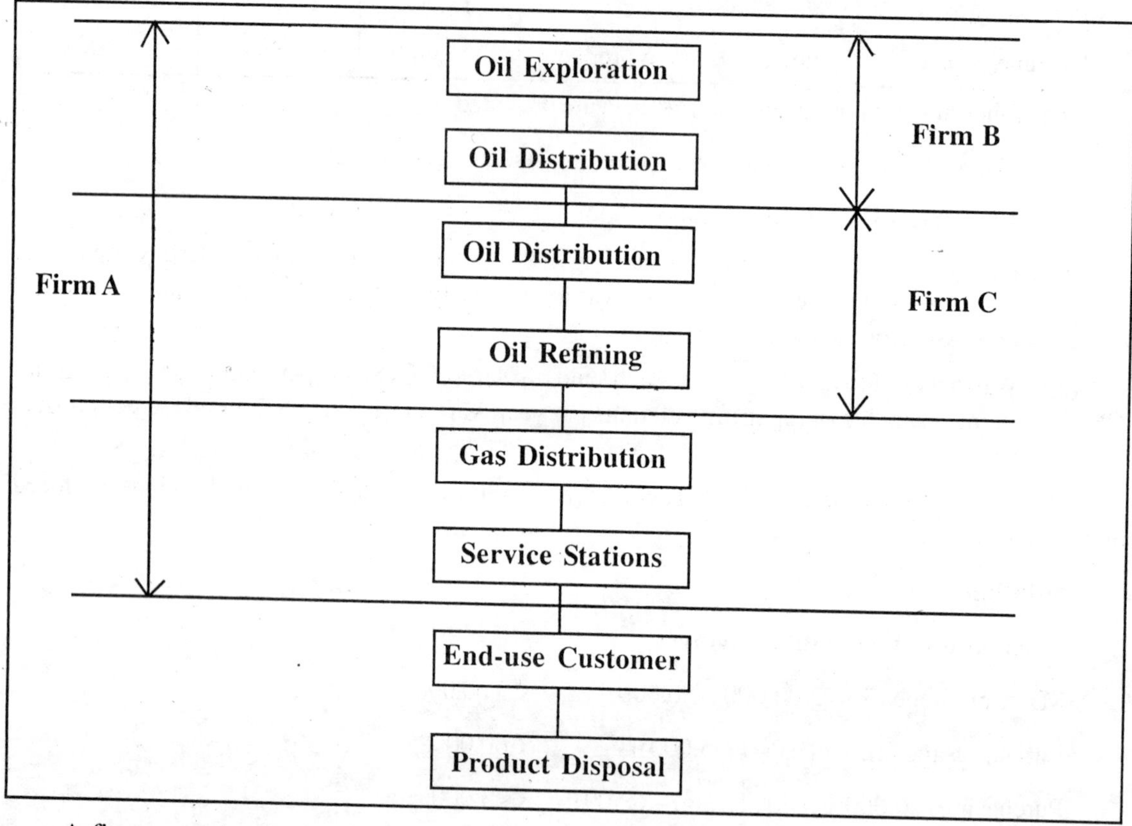

A firm operating in the oil industry may not span the entire value chain. The above exhibit illustrates that different firms participate in different portions of the value chain. Most large oil firms are involved in the value chain from exploration to service stations. These oil giants even purchase oil from other producers and supply gasoline to service stations or outlets that are owned by others. There are many oil firms that are engaged exclusively in smaller segments of the chain such as exploration and production or refining and distribution. Thus, regardless of its position in the value chain to create and sustain a competitive advantage, a firm must understand the entire value chain and not just the portion in which it operates.

The value chain system also includes value chain activities that are performed by suppliers and buyers. A firm cannot ignore the interaction between its own value chain activities and those of its suppliers and buyers. Linkages with activities external to the firm can also be exploited. Exploiting external linkages means managing these linkages so that both the company and the external parties receive an increase in benefits.

Suppliers provide inputs and as a consequence, can have a significant effect on a user's strategic positioning. If a company adopts a total quality control approach to managing quality that demands the production of defect-free products, reducing defects in turn reduce the total costs spent on quality activities. If the components are delivered late and are of low quality, there is no way the buying company can produce high quality products and deliver them on time to its customers. Thus, to achieve defect-free state of products, a company is strongly dependent on its supplier's ability to provide defect-free parts. Once this linkage is understood, then a company can work closely with its suppliers so that the product being purchased meets its need. The partnership fosters a sense of interdependence between purchaser and supplier including a sense of trust and ethical treatment.

Every manufacturing firm can manage its procurement costs with the value chain analysis. In order to avoid weakening of its strategic position, a firm must carefully choose its suppliers. To encourage purchasing managers to choose suppliers whose quality, reliability and delivery performance are acceptable, two essential requirements have been identified. First, a broader view of component costs is needed. Functional based costing systems typically reward purchasing managers solely on purchase price. A broader view means that the costs associated with quality, reliability and late deliveries are added to the purchase costs. Purchasing managers are required to evaluate suppliers based on total cost and not just purchase price. Second, the supplier costs are assigned to products using casual relationships.

Activity based costing is the key to satisfying both the requirements. To satisfy the first requirement, suppliers are defined as a cost object and costs relating to purchase, quality, reliability and delivery performance are traced to suppliers. In the second case, products are the cost objects and supplier costs are traced to specific products. By tracing supplier costs to products, managers can see the effect of large numbers of unique components requiring specialty suppliers versus products with only standard components. Knowing the costs of more complex products helps product designers better evaluate the trade-offs between functionality and cost as they design new products. Additional functions should provide more benefits than costs. By accurately tracing supplier costs to products, a better understanding of product profitability is produced and product designers are more capable of choosing among competing product designs.

Illustration 4.2: Purchasing Manager of MIRC Electronics uses two suppliers, Soni Electronics and Omega Ltd., as the source of two electronics components X and Y. The Purchasing Manager prefers Soni Electronics to use because it provides the components at a lower price. The Omega Ltd. is also used as well to ensure a reliable supply of these components. There are two activities to be carried out in the company, i.e., reworking and expediting products. Reworking products occur because of component failure or process failure. Expediting products takes place due to late delivery of components or process failure. Component failure and late delivery are attributable to suppliers. The process failure costs are attributable to internal proceses. Reworking costs are attributable to component failure and assigned to suppliers using the number of failed components as the driver. The costs of expediting attributable to late deliveries are assigned testing the number of late shipments as the driver. The activity cost data are given below:

(i) Activity costs:

Activity	*Component failure/ Late delivery (₹)*	*Process failure (₹)*
Reworking products	20,000	40,000
Expediting products	25,000	10,000

(ii) Supplier data:

Particulars	*Soni Electronics*		*Omega Ltd.*	
	X	*Y*	*X*	*Y*
Purchase price per unit (₹)	10	25	12	30
No. of units purchased	4,000	2,000	500	500
Failed units	80	10	5	5
Late shipments	30	20	0	0

You are required to compute: (a) the activity rates for assigning costs to suppliers and (b) the purchasing cost per unit.

Solution:

(a)(i) Calculation of Reworking Rate:

$$= \frac{\text{Reworking Costs}}{\text{Failed Units}}$$

$$= \frac{20{,}000}{200}$$

= ₹ 100 per failed component

Failed units = 80 + 10 + 5 + 5 = 100 units

(ii) Calculation of Expediting Rate

$$= \frac{\text{Expediting Costs}}{\text{Late Shipments}}$$

$$= \frac{25{,}000}{50}$$

= ₹ 500 per late delivery

Late shipments = 30 + 20 = 50

(b) Calculation of Purchasing Cost per unit:

Particulars	*Soni Electronics*		*Omega Ltd.*	
Products	(₹) *X*	(₹) *Y*	(₹) *X*	(₹) *Y*
Purchase costs	40,000	50,000	6,000	15,000
Reworking costs	8,000	1,000	500	500
Expediting costs	15,000	10,000	–	–
Total costs	63,000	61,000	6,500	15,500
No. of units	4,000	2000	500	500
Cost per unit	15.75	30.50	13.00	31.00

4.6 EXPLOITING CUSTOMER LINKAGES

Customers have a significant influence on a firm's strategic position. Choosing market segments is one of the principal elements that define strategic position. Selling a middle level quality product to low-end dealers for a special low price because of idle capacity could threaten the main channels of distribution for the product. This is true even if the dealers apply their own private labels to the product. Selling the product to low-end dealers creates a direct competitor for its regular, medium level dealers. Potential customers of the regular retail outlets could switch to the lower-end outlets because they can buy the same quality for a lower price. The long-term damage to the company's profitability may be much greater than any short-run benefit from selling the special order.

A key objective for strategic costing is the identification of a firm's sources of profitability. In a functional based costing system, selling and general administrative costs are usually treated as period costs. If these costs are assigned to the customers, they are typically assigned in proportion to the revenues generated. The message of functional based costing is that servicing customers either at no cost or they all appear to cost the same percentage of their sales revenue. If customer servicing costs are significant, then failure to assign them at all or to assign them accurately will prevent sales representatives from managing the customer mix effectively. The reason is that the sales representatives will not be able to distinguish between customer who place significant demands on servicing resources and those who place virtually no demand on these resources. The lack of knowledge can lead to actions that will weaken a firm's strategic position. To avoid this outcome and encourage actions that strengthen strategic position, customer related costs should be assigned to customers using activity based costing. Accurate assignment of customer related costs allows the firm to classify customers as profitable customers.

Once the customers are identified as profitable, action can be taken to strengthen the strategic position of the firm. For profitable customers, an organisation can undertake efforts to increase satisfaction by offering higher levels of service, lower prices, new services or some combinations of the three. For unprofitable customers, an organisation can attempt to deliver the customer services more efficiently and increase prices to reflect the cost of the resources being consumed, encourage unprofitable customer to leave or some combinations of the three actions. For example, about

50 per cent of large banks are now using customer profitability data to engage in exactly the kinds of actions. According to Market Line Associates, USA, the top 20 per cent of bank customers generate 150 per cent of overall profit, while the bottom 20 per cent drain about 50 per cent of overall profit. One of the largest banks in the United States uses a computerised colour-coded information system that reveals information about customer profitability to bank employes who service the customers. Customers asking for specific services get a yes or no answer depending on their colour code ranking. A red code means the customer is losing money for the bank and a green colour code means the customer is a source of significant profits for the bank. A yellow colour code is for in-between customers. Green colour code customers who request a lower credit card interest rate or a fee waved for a bounced cheque get a positive answer. The customers with a red colour code almost always receive a negative answer, while customers with a yellow colour code have a chance to negotiate. The company estimates that this type of approach will increase its annual revenue by millions. About half of this revenue is from extra fees and other funds collected from unprofitable customers and from the increased deposits gained by returning preferred customers who have been receiving more services.

Illustration 4.3: Thomas Cook produces precision parts for 11 major buyers. An activity based costing system is used to assign manufacturing costs to products. The company charges each customer's order by adding order-filling costs to manufacturing costs and then adding a 20 per cent markup to cover administrative costs and profits. Order-filling costs are ₹ 6,06,000 and are currently assigned in proportion to sales volume. Of the 11 customers, one accounts for 50 per cent of sales, with the other 10 accounting for the remaining. The 10 smaller customers purchase parts in roughly equal quantities. Orders placed by the smaller customers are also about the same size. The data relating to Thomas Cook's current activities are given below:

Particulars	*One large customer*	*10 smaller customers*
Units purchased	5,00,000	5,00,000
Orders placed	2	200
Manufacturing cost (₹)	₹ 30,00,000	30,00,000
Order-filling costs allocated (₹)	₹ 3,03,000	3,03,000
Order cost per unit	₹ 0.610	0.610

Order-filling capacity is purchased in blocks of 45 and each block costing ₹ 40,400 variable order-filling activity costs are ₹ 2,000 per order. The activity capacity is 225 orders. Therefore, the total order-filing cost is ₹ 6,06,000 (5 × 40,400) + (2,000 × 202). This total is allocated in proportion to the units purchased and the large customer receives half of the total cost.

The large size customer complains about the price being charged higher and threatens to take his business elsewhere. The customer reveals a bid from Thomas Cook competitor that is ₹ 0.50 per part less than the company charges. Decide with the help of exploiting customer linkages.

Solution:

The company investigates that the assignment of order-filling costs and discovers that the number of orders processed is a much better cost driver than number of parts sold. Thus, activity demand is measured by the number of sales order and ordering cost should be assigned to customers using an activity rate of ₹ 3,000 per order as follows:

$$\text{Activity Rate} = \frac{\text{Order} - \text{filling Cost}}{\text{Orders Placed}}$$

$$= \frac{₹3{,}03{,}000 + 3{,}03{,}000}{2 + 200}$$

$$= \frac{₹6{,}06{,}000}{202}$$

$$= ₹\ 3000 \text{ per order}$$

Using this rate, the large customer should be charged ₹ 6,000 for order-filling (2 × 3,000) costs. Thus, the large customer is being overcharged ₹ 2,97,000 each year. This comes to ₹ 0.59 per unit as follows:

$$\frac{2{,}97{,}000}{5{,}00{,}000} = ₹\ 0.59$$

This overcharging is compounded by the 20 per cent markup, producing a price that is about ₹ 0.71 which is too high. On the basis of this analysis, the management of Thomas Cook immediately offers to reduce the price charged to its large customers by at least ₹ 0.50 per unit.

This gives benefit to the large customers because the price is reduced. This also benefits the company because the price correction is needed to maintain half of its current business. Thus, identifying the right cost driver reveals a linkage between order-filling activity and customer behaviour. Larger and less frequent orders will also reduce the demand on other internal activities such as setting up equipment and materials handling. Reduction in other activity demands could produce further cost reductions and additional price cuts, making the company more competitive. Thus, exploiting customer linkages can make both the seller and buyer better off.

4.7 VALUE CHAIN FRAMEWORK

Choosing an optimal strategic position requires managers to understand the activities that contribute to its achievement. Successful pursuit of a sound strategic position mandates an understanding of the industrial value chain. The industrial value chain is the linked set of value-creating activities from basic raw materials to the disposal of finished product by end-use customers. Breaking down the value chain into its strategically relevant activities is basic to successful implementation of cost leadership and differential strategies. Thus, a value chain framework is a compelling approach to understanding a firm's strategically important activities. Fundamental to a value chain framework is the recognition that there exists complex linkages and interrelationships among activities both within and beyond the firm. A company cannot ignore supplier and customer linkages and expect to establish a sustainable competitive advantage. Therefore, a company needs to understand its relative position in the industrial value chain.

An assessment of the economic strength and relationships of each stage in the entire value chain system can provide a company with several significant strategic insights. Thus, knowing revenues and costs of the different stages may reveal the need to forward or backward integration to increase overall economic performance. Otherwise, it may reveal that divestiture and a narrowing of participation in the industrial value chain is a good strategy. Knowing the supplier power and buyer power can have a significant effect on how external linkages are exploited. Supplier and buyer power can be assessed for a company by comparing the percentage of profits earned in the industrial value chain with the percentages earned by suppliers and customers.

Illustration 4.4: BPCL is an independent refiner and producer of gasoline in Mumbai. The company earns profit of ₹ 45 per gallon. However, the profit earned by its network of service stations that buy the gasoline is ₹ 15 per gallon. The selling price per gallon is ₹ 150. Determine the supplier and buyer power.

Solution:

(a) The percentage of profit earned by the company, i.e., Independent Refiner is

$$= \frac{45}{150} \times 100 = 30\%.$$

(b) The percentage of profit earned by the downstream stage is $= \frac{15}{150} \times 100 = 10\%$.

(c) The buyer power is weak relative to the refiner and producer. If the return on investment being earned by the service stations is high, this may reveal that integrating forward is both desirable and possible.

In order to exploit a firm's internal and external linkages, we must identify the firm's activities and select those that can be used to produce a competitive advantage. Therefore, for strategic analysis, activities should be classified as organisational activities and operational activities. The cost of these activities are to be determined by organisational and operational cost drivers.

4.8 ORGANISATIONAL ACTIVITIES AND COST DRIVERS

There are two types of organisational activities — structural and executional. Structural activities are those activities which determine the underlying economic structures of the organisation. Executional activities are the processes and capabilities of an organisation and are directly related to the ability of an organisation to execute successfully. Organisational cost drivers are structural and executional factors that determine the long-term cost structure of an organisation. Structural and executional activities with their cost drivers are given below:

(a)	**Structural Activities**	**Structural Cost Drivers**
	Building Plants	Number of plants, scale, degree etc.
	Management Structuring	Management style and philosophy
	Grouping Employees	Number and type of work units
	Complexity	Number of product lines
	Vertical Integrating	Scope, Buying Power, Selling Power
	Selecting and Using Process Technologies	Types of Process Technologies
(b)	**Executional Activities**	**Executional Cost Drivers**
	Using Employees	Degree of involvement
	Providing Quality	Quality Management approach
	Providing Plant Layout	Plant Layout Efficiency
	Designing and Producing	Product Configuration
	Providing Capacity	Capacity Utilisation

The above classification shows that, it is possible that a given organisation activity can be driven by more than one driver. For example, the cost of building plant is affected by number of plants, scale and degree of centralisation. Companies that have a commitment to a high degree of centralisation can build larger plants so that there can be more geographic concentration and greater control. Complexity may be driven by number of different products, number of unique processes and number of unique parts.

Organisational drivers are factors that affect an organisation's long-term cost structure. Among the structural drivers, the familiar one are drivers of scale, scope, experience, technology and complexity. Economies and diseconomies of scale are well-known economic phenomena and the learning curve effect is also well documented. An interesting property of structural cost drivers is that more is not always better. Moreover, the efficient level of a structural driver can change. Changes in technology can affect the scale driver by changing the optimal size of a plant. In the steel industry, minimal technology has eliminated scale economies as a competitive advantage. Plants of much smaller scale can achieve the same level of efficiency once produced only by larger steel plants.

Executional drivers have more emphasis in recent years. Considerable managerial effort is being expended to improve how things are done in an organisation. Continuous improvement and its many faces are what executional efficiency is all about, for example, employee involvement and empowerment. The cost of using employees decreases as the degree of involvement increases. Employee involvement refers to the culture, degree of participation and commitment to the objective of continuous improvement.

4.9 OPERATIONAL ACTIVITIES AND DRIVERS

Operational activities are day-to-day activities performed as a result of the structure and processes selected by the organisations. For example, receiving and inspecting incoming parts, moving materials, shipping products, testing new products, servicing products and setting up equipments. Operational cost drivers are those factors that drive the cost of operational activities. For example, number of parts, number of moves, number of products, number of customer orders and number of returned products. Operational activities and drivers are the focus of activity based costing. Possible operational activities and their drivers are shown below:

	Activities	Drivers
(a)	**Unit Level Activities**	**Unit Level Drivers**
	Grinding parts	Grinding machine hours
	Assembling parts	Assembly labour hours
	Drilling holes	Drilling machine hours
	Using materials	Material amount
	Using power	No. of kilowatt hours
(b)	**Batch Level Activities**	**Batch Level Drivers**
	Setting up equipment	Number of setups
	Moving batches	Number of moves
	Inspecting batches	Inspection hours
	Reworking products	Number of defective units
(c)	**Product Level Activities**	**Product Level Drivers**
	Redesigning products	Number of change orders
	Expediting	Number of late orders
	Scheduling	Number of different products
	Testing products	Number of procedures

If an organisation decides to produce more than one product at a facility, then this structural choice produces a need for scheduling a product level activity. Similarly, providing a plant layout defines the nature and extent of the materials handling activity. Although organisational activities define operational activities, an analysis of operational activities and drivers can be used to suggest strategic choices of organisational activities and drivers. Knowing that the number of moves is a measure of consumption of the materials handling activity by individual, products may suggest that resource spending can be reduced if the plant layout is redesigned to reduce the number of moves needed. Operational and organisational activities and their associated drivers are strongly interrelated.

4.10 VALUE CHAIN ANALYSIS AND TRADITIONAL COST MANAGEMENT

The information generated from traditional management accounting system can be very successfully used in value chain analysis. Traditional costing overemphasises manufacturing cost. It works on the premise that cost reduction is to be found in value-added process. However, value-added approach ignores linkage with suppliers or customers. Value chain approach is not confined to internal or external data. It uses appropriate cost drivers for major value-creating processes. It focuses on defining company's strategic competitive advantage. Conventional costing is based on single cost driver approach. In value chain, multiple cost drivers are used. It is common to ask strategic questions such as make or buy and forward or backward integration. Thus, the focal point and perspective under traditional costing differs from value chain analysis substantially.

4.11 THE ROLE OF MANAGEMENT ACCOUNTANT

A Management Accountant has to play a strategic role in implementing value chain analysis. He uses ABC analysis, benchmarking, target costing, life cycle costing, economic value added for decision-making. He has to coordinate with different groups like engineering, market, distribution and identify strengths and weaknesses in value chain analysis system. The management accountant can enhance the firm's value by emphasising the value chain analysis. It highlights the value contribution to specific activities. It can also demonstrate the value of finance function in firm's growth and survival. The value chain analysis can expose to some interesting opportunities as follows:

(i) To fashion a major reconstruction of the industry value chain.

(ii) To enhance current value chain position by making the firm run lean and fast.

(iii) To revalue the firm's investment intensity at the various levels of the industry value chain.

(iv) To build greater differentiation through an enhanced role in the buyer's value chain.

(v) To expand value chain position through acquisition, joint venture or other alliances.

Value chain analysis can be best performed on a regular basis. The dynamic nature of some industries require close monitoring. All industries, mature or emerging, are in a dynamic state. Most firms concentrate their analysis on their immediate market. The challenge is to expand the horizon to include the total industry. Some firms regularly reinvent themselves using reengineering and other techniques to evaluate their processes. Many firms challenge the current state of their firm value chain and seek to find a better route to the customer through the industry value chain. The value chain analysis is conceptually straightforward. It requires a sound understanding of company and industry. The Management Accountant should be comfortable with making reasonable estimates of market and financial results. Good value chain analysis is driven by good information and industry intelligence.

4.12 LONG-TERM COST MANAGEMENT

Costs influence prices because they affect supply. As companies supply more product, the cost of producing each additional unit initially declines but then eventually increases. Companies supply products so long as the additional revenue from selling one more unit exceeds the additional cost of producing it. The lower the cost of producing a product, the greater the quantity of product the company is willing to supply. Managers who understand the cost of producing their companies products set prices that make the products attractive to customer while maximising their companies operating incomes, in computing the relevant costs in all business functions of the value chain, from R&D to customer service.

Short-run pricing decisions typically have a time horizon of less than a year and include decisions such as pricing a one-time only special order with no long-run implications and adjusting product mix and output volume in a competitive market. Long-run pricing decisions have a time horizon of a year or longer and include pricing a product in a major market in which there is some leeway in setting price. Two key differences affect pricing for the long run versus short run are:

(i) Costs that are often irrelevant for short-term pricing decisions are generally in the long run because costs can be altered in the long run.

(ii) Profit margins in long-run pricing decisions are often set to earn a reasonable return on investment.

Long-run pricing is a strategic decision designed to build long-run relationship with customers, based on stable and predictable prices. Buyers typically prefer stable and predictable prices over a long time horizon. A stable price reduces the need for continuous monitoring of supplier's prices, improves planning and builds long-run buyer-seller relationships. But to charge a stable price and earn the target long-run return, a company should know and manage its costs of supplying products to customers. Thus, the relevant costs for long-run pricing decisions include all future fixed and variable costs. The management should observe that:

(i) Direct material costs vary with number of units produced.

(ii) Direct labour costs vary with number of direct manufacturing labour hours used.

(iii) Direct machining costs, such as rentals do not vary with number of machine hours used over this time horizon. So, they are fixed in the long run.

(iv) Ordering and receiving, testing and inspection and rework costs vary with the quantity of their respective cost driver. Ordering and receiving costs vary with the number of orders. Staff members responsible for placing orders can be reassigned or laid off in the long run, if fewer orders need to be placed or the number of staff members can be increased in the long-run process more orders.

Illustration 4.5: Provoge Ltd. provides the following details of their activities for the year ended 31st March, 2012.

Solution:

Output 1,50,000 units

Sr. No.	*Cost*	*Cost Driver*	*Cost Driver Quantities Output*	*Total Quantity of Cost Driver*	*Cost per Unit of Cost Driver*
1	Direct Materials	No of kits – 1	1,50,000	1,50,000	460
2	Direct Labour	Hours 3.2 Per unit	1,50,000	4,80,000	20
3	Direct Machining (fixed)	Hours	–	3,00,000	38
4	Ordering and Receiving	No. of orders 50	450 Components	22,500	80
5	Testing and Inspection	Testing Hour 30	1,50,000 8% Defect	4,50,000	2
6	Reworks	Hours 2-5	12,000	30,000	40

You are required to calculate the total cost of manufacturing and manufacturing cost per unit.

Solution:

Sr. No.	*Particulars* *Output 1,50,000 units*	*Manufacturing Cost (₹)*	*Cost Per Unit (₹)*
1	Direct Materials	6,90,00,000	460
2	Direct Labour	96,00,000	64
3	Direct Machining	1,14,00,000	76
	Direct Manufacturing	9,00,00,000	600
4	Manufacturing Overheads:		
	Ordering and Receiving	1,80,0000	12
	Testing and Inspection	90,00,000	60
	Rework Costs	12,00,000	8
	Total Overheads	120,00,000	80
	Total Manufacturing cost	10,20,00,000	680

Working:

1. Direct Material Cost = 1,50,000 units @ ₹ 460 per unit = ₹ 6,90,00,000
2. Direct Labour Cost = 4,80,000 labour hours @ ₹ 20 per hour = ₹ 96,00,000
3. Direct Machining Cost = 3,00,000 machine hours @ ₹ 38 each = ₹ 1,14,00,000
4. Ordering and Receiving Cost = 22,500 orders @ ₹ 80 per order = ₹ 18,00,000
5. Testing and Inspection Cost = 45,00,000 hours @ ₹ 2 per hour = ₹ 90,00,000
6. Rework Costs = 30,000 hours @ ₹ 40 each = ₹ 1,20,000

Long-run pricing approaches can be market-based or cost-based. The market-based approach to pricing starts by management asking what price should be charged? The cost-based approach to pricing starts by management asking what price should we charge to recoup our costs and achieve a target return on investment. Companies operating in one competitive market use the market-based approach. The products manufactured by one company are very similar to products produced by other companies. The companies in these markets should accept the prices set by the market. On the other hand, companies operating in the less competitive markets offering products or services that differ from each other can use either the market-based or cost-based approach as the starting point for decisions. Some companies first look at costs and then consider customers or competitors, i.e., the cost-based approach. Other companies start by considering customers and competitors and then look at costs, i.e., the market-based approach. Only their starting point differs. The management should always keep in mind market forces regardless of which pricing approach is used. For example, a price set via cost plus thinking may simply be unacceptable to customers, because a competitor has introduced a new, lower priced product. Therefore, the 'plus' in cost plus is reduced to a price acceptable to the market. Companies operating in markets that are not competitive favour cost-based approaches; because these companies do not need to respond or react to competitor's prices.

Market-based pricing starts with a target price. A target price is the estimated price for a product or service that potential customers will pay. This estimate is based on an understanding of customer's perceived value for a product or service and how competitor will price competing products or services. Having this understanding of customers and competitors has become important for the following reasons:

1. Competition from lower cost producers has meant that prices cannot be increased.
2. Products are on the market for shorter periods of time leaving less time and opportunity to recover from pricing mistakes.
3. Customers have become more knowledgeable and demand quality products at reasonable prices.

A company's sales and marketing department through close contact and interaction wish customers is usually in the best position to identify customer's needs and their perceived value for a product or service. Companies also conduct Market Research studies about product features that customers want and the prices they are willing to pay for those features.

To judge how competitors might react to prospective price, a company needs to understand competitor's technologies, products or services, costs and financial conditions. Knowing competitor's technologies and products helps a company:

(a) to evaluate how distinctive its own products or services will be in the market.

(b) to determine the prices it will be able to charge as a result of being distinctive. Usually, the companies obtain information about its competitors from customers, suppliers and employees of competitors. Another source is reverse engineering, i.e., disassembling and analysing competitor's products to determine product design, materials and to become acquainted with the technologies used by the competitors. The following steps are followed for developing target prices and target costs:

1. Develop a product that satisfies the needs of potential customers.
2. Choose a target price.
3. Derive a target cost per unit by subtracting target operating income per unit from the target price.
4. Perform cost analysis.
5. Perform value engineering to achieve target cost.

Illustration 4.6: Tata Motors Ltd. has provided you the following information:

Number of units produced and sold	15,0000
Cost of manufacture	₹ 680 per unit
Other operating expenses	₹ 220 per unit
Total cost per unit	₹ 900

To earn the target return on capital invested in the business, a company needs a 10% target operating income on target revenues. The long-term target revenues are ₹ 800 per unit from 2,00,000 units. You are required to determine the target cost per unit.

Solution:

Total Target Revenues $= 800 \times 2{,}00{,}000 =$ ₹ 16,00,00,000

Total Operating Income = 10% of 16,00,00,000

= ₹ 1,60,00,000

$\therefore$ Target Operating Income per unit $= \dfrac{1{,}60{,}00{,}000}{2{,}00{,}000} =$ ₹ 80 per unit

$\therefore$ Target Cost per unit = Target Revenue – Operating Income

= ₹ 800 – ₹ 80

= ₹ 720 per unit

The company's Target Cost per unit is ₹ 720 which is well below its existing unit cost of ₹ 900. Thus, the company should reduce its unit cost by ₹ 180 to reach its goal. Thus, cost reduction efforts need to extend to all parts of the value chain including seeking lower prices from suppliers for materials and components.

Illustration 4.7: The Engineers of 'A' Ltd. have redesigned that uses a 12% markup on the full unit cost of the product in developing the prospective selling price. The details are as follows:

Unit cost of product	₹ 720
Invested capital	₹ 960 lakhs
Target rate of return on investment	18%
Number of units produced	20,00,000

You are required to calculate the prospective selling price per unit.

Solution:

(a) Target Annual Operating Income = 18% of ₹ 960 lakhs = ₹ 172.80 lakhs

$$\text{Target Operating Income per unit} = \frac{172.80}{2} = ₹\ 86.40$$

(b) Prospective Selling Price = Cost Per Unit + Target Operating Income

= ₹ 720 + ₹ 86.40

= ₹ 806.40 per unit

OR

(c) Prospective Selling Price = Unit Cost Price + Markup Component

= ₹ 720 + 12% of 720

= ₹ 720 + 86.40

= ₹ 806.40

Illustration 4.8: Walchandnagar Industries Ltd. manufactures and sells a speciality product used white water rafting. In 2011, it reported the following:

Units produced and sold	20,000
Investment	₹ 24,00,000
Full cost per unit	₹ 300
Rate of return on investment	20%

Markup percentage on variable cost 50%

Required:

(a) What was the selling price per unit in 2011?

(b) The company is considering raising its selling price to ₹ 348. However, at this price, its sales volume is predicted to fall by 10%. If the cost structure remains the same and its demand forecast is accurate, should it raise the selling price?

(c) In 2012, due to increased competition, the company must reduce its selling price to ₹ 315 in order to sell 20,000 units. The manager of the division is ready to reduce annual investment to ₹ 21 lakhs but still demands a 20% target rate of return on investment. If fixed costs cannot change in this time frame, what is the target variable cost per unit?

Solution:

(a) Calculation of Selling Price per unit:

Full Cost per unit	₹ 300
Markup Component	24
Selling Price	324

Calculation of Variable Cost per unit:

V + 50% = ₹ 324

1.5V = ₹ 324

$\therefore$ V $= \frac{324}{1.5}$ = ₹ 216

(b) Statement of Profit:

Particulars	***2011***	***2012***
No. of units sold	20,000	10,000
	₹	₹
Sales	64,80,000	62,64,000
(–) Variable cost	43,20,000	38,88,000
Contribution	21,60,000	23,76,000
(–) Fixed cost	16,80,000	16,80,000
Profit	4,80,000	6,96,000
Investment	24,00,000	24,00,000
ROI	20%	29%

As the Return on Investment is increased from 20% to 29%, the company can raise its selling price.

(c) Calculation of Target Variable Cost:

	₹
Investment	21,00,000
(+) Return on Investment (20%)	42,00,000
Sales	63,00,000
(–) Return on Investment	4,20,000
Cost of Sales	58,80,000
(–) Fixed cost	16,80,000
Variable cost	42,00,000

$$\text{Variable cost per unit} = \frac{42{,}00{,}000}{20{,}000} = ₹\,210$$

Illustration 4.9: Mr. Lalit is the managing partner of a business that has just finished building a 60-room motel. Lalit anticipates that he will rent these rooms for 16,000 nights next year (or 16,000 room-nights). All rooms are similar and will rent for the same price. Mr. Lalit estimates the following operating costs for the next year:

Variable Operating Costs	₹ 3 per Room-night
Fixed Costs:	
Salaries and Wages	₹ 1,75,000
Maintenance	37,000
Administrative Costs	1,40,000
Total	3,52,000

The capital invested in the motel is ₹ 9,60,000. The partnership's target return on investment is 25%. Mr. Lalit expects demand for rooms to be uniform throughout the year. He plans to price the rooms at full cost plus a markup on full cost to earn the target return on investment.

Required:

(a) What price should Mr. Lalit charge for a room-night? What is the markup as a percentage of the full cost of a room-night?

(b) Mr. Lalit's market research indicates that if the price of a room-night determined in the above case is reduced by 10%, the expected number of room-nights Mr. Lalit could rent could increase by 10%. Should Mr. Lalit reduce prices by 10%?

Solution:

(a) Calculation of Price per room-night:

Variable cost	₹ 3	per room night
Fixed cost	₹ 22	per room night
Return on Investment	₹ 15	per room night
Total	₹ 40	

$$\text{Fixed Cost per unit} = \frac{1,75,000+37,000+14,000}{16,000} = ₹\ 22$$

Return on Investment per Room:

Investment	₹ 9,60,000
Target ROI = (25%)	₹ 2,40,000

$$\text{ROI per Room} = \frac{2,40,000}{16,000} = ₹\ 15$$

$$\text{Calculation of Markup} = \frac{\text{ROI}}{\text{Full cost}} \times 100$$

$$= \frac{2,40,000}{4,00,000} \times 100$$

$$= ₹\ 60\%$$

Full cost = Variable Cost + Fixed Cost

$= 3 \times 16,000 + 3,52,000$

$= ₹\ 48,000 + 3,52,000$

$= ₹\ 4,00,000$

(b) Statement of Profit:

	₹
Total Revenue (36 × 17,600)	6,33,600
(–) Variable cost (3 × 17,600)	52,800
Contribution	5,80,800
(–) Fixed cost	3,52,000
Profit	2,28,800

$$ROI = \frac{Profit}{Investment} \times 100$$

$$= \frac{2,28,800}{9,60,000} \times 100$$

$$= 23.83\ \%$$

Note: 1. Revised Price = ₹ 40 × 0.90 = ₹ 36

2. Number of Rooms = 16,000 × 1.10 = 17,600

As the Return on Investment is reducing from 25% to 23.83%, Mr. Lalit is advised not to reduce the price of rooms.

Illustration 4.10: Starlite Ltd. cans peaches for sale to food distributors. All costs are classified as either manufacturing or marketing. Starlite prepares monthly budgets. The budgeted income statement of March 2012 is given below:

Revenues (1,000 crates @ ₹ 100 each)	₹ 1,00,000
Cost of goods sold	₹ 60,000
Gross margin	₹ 40,000
Marketing costs	₹ 30,000
Operating Income	₹ 10,000

Normal markup percentage is 66.7% of Absorption cost (40,000 ÷ 60,000 × 100)

Monthly costs are classified as fixed or variable with respect to the number of crates produced for manufacturing costs and with respect to number of crates sold for marketing costs.

Costs	**Fixed**	**Variable**
Manufacturing	₹ 20,000	₹ 40,000
Marketing	₹ 16,000	₹ 14,000

Starlite has capacity to can 1,500 crates per month. The relevant range in which monthly fixed manufacturing costs will be fixed is from 500 to 1,500 crates per month.

Required:

(a) Calculate the markup percentage based on total variable cost.

(b) A new customer approaches to buy 200 crates at ₹ 55 per crate for cash. The customer does not require any marketing effort. Additional manufacturing costs of ₹ 2,000 (for special packing) will be required. Starlite believes that this is a one-time-only special order because the customer is discontinuing business in six week's time. The company is reluctant to accept this 200 crate special order because the ₹ 55 per crate is below the ₹ 60 per crate absorption cost. Do you agree with this reasoning?

(c) The new customer decides to remain in business. How would this longevity affect your willingness to accept ₹ 55 per crate offer?

Solution:

(a) Calculation of Markup Percentage:

Revenues		₹ 1,00,000
(–) Variable cost:		
Manufacturing	40,000	
Marketing	14,000	54,000
Contribution		46,000
(–) Fixed cost		36,000
Profit		10,000

$$\therefore \text{Markup percentage on total variable cost} = \frac{\text{Profit}}{\text{Variable Cost}} \times 100$$

$$= \frac{10,000}{54,000} \times 100$$

$$= 18.52\%$$

(b) Statement of income when special affer is accepted:

Revenue (200 × 55)	₹ 11,000
(–) Variable Cost (Manufacturing) (200 × 40)	8,000
Contribution	3,000
(–) Special packing	2,000
Profit	1,000

$$\text{Profit per crate} = \frac{1,000}{200} = ₹\ 5$$

Alternatively, marginal cost can be determined as follows:

Variable Mfg. cost per crate	₹ 40
Additional Mfg. cost per crate	₹ 10
Marginal cost	₹ 50

We cannot agree with the reasoning of the company because in this case marginal cost is important for decision making and not the absorption cost. The company should accept this one-time offer because it generates profit of ₹ 1,000 (₹ 5 per crate).

(c) At present, the company is producing 1,000 crates. The capacity is 1,500 crates per month. Even if the new customer decides to remain in business, the company should accept this offer because it will be benefited in the long run.

4.13 EXERCISES

1. What is Value Chain Analysis? What role does it play in Strategic Cost Analysis?
2. What does it mean to exploit internal and external linkages?
3. What is an industrial value chain? Explain why a firm's strategies are tied to what happens in the rest of the value chain.
4. What does it mean to obtain a competitive advantage? What role does the cost management system play in helping to achieve this goal?
5. What is long-term cost management?
6. What are target costs? What are the steps in developing a target cost?
7. Johnson Ltd. manufactures computerised manufacturing equipment. It produces all the parts necessary for the production of its products except for one electronic component. This component is purchased from two local suppliers — Bombay Electronics and Plaza Ltd. Both suppliers are reliable and seldom deliver late. However, Bombay Electronics sells the component for ₹ 48 per unit, while Plaza Ltd. sells the same component for ₹ 43. Because of the lower price, Johnson Ltd. purchases 80 per cent of its components from Plaza Ltd. The total annual demand is 10,00,000 components.

   Bombay Electronics' sales manager is pushing Johnson Co. to purchase more of its units arguing that their component is of much higher quality and so should prove to be less costly than its competitors' lower quality component. Bombay Electronics has sufficient capacity to supply all the components needed and is asking for a long-term contract with a five-year contract for 8,00,000 or more units, it will sell the components for ₹ 45 each with a contractual provision for an annual product-specific inflationary adjustment. Johnson's purchasing manager is intrigued by the offer and wonders if the higher quality component actually costs less than the lower quality Plaza component. To help assess the cost effect of two components, the following data were collected for quality related activities and suppliers.

(a) Activity data:

Activity	*Cost ₹*
Inspecting components (sampling only)	1,20,000
Reworking products	7,60,500
Warranty work	24,00,000

(b) Supplier data:

	Bombay Electronics	*Plaza Ltd.*
	₹	₹
Unit purchase price	48	43
Units purchased	2,00,000	8,00,000
Sampling hours	20	980
Rework hours	90	1,410
Warranty hours	200	3,800

You are required to:

(i) Calculate the cost per component for each supplier, taking into consideration the cost of the quality related activities and using the current prices and sales volume.

(ii) What do you think the purchasing manager ought to do?

8. Cairan Ltd. sells machine parts to industrial equipment manufacturing company for an average price of ₹ 30 per part. There are two types of customers: those who place small, frequent orders those who place larger, less frequent orders. Each time an order is placed and processed, a setup is required. Scheduling is also needed to coordinate the different orders that come in and place demands on the plant's manufacturing resources. The company also inspects a sample of the products each time a batch is produced to ensure that the customer's specifications have been met. Inspection takes essentially the same time regardless of the type of part being produced. The company's cost accounting department has provided the following budgeted data for customer-related activities and costs, i.e., the amounts expected for the coming year.

Particulars	***Frequently ordering customers***	***Less frequently ordering customers***
Sales orders	8,000	800
Average order size	2,000	20,000
Number of setups	5,000	1,000
Scheduling hours	7,000	1,000
Inspections	5,000	1,000
Average unit cost (₹)	20	₹ 20

Average unit cost does not include the cost of the customer-related activities listed below:

Customer-related activity costs:

Processing sales orders	₹4,40,000
Scheduling production	₹2,40,000
Setting up equipments	₹7,20,000
Inspecting batches	₹9,60,000
Total	₹23,60,000

You are required to:

(a) assign the customer-related activity costs to each category of customers in proportion to the sales revenue earned by each customer type and calculate the profitability of each customer type.

(b) Assign the customer-related activity costs to each customer type using activity rates and calculate the profitability of each customer category.

9. Bharat Engineers Ltd. specialises in assembling and turning mass-produced musical instruments. Glaxo, a large distributor, has asked Bharat Engineers to bid on the assembly of 5,000 instruments. Glaxo will supply all the necessary materials. The information about Bharat Ltd. is as follows:

(i) Assembly rate – ₹ 4 per direct labour hour

(ii) Variable manufacturing labour – ₹ 60 per direct labour hour

(iii) Variable overheads – ₹ 20 per direct labour hour

(iv) Fixed overheads – ₹ 50 per direct labour hour

(v) Administrative costs – ₹ 10,000

You are required to calculate:

(a) Minimum price per instrument Bharat Engineers should bid.

(b) Glaxo Ltd. offers to pay full cost plus a maximum of 20% markup.

(c) Glaxo Ltd. will entertain highest bid of ₹ 33 per instrument. What factors should Bharat Engineers consider in making a decision about whether to put in a bid at that price?

10. Avinash Brothers, a large labour contractor supplies contract labour to building-construction companies. The firm has budgeted to supply 80,000 hours of contract labour for 2013. Its variable costs are ₹ 12 per hour and fixed costs are ₹ 2,40,000. The General Manager has proposed a cost plus approach for pricing labour at full cost plus 20%.

You are required to:

(a) Calculate the price per hour to the charged and

(b) The Marketing Manager supplies the following information on demand levels at different prices:

Price Per Hour (₹)	*Demand (Hours)*
16	1,20,000
17	1,00,000
18	80,000
19	70,000
20	60,000

Avinash Brothers can meet any of these demand levels. Fixed costs will remain unchanged for all the demand levels. Calculate the price per hour that Avinash Brothers should charge to maximise operating income.

Chapter

5

Objective Based Costing

STRUCTURE:

5.1 Introduction

5.2 Meaning of Activity Based Management

5.3 Process Value Analysis

5.4 Kaizen Standards

5.5 Benchmarking

5.6 Activity Based Management

5.7 Exercises

5.1 INTRODUCTION

Activity based management is an effective means of helping the organisation to use scarce resources more effectively. Identifying activities and the resources they consume can provide significant insights concerning potential ways to save money and increase an organisation's efficiency. It can benefit both service and manufacturing organisations. Many firms operate in rapidly changing environments. These firms face stiff national and international competition. The stringent competitive environment demands that firms offer customised products and services to diverse customer segments. This means that firms should find cost-efficient ways of producing high-variety-low-volume products. Improving performance translates into constantly searching for ways to eliminate waste. This process is known as continuous improvement. Activity based costing and activity based management are important tools in this ongoing improvement efforts. Activity based management is a form of responsibility accounting. It tells how it differs from financial based responsibility accounting.

5.2 MEANING OF ACTIVITY BASED MANAGEMENT

Activity based management is a systemwide integrated approach that focuses management's attention on activities with the objective of improving customer value and the profit achieved by providing this value. Thus, the activity based management model has two dimensions: a cost dimension and a process dimension. The model is presented below.

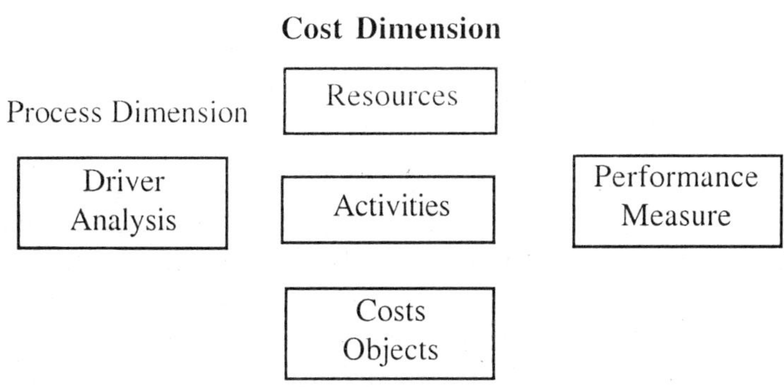

Activity Based Management Model

The cost dimension provides cost information about resources, activities and cost objects of interests such as products, customers, suppliers and distribution channels. The objective of cost dimension is improving the accuracy of cost assignments. The cost of resources is traced to activities and then the cost of activities is assigned to cost objects. This activity based costing dimension is useful for product costing, strategic cost management and tactical analysis. The process dimension provides information about the activities to be performed and the way these activities will be performed. This dimension's objective is to reduce cost. This dimension provides the ability to engage in and measure continuous improvement.

5.3 PROCESS VALUE ANALYSIS

Process value analysis is fundamental to activity based responsibility accounting. It focuses on accountability for activities rather than costs. It also emphasises the maximisation of systemwide performance instead of individual performance. Process value analysis moves activity management from a conceptual basis to an operational basis. Process value analysis is concerned with driver analysis, activity analysis and performance measurement.

(a) Driver Analysis: Managing activities requires an understanding of factors which cause activities. It also causes activity costs to change. Activities consume inputs (resources) and produce outputs. An activity output measure is the number of times the activity is performed. It is the quantifiable measure of the output. The output measure calculates the demands placed on an activity and is an activity driver. As the demand for an activity changes, the cost of an activity can also change. However, output measures may not correspond to the root causes of activity costs. They are also consequences of activity performance. Thus, the purpose of driver analysis is to reveal the root causes. The driver analysis is the effort expanded to identify those factors that are the root causes of activity costs. Several activities may have the same root cause.

(b) Activity Analysis: The heart of process value analysis is activity analysis. It is the process of identifying, describing and evaluating the activities an organisation performs. Activity analysis should produce four outcomes as follows:

(i) what activities are performed

(ii) how many people perform the activities

(iii) the time and resources required to perform the activities

(iv) an assessment of the value of the activities to the organisation including a recommendation to select and keep only those that add value.

The activities can be classified as value-added and non-value-added activities. Value-added activities are those activities necessary to remain in business. Value-added activities contribute to customer value and help to meet an organisation's needs. Activities that comply with legal mandates are value-added because they exist to meet organisational needs. Even though mandated activities are necessary, customers should insist that they be performed as efficiently as possible to reduce the cost impact on goods and services. Classifying discretionary activities as value-added is more of an art than a science and depends heavily on subjective judgement. The conditions to be fulfilled to classify a discretionary activity are:

(i) the activity produces a change of state

(ii) the change of state was not achievable by preceeding activities

(iii) the activity enables other activities to be performed.

Once value-added activities are identified, the value-added costs can be defined. Value-added costs are the costs to perform value-added activities with perfect efficiency.

Non-value-added activities are unnecessary and are not valued by internal or external customers. Non-value-added activities are often those that fail to produce a change in state or those that replicate work because it was not done correctly the first time. Inspection is a state-detection activity and not a state-changing activity. As a general rule, state-detection activities are not value-added activities. Non-value-added costs are costs that are caused either by non-value-added activities or the inefficient performance of value-added activities. Firms have been attempting to eliminate non-value-added activities and non-essential portions of value-added activities because they add unnecessary costs and impede performance. Thus, activity analysis attempts to identify and eventually eliminate all unnecessary activities and increase the efficiency of necessary activities.

Assessing the value content of activities enables managers to eliminate waste. As waste is eliminated, the costs are reduced. Thus, cost reduction follows the elimination of waste. Increasing the efficiency of a non-value-added activity is not a good long-term strategy. The examples of non-value-added activities are scheduling, moving, waiting, inspecting and storing. None of these activities adds value for the customer.

(c) Performance Measurement: Activity performance measurement is designed to assess how well an activity is performed and the results are achieved. Measures of activity performance are both financial as well as non-financial and cater on three major dimensions — Efficiency, Quality and Time. Efficiency is concerned with the relationship of activity outputs to activity inputs. If the cost trend is downward, it indicates that the activity efficiency is improving. Quality is concerned with doing the activity right the first time it is performed. If the activity output is defective, then the activity may need to be repeated causing unnecessary cost and reduction in efficiency. The time required to perform an activity is also critical. Longer time usually mean more resource consumption and less ability to respond to customer demands. Time measures of performance tend to be non-financial, whereas efficiency and quality measures are both financial and non-financial.

Illustration 5.1: Ashok Engineers Ltd. has four production activities for manufacturing Engines: purchasing materials, moulding, inspecting moulds and grinding imperfect moulds. Purchasing and moulding are necessary activities while inspection and grinding are unnecessary activities. The following data pertain to the four activities for a period:

Activity	*Activity Driver*	*Standard Quantity*	*Actual Quantity*	*Standard Price (₹)*
Purchasing	Purchasing hours	20,000	23,000	20
Moulding	Moulding hours	30,000	34,000	12
Inspecting	Inspection hours	—	6000	15
Grinding	Number of units	—	5000	06

The value-added standards for inspection and grinding call for their elimination. You are required to determine the value-added costs and non-value-added costs as well as actual costs.

Solution:

Calculation of Value-added and Non-value-added Costs

Activity	*Value-added costs (₹)*	*Non-valued-added costs (₹)*	*Actual Costs (₹)*
Purchasing	4,00,000	60,000	4,60,000
Moulding	3,60,000	48,000	4,08,000
Inspecting	—	90,000	90,000
Grinding	—	30,000	30,000
Total	**7,60,000**	**2,28,000**	**9,88,000**

Working:

(1) Value-added costs = SQ × SP

Purchasing = 20,000 × 20 = ₹ 4,00,000

Moulding = 30,000 × 12 = ₹ 3,60,000

(2) Non-value-added costs = SP (AQ – SQ)

Inspecting = 15 (6,000 – 0) = ₹ 90,000

Grinding = 06 (5,000 – 0) = ₹ 30,000

Ideally, there should be no defective moulds. In improving quality and changing production, processes, inspection and grinding can be eventually eliminated.

Illustration 5.2: The trend of non-value-added costs of Chirag Ltd. is given below:

Activity	*2010* (₹)	*2011* (₹)
Purchasing	60,000	30,000
Moulding	48,000	36,000
Inspecting	90,000	50,000
Grinding	30,000	20,000

You are required to calculate the reduction in non-value-added cost over the period and offer your comments.

Solution:

(a) Non-value-added Costs

Activity	*2010 (₹)*	*2011 (₹)*	*Reduction in Cost (₹)*
Purchasing	60,000	30,000	30,000
Moulding	48,000	36,000	12,000
Inspection	90,000	50,000	40,000
Grinding	30,000	20,000	10,000
Total	2,28,000	1,36,000	92,000

(b) Comparing the costs for each activity over time, managers can take actions to improve activities. The goal is activity improvement as measured by cost reduction. There is a decline in non-value-added costs from 2010 to 2011. This shows that activity improvement initiatives are effective.

5.4 KAIZEN STANDARDS

Kaizen costing is concerned with reducing the costs of existing products and processes. This helps to reduce non-value-added costs. Controlling non-value-added costing process can be made with the help of Kaizen and maintenance cycle. If a company is emphasising the reduction of non-value-added costs, the amount of improvement planned for the coming period is to be set.

The Kaizen standard reflects the planned improvement for the upcoming period. It is a sub-cycle defined by a Plan-Do-Check-Act sequence. The process is as follows:

(i) **Plan** – the amount of improvement for the coming period.

(ii) **Do** – actions are taken to implement the planned improvements.

(iii) **Check up** – actual results are compared with the Kaizen standard to provide a measure of level of improvement attained.

(iv) **Act** – the new level is set as a minimum standard for future performance checks in the realised improvements and simultaneously initiates the maintenance cycle and a search for additional improvement opportunities. Thus, the Kaizen cost reduction process is shown in the following diagram:

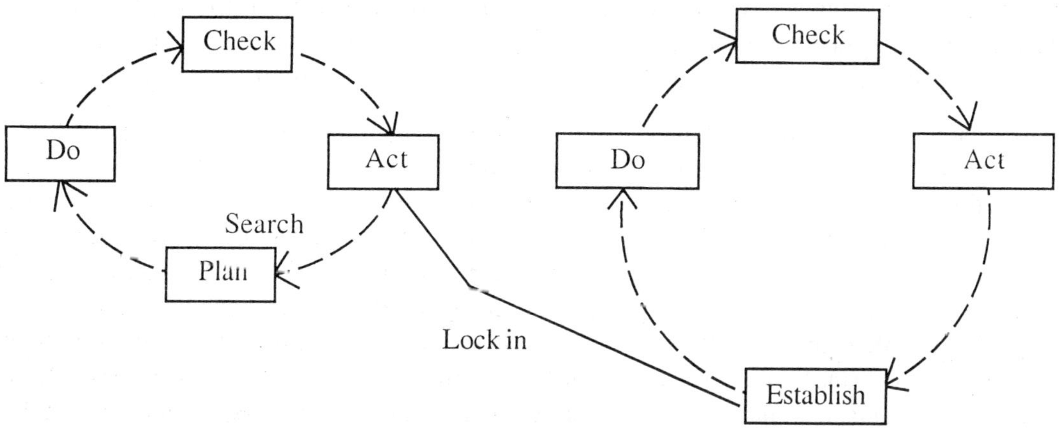

Kaizen Cost Reduction Process

The maintenance cycle follows a traditional Establish-Do-Check-Act sequence. A standard is set based on prior improvements. The actions are taken and the results are checked to ensure that performance confirms to the new level. Otherwise corrective actions are taken to restore performance.

Illustration 5.3: An automotive parts division of Hind Motors engages in a setup activity for the sub-assemblies that it produces. The value-added standard for this activity calls for zero setup hours with a cost of zero per batch sub-assemblies. The company used 8 hours to set up each batch at a cost of ₹ 20 per hour in the past year. This was also the non-value-added cost. The company has been planning in implementing a new setup method deployed by its industrial engineers that is expected to reduce setup time by 50 per cent. Calculate the planned cost reduction per batch.

Solution:

(i) The actual setup cost per batch in the last year

= ₹ 20 × 8 = ₹ 160

(ii) The planned cost for the future

= ₹ 20 × 4 = ₹ 80

(iii) Planned cost reduction per batch

= ₹ 160 – ₹ 80 = ₹ 80

If the actual cost achieved after implementing the new production process is ₹ 80, the actual improvements expected will materialise and the new Kaizen standard will be ₹ 80 per batch.

5.5 BENCHMARKING

Benchmarking uses best practices found within and outside the organisation as the standard for evaluating and improving activity performance. The objective of benchmarking is to become the best at performing activities and processes. It is complimentary to Kaizen costing and activity based management. It can be used as a search mechanism to identify opportunities for improvement.

Benchmarking may be internal or external. Benchmarking against internal operations is called internal benchmarking. The different units that perform the same activities are compared within an organisation. The unit with the best performance for a given activity sets the standard. Other units have a target to meet or exceed. The best practices unit can share information with other units on how it has achieved its superior results. Internal benchmarking has general advantages. A significant amount of information is often readily available that can be shared throughout the organisation. Immediate cost reductions are often realised. The best internal standard that spread throughout the organisation become the benchmark for comparison against external benchmarking patterns. However, the major disadvantage of internal benchmarking is that the best internal performance may fall short of particularly in direct comparisons. The internal benchmarking does not have to be restricted to cost management.

The benchmarking that involves comparisons with others is called as external benchmarking. The different types of external benchmarking are competitive benchmarking, functional benchmarking and generic benchmarking. Competitive benchmarking is a comparison of activity performance with direct competitors. Functional benchmarking is a comparison with firms that are in the same industry but do not compete in the same markets. Generic benchmarking studies the best practices of non-competitors outside a firm's industry. Certain activities and processes are common to all organisations. If superior external best practice can be identified, it can be used as standard to motivate internal improvements.

Activity flexible budgeting is the prediction of what activity costs will be as activity output changes. Variance analysis within an activity framework makes it possible to improve traditional budgetary performance reporting. It enhances the ability to manage activities. In a functional based approach, budgeted costs for the actual level of activity are obtained by assuming that a single unit based driver drives all costs. A cost formula is developed for each cost item as a function of units produced or direct labour hour. If costs vary with respect to more than one driver and the drivers are not highly correlated with direct labour hours, then the predicted costs can be misleading. The solution is to build flexible budget formulas for more than one driver. Cost estimation procedure can be used to estimate and validate the cost formulas for each activity. The variable cost component for each activity should correspond to resources acquired in advance of usage. This multiple formula approach allows managers to predict more accurately the costs for different levels of activity usage as measured by the activity output measure. These costs can be compared with the actual costs to help assess budgetary performance.

Illustration 5.4: The details about budgeted costs of X Ltd. are given below:

Particulars	*Cost Formula*		*Direct Labour Hours*	
	Fixed (₹)	*Variable* (₹)	*10,000* (₹)	*20,000* (₹)
Direct Materials	—	10	1,00,000	2,00,000
Direct Labour	—	8	80,000	1,60,000
Maintenance	20,000	3	50,000	80,000
Machining	15,000	1	25,000	35,000
Inspections	1,20,000	—	1,20,000	1,20,000
Setups	50,000	—	50,000	50,000
Purchasing	2,20,000	—	2,20,000	2,20,000
Total	4,25,000	22	6,45,000	8,65,000

The budgeted amounts for other items differ significantly from the traditional amounts as the activity output measures differ. If the actual fixed inspection cost are ₹ 82,000 and the actual variable inspection costs are ₹ 43,500, calculate the variable and fixed budget variances for the inspection activity. The actual levels of drivers: 10,000 direct labour hours, 8,000 machine hours, 25 setups and 15,000 orders.

Solution:

(a) Driver: Direct Labour Hours

	Formula		Level of Activity
	Fixed	Variable	10,000
Direct Materials	—	10	1,00,000
Direct Labour	—	8	80,000
Total		18	1,80,000

(b) Driver: Machine Hours (8,000)

Maintenance	20,000	5.50	64,000
Machining	15,000	2.00	31,000
Total	35,000	7.50	95,000

(c) Driver: Number of Setups (25)

Inspections	80,000	2,100	1,32,500
Setups	—	1,800	45,000
Total	80,000	3,900	1,77,500

(d) Driver: Number of Orders (15,000)

Purchasing	2,11,000	1	2,26,000

(e) Budgeted Cost (25 setup levels)

Activity	*Actual cost* ₹	*25 setup levels* ₹	*Variance* ₹
Inspection:			
Fixed	82,000	80,000	2,000 A
Variable	43,500	52,500	9,000 F
Total	1,25,500	1,32,500	7,000 F

Breaking each variance into fixed and variable components provides more insight into the source of the variation in planned and actual expenditure.

5.6 ACTIVITY BASED MANAGEMENT

Activity Based Management (ABM) is a systemwide integrated approach that focuses management's attention on activities with the objectives of improving customer value and the profit achieved by providing this value. ABC is the major source of information for activity based management. It can benefit both service and manufacturing organisations. NASA's Lewis Research Center has found that activity based management is an effective means of helping it use scarce resources dollars more efficiently. Identifying activities and the resources they consume can provide significant insights concerning potential ways to save money and increase an organisation's efficiency.

Many firms operate in rapidly changing environments. This stringent competitive environment demands that firms offer customised products and services to diverse customer segments. This, in turn, means that firms must find cost-efficient ways of producing high-variety-low-volume products. To find ways to improve performance, firms operating in this kind of environment not only must know what it currently costs to do things but they must also evaluate why and how they do things. Improving performance translates into constantly searching for ways to eliminate waste. Activity based costing and Activity based management are important tools in this ongoing improvement effort.

Activity based management is a more comprehensive system than an ABC system. ABM adds a process view to the cost view of ABC. ABM encompasses ABC and uses it as a major source of information. ABM can be viewed as an information system that has the broad objectives of improving decision-making by providing accurate cost information and reducing costs by encouraging and supporting continuous improvement efforts.

5.6.1 ABM Implementation

The overall objective of ABM is to improve the firm's profitability. It is an objective achieved by identifying and selecting opportunities for improvement and using more accurate information to make better decisions. Root cause analysis reveals opportunities for improvement. By identifying non-value-added costs, priorities can be established based on the initiatives that offer the most cost reduction. The potential cost reduction itself is measured by ABC calculations. The two common steps in ABM implementation are:

(a) Systems Planning: It provides the justification for implementing ABM and address the following issues:

(i) The purpose and objectives of the ABM system

(ii) The organisation's current and desired competitive position

(iii) The organisation's business processes and product mix

(iv) The timeline, assigned responsibilities and resources required for implementation

(v) The ability of the organisation to implement, learn and use new information

(b) Activity Identification, Definition and Classification: Identifying, defining and classifying activities requires more attention for ABM. The activity should define a detailed listing of the tasks that define each activity. Knowing the tasks that define an activity can be very helpful for improving the efficiency of value-added activities. Classification of activities allows ABM to connect with other continuous improvement initiatives such as Just in Time, Total Quality Management and total environmental quality cost management. It is important to realise that successful implementation requires time and patience. This is specially true when it comes to using the new information provided by Activity Based Management System.

ABM can fail as a system. One of the major reasons for failure is the lack of support of higher-level management. This support should be obtained before undertaking an implementation project and it should be maintained. Loss of support can occur if the implementation takes too long or the expected results do not materialise. Results may not occur as expected because operating and sales managers do not have the expertise to use the new activity information. Involving non-financial managers in the planning and implementation stage may reduce resistance and secure the required support. The probability of success is increased if the ABM system is not in competition with other improvements programme. Therefore, it is important to communicate the concept that ABM complements and enhances other improvement programmes. The ABM should be integrated to the point that activity costing outcome are not in direct competition with the traditional accounting numbers.

5.6.2 Activity Based Responsibility Accounting

Responsibility accounting is a fundamental tool of managerial control and it is defined by four essential elements as under:

(i) Assigning responsibility

(ii) Establishing performance measures

(iii) Evaluating performance

(iv) Assigning rewards

The objective of responsibility accounting is to influence behaviour in such a way that individual and organisational initiatives are aligned to achieve a common goal.

A particular responsibility accounting system is defined by how these four elements are defined. Three types of responsibility accounting systems have evolved over time. These are financial based, activity based and strategic based. These are practiced today. Normally, firms choose the responsibility accounting system that is compatible with the requirements and economics of their particular operating environment. Firms that operate in a stable environment, with standardised products and processes and low competitive pressures are likely to find the less complex, financial based responsibility accounting systems to be quite adequate. As organisational complexity increases and the competitive environment becomes much more dynamic, activity based and strategic based systems are likely to be more stable.

The responsibility accounting system for a stable environment is referred to as financial based responsibility accounting. A financial based responsibility accounting system assigns responsibility to organisational units and expresses performance measures in financial terms. It emphasises a financial perspective. Activity based responsibility accounting is the responsibility accounting system developed for those firms operating in continuous improvement environments. Activity based responsibility accounting assigns responsibility to processes and uses both financial and non-financial measures of performance emphasising both financial and process perspectives.

(i) Assigning Responsibility: First of all, a responsibility centre is identified. It is an organisational unit such as plant, production line or department. The responsibility is assigned to the individual in charge. Responsibility is defined in financial terms that is costs emphasis is on achieving optimal financial results at the local level. In any activity or process based responsibility system, the focal point changes from units and individuals to processes and teams. In a continuous improvement environment, the financial perspective translates into continuously enhancing revenues, reducing costs and improving asset utilisation. Creating this continuous growth and improvement requires an organisation to constantly improve its capabilities of delivering value to customers and shareholders.

(ii) Establishing Performance Measures: Performance measures should be identified and standards should be set to serve as benchmarks for performance measurement. Budgeting and standard costing are the cornerstones of the benchmark activity for a financial based system. This implies that performance measures are objective and financial in nature. Performance measures are process-oriented and must be connected with process attributes such as process time, quality and efficiency. Performance measurement standards are structured to support change. Optimal standards assume a vital role. They set the ultimate achievement target and identify the potential for improvement. The standards should reflect the value added by individual activities and processes. It expands control to include the entire organisation.

(iii) Evaluating Performance: In a financial based framework, performance is measured by comparing actual outcomes with budgeted outcomes. Individuals are held accountable only for those items over which they have control. Financial performance measured by the ability to meet or beat a stable financial standard is strongly emphasised. In the activity based framework, performance is concerned with more than just the financial perspective. The process perspective adds time, quality, and efficiency as critical dimensions of performance. Decreasing the time a process takes to deliver its output to customers is viewed as a vital objective. Non-financial process-oriented measures also become important. Performance is evaluated by gauging whether these measures are improving over time. It is time for measures relating to quality and efficiency. Improving a process translates into better financial results. Measures of cost reduction achieved, trends in cost and cost per unit of output are all useful indicators of whether a process has improved or not. Thus, the objective is to provide low-cost, high quality products to be delivered on a timely basis.

(iv) Assigning rewards: Progress rewards achieving optimal standards and interim standards need to be measured. Individuals should be rewarded or penalised according to the policies and direction of top management. Some of the financial instruments are used to provide rewards for good performance. It includes bonus, profit-sharing and promotions. The nature of the incentive structure differs in each system. For the activity based reward system, rewarding individual is more complicated than it is in a functional based setting. Individuals simultaneously have accountability for team and individual performance. Process related improvements are mostly achieved through team efforts, Group based rewards are more stable than individual rewards. Bonuses are awarded to the team whenever performance is maintained on all measures and improves on at least one measure. Profit-sharing is a global incentive designed to encourage employees to contribute to the overall financial well-being of the organisation. Employees are allowed to share in gains related to specific improvement projects.

Illustration 5.5: Ponds Ltd. has developed value-added standards for its activities including material usage, purchasing and inspecting. The value-added output levels for each of the activities, their actual levels achieved and the standard prices are as follows:

Activity	*Activity Driver*	*Standard Quantity*	*Actual Quantity*	*Standard Price (₹)*
Using lumber	Board feet	24,000	30,000	10
Purchasing	Purchase orders	800	1000	50
Inspecting	Inspection hours	0	4000	10

Assume that material usage and purchasing costs correspond to flexible resources and that inspection uses resources that are acquired in blocks or steps of 2,000 hours. The actual prices paid for the inputs equal the standard prices.

Required:

(a) Assume that continuous improvement efforts reduce the demand for inspection by 30 per cent during the year. Calculate the volume and unused capacity variances for the inspection activity.

(b) Prepare a cost report that shows the value-added and non-value-added costs.

(c) Assuming that the company wants to reduce all non-value-added costs by 30 per cent in the coming year, prepare the Kaizen standards that can be used to evaluate the company's progress towards this goal.

Solution:

(a) (i) Volume Variance = Standard Price × Actual Quantity

= ₹ 10 × 4,000

= ₹ 40,000

(ii) Capacity Variance = Standard Price × Actual Usage

= ₹ 10 × 2,800

= ₹ 28,000

Unused Capacity Variance = ₹ 40,000 – ₹ 28,000

= ₹ 12,000

(b) Cost Report

Particulars	*Value-added*	*Non-value-added*	*Total*
Using lumber	2,40,000	60,000	3,00,000
Purchasing	40,000	10,000	50,000
Inspecting	0	40,000	40,000
Total	2,80,000	1,10,000	3,90,000

(c) Kaizen Standards

Particulars	**Quantity**	**Cost (₹)**
Using lumber	28,200	2,82,000
Purchasing	940	47,000
Inspecting	2,800	28,000

If the standards are met, then the savings will be as follows:

Using lumber (10 × 1,800)	₹ 18,000
Purchasing (50 × 60)	₹ 3000
Savings	₹ 21,000

Notes:

(1) There is no reduction in resource spending for inspection activities because it must be purchased in increments of 2,000 and only 1,200 hours can be saved. Another 800 hours must be reduced before any reduction in resource spending is possible. The unused capacity variance should reach ₹ 24,000 before resources spending can be reduced.

(2) Inspecting (AQ) hours = 4,000 – 1,200 = 2,800 hours

(3) Reduction in Purchasing orders (AQ) = 30% (1,000 – 8,000) = 200 × 30% = 60

(4) Reduction in lumber = 30% (30,000 – 24,000)

= 30% × 6,000

= 1,800

5.7 EXERCISES

1. What is Activity Based Management? What are the two dimensions of the activity based management model?
2. What is Driver Analysis? What role does it plan in process value analysis?
3. What is Activity Analysis? Why is this approach compatible with the goal of continuous improvements?
4. What are value-added activities and costs?
5. What are non-value-added activities and costs?
6. Explain four different ways to manage activities so that costs can be reduced.
7. Explain how value-added standards are used to identify value-added and non-value-added costs.
8. What is Kaizen Standard? Explain the Kaizen and maintenance subcycles.
9. What is Benchmarking? Explain how Benchmarking can be used to improve activity performance.
10. What are some of the planning considerations in implementing an ABM system?
11. What are the reasons for the failure of the ABM implementation?
12. Explain the activity based responsibility accounting system. How does it differ from financial based responsibility accounting?
13. Siemens Ltd. has been experiencing competitive difficulties. It sells its products on a cost plus basis and has lost a number of bids on its high-volume products. The average losing bid was ₹ 600 more than the warming bid. Bill Lorry, a consultant, has indicated that poor

overhead costing assignments may be causing the company's bidding problems. The company has two overhead activities, setup and machining. The two activities, their costs and practical capacities are given below:

Activity	*Cost (₹)*	*Practical (Capacity)*
Setup	12,00,000	40,000 setup flours
Machining	18,00,000	1,50,000 machine hours

Siemens Ltd. assigns overhead costs to jobs using a plantwide rate based on machine hours. Setup time for a job involving a high-volume product is usually half that of jobs for low-volume speciality products (20 hours versus 40 hours). On the other hand, a typical high-volume product job was 100 machine hours and a typical low-volume product job uses 20 machine hours. Prime costs for a typical high-volume product job are ₹ 2,000. The company management indicated that the markup on jobs is cost plus 50 per cent.

You are required to calculate the cost of a typical job for a high-volume product using machine hours to assign overhead costs.

14. Hindustan Zinc Ltd. has 20 clerks who work in the accounts department. A study revealed the following activities and the relative time demanded by each activity:

Activity	*% of Clerical Time*
(i) Comparing purchase orders and receiving orders and invoices	15%
(ii) Resolving discrepancies among the three documents	70%
(iii) Preparing cheques for supplies	10%
(iv) Making journal entries and mailing cheques	5%

The average salary of clerk is ₹ 30,000 per month.

You are required to classify the four activities as value-added and non-value-added and calculate the clerical cost of each activity.

15. Raymonds produces a variety of cell phones. The company is implementing an activity based management due to competitive pressures. The objective is to reduce costs. ABM focuses attention on processes and activities. Receiving was among the processes (activities) that were carefully studied. The study revealed that the number of reciving order was a good driver for purchasing costs. During the last year, the company incurred fixed receiving costs of ₹ 2,80,000 which includes the salary of 8 employees. The fixed costs provide a capacity of processing 32,000 orders with practical capacity of 4,000 per employee. Management decided that the value-added standard number of purchase orders is 16,000. The number of actual orders processed in the period was 28,000.

You are required to calculate the volume and unused capacity variances for receiving.

16. Suzlon Ltd. has developed value-added standards for its four activities: receiving parts, inspecting parts, moving parts and assembling parts. The activities, the activity drivers, the standard and actual quantities and the price standards for 2012 are as follows:

Activities	*Activity Driver*	*SQ*	*AQ*	*SP (₹)*
Receiving Parts	Orders	1,000	1,400	150
Inspecting Parts	Inspection Hours	0	8,000	15
Moving Parts	No. of Moves	0	800	100
Assembling Parts	Labour Hours	20,000	24,000	12

The actual prices paid per unit of each activity driver were equal to the standard prices.

You are required to prepare a Cost Report that lists the value-added, non-value-added and actual costs for each activity.

Chapter

Balance Scorecard Concept

STRUCTURE:

6.1 Introduction

6.2 Balanced Scorecard

6.3 Four Basic Business Perspectives

6.4 Components and Measures of Performance

6.5 Evaluation of Responsibility Centres

6.6 Exercises

6.1 INTRODUCTION

The Balanced Scorecard is a collection of critical performance measures that have some special properties. The performance measures are derived from a company's vision, strategy and objectives. To link measures to a strategy, they must be derived from strategy. The performance measures should be chosen so that they are balanced between outcome and lead measures. Outcome measures are such as profitability, return on investment, market share trend to be generic common to most strategies and organisations. Performance drivers make things happen consequently. Lead measures are indicators of how the outcomes are going to be realised. Lead measures usually distinguish one strategy and other. The lead measures are often unique to a strategy and because of this uniqueness support the objective of linking measures to strategy. Thus, all scorecard measures should be linked by cause and effect relationships.

Delivering goods on time to customers is an important performance driver. The customer satisfaction increases if the goods are delivered on time. More goods can be produced and sold if customer satisfaction increases. More revenue is generated if goods are sold more. Thus, recognising and managing these kinds of cause and effect relationships is a key feature of the balanced scorecard.

Many firms operate in an environment where change is rapid. Products and processes are constantly being recognised and improved. There are stiff national and international competitors. The competitive environment demands that firms offer customised products and services to diverse customer segment. This means that firms should find cost-effective ways of producing high variety low volume products. More attention is paid to linkages between the firm and its suppliers and customers with the goal of improving cost, quality and response times for all parties in the value chain. Product life cycles are shrinking for many industries, placing greater demands on the need for innovation. Thus, organisations operating in a dynamic, rapidly changing environment are finding that adaption and change are essential for the survival.

6.2 BALANCED SCORECARD

Balanced Scorecard: The linking of financial and non-financial measures of performance and identification of key performance measures help to devise the balance scorecard, a set of measures that give top managers a fast but comprehensive view of the business. The failure of traditional cost systems to remain useful in the changing environment is evidenced by the following factors:

(i) Organisations often fail to link performance measurement to the strategic initiatives of organisations.

(ii) Extra emphasis is laid down on accounting for external reporting rather than reports useful for internal decision making.

(iii) The traditional approaches failed to account for advances in technology that change how manufacturing firms operate in new environment.

(iv) The growing importance of service industries and increased global competition has intensified the need for alternative control and performance measures for organisations seeking to remain competitive.

The balanced scorecard is defined as "an approach to the provision of information to the management to assist strategic policy formulation and achievement". It emphasises the need to provide the user with a set of information, which addresses all relevant areas of performance in an objective and unbiased fashion. Thus, balanced scorecard is a set of measures that gives top management a fast but comprehensive view of the organisational unit. The aim of balanced scorecard is to provide a comprehensive framework for translating a company's strategic objectives into a coherent set of performance measures. The balanced scorecard is a performance measurement system that focuses employee's behavior on actions that directly or indirectly relate to achieving business-unit strategic objectives.

The term balanced scorecard became popular after Robert Kaplan and David Norton published an article in the *Harvard Business Review* in 1992. They have developed four concepts supporting balanced scorecard which are given below:

(i) A balanced scorecard should focus on strategies appropriate for each business unit.

(ii) By assessing on lag indicators, an organisation can identify cause and effect relationships. This, in turn, suggests financial and non-financial performance measures, that can be included on scorecards for both individuals and business units.

(iii) The inclusion of financial and non-financial measures in balanced scorecard encourages employees to pay attention to actions that improves the long-term benefits for a business unit.

(iv) Communicating the specific details of a balanced scorecard to employees helps them to embrace the performance measures, because they will better understand how they can contribute to the organisation's success.

The balanced scorecard permits an organisation to create a strategic focus by translating an organisation's strategy into operational objectives and performance measures for different perspectives. It is an effective way of implementing and managing a company's strategy. Many companies attribute their recent financial success to this strategic performance management system. Strategy is defined as choosing the markets and customer segments the business unit intends to serve. It is also identifying the critical internal and business processes that the unit must excel at to deliver the value propositions to customers in the targeted market segments and selecting the individual and organisational capabilities required for the internal customer and financial objectives. Strategy is again, identifying and defining management's desired relationships among the different perspectives. Strategy translation means specifying objectives, measures, targets and initiatives for each perspective.

6.3 FOUR BASIC BUSINESS PERSPECTIVES

Kaplan and Norton classified performance measures into four business perspectives as shown in Chart 6.1:

Chart 6.1: Financial Perspective

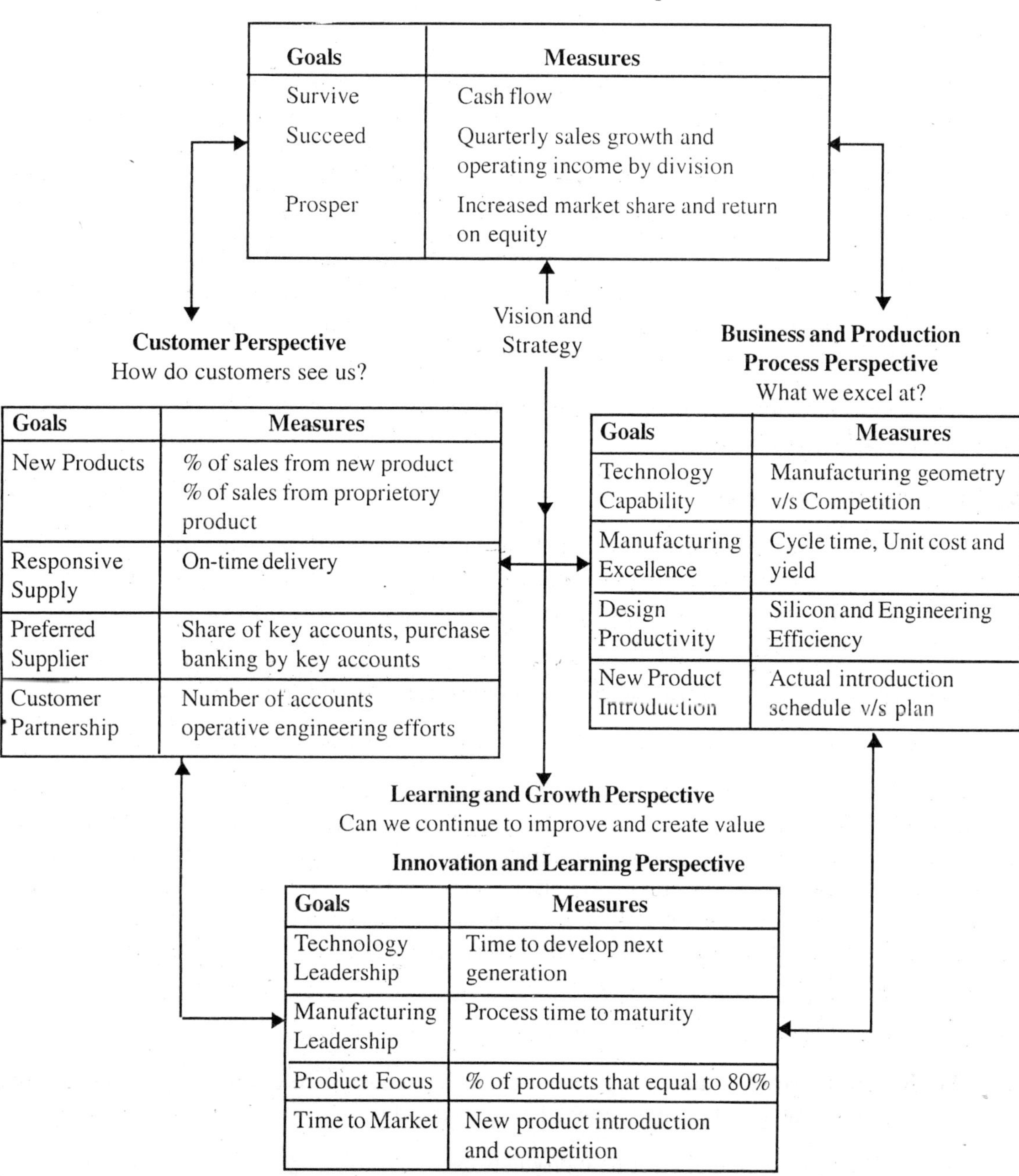

Goals	Measures
Survive	Cash flow
Succeed	Quarterly sales growth and operating income by division
Prosper	Increased market share and return on equity

Vision and Strategy

Customer Perspective
How do customers see us?

Goals	Measures
New Products	% of sales from new product % of sales from proprietory product
Responsive Supply	On-time delivery
Preferred Supplier	Share of key accounts, purchase banking by key accounts
Customer Partnership	Number of accounts operative engineering efforts

Business and Production Process Perspective
What we excel at?

Goals	Measures
Technology Capability	Manufacturing geometry v/s Competition
Manufacturing Excellence	Cycle time, Unit cost and yield
Design Productivity	Silicon and Engineering Efficiency
New Product Introduction	Actual introduction schedule v/s plan

Learning and Growth Perspective
Can we continue to improve and create value

Innovation and Learning Perspective

Goals	Measures
Technology Leadership	Time to develop next generation
Manufacturing Leadership	Process time to maturity
Product Focus	% of products that equal to 80%
Time to Market	New product introduction and competition

From the above diagram, we can see that it allows managers to look at the business from four different perspectives by seeking to provide answers to the following four basis questions:

(i) How do customers see us?

(ii) What must we excel at?

(iii) Can we continue to improve and create value?

(iv) How do we look to shareholders?

The aim of the scorecard is to provide a comprehensive framework for translating a company's strategic objectives into a coherent set of performance measures. By providing all this information in a single report, management is able to assess the impact of particular actions on all perspectives of the company's activities. Determining the specific items to include in a balanced scorecard requires a business to examine its operations carefully.

The organisations should articulate the major goals for each of the four perspectives and then translate these goals into specific performance measures. Each organisation should decide what its critical performance measures are. The choice will vary over time and should be linked to the strategy that the organisation is following.

The process of establishing objectives and performance measures in each of the four scorecard perspectives are given below:

A. Financial Perspective

Business has to be viewed first of all from financial perspective. Examining strategic initiatives from a financial perspective leads to determining whether these initiatives are being met. Financial measures remain the central focus of most balanced scorecard programmes. The financial objectives chosen serve two purposes:

(i) To provide definite performance expectations from chosen strategies, and

(ii) To provide a focus for objectives and measures in each of the three perspectives.

The financial perspective indicates whether the company's strategy and operations add value to shareholders. The balanced scorecard uses financial performance measures such as net income and return on investment because they are universally used in for-profit organisations. Financial performance measures provide a common language for analysing and comparing companies. Financial measures are important but are not sufficient to guide performance in creating value. The balanced scorecard looks for a balance of multiple performance measures both financial and non-financial to guide organisational performance towards success.

The financial perspective has three strategic themes as under:

(1) Revenue growth: Increasing revenue can be achieved in a variety of ways and the potential strategic objectives reflect these possibilities:

(i) Increase the number of new products.

(ii) Create new application for existing products.

(iii) Develop new customers and markets.

(iv) Adopt new pricing strategy.

Performance measures can be designed once operational objectives are known. Possible measures for the preceding list of objectives are percentages of revenue from new products, new applications and from new customers and market segments.

(2) Cost Reduction: The cost reduction objectives may be to reduce cost per unit of product or customer or distribution channel. The appropriate measures are obvious: The cost per unit of the particular cost object. Trends in these measures will indicate whether or not the costs are being reduced. For these objectives, the accuracy of cost assignments is especially important. Activity based costing can play an important role especially for selling and distribution costs and administrative costs.

(3) Asset Utilisation: Financial measures such as return on investment and economic value added are used to improve asset utilisation. Both these measures are based on the asset utilisation.

Managing the risk associated with the adopted strategy is critical strategic theme. It is common to the three strategic financial themes. Diversification of customer types product lines and suppliers are common means of lowering risk. Again sourcing materials from only one supplier may lower costs, but it may also affect the firms performance if something goes wrong with the supplier. Similarly, revenues may be increased by relying on one very large customer. But if the customer decides to buy from other firm, there will be a risk to this firm. Thus, strategic initiative must be balanced with careful consideration of the risk involved.

B. Customer Perspective

The balanced scorecard makes efforts to ascertain the customer's perspective about the business unit. The companies identify customers and market segment in which they compete. In identifying why customers chose a particular business unit, managers identify lead indicators for the customer perspectives. If customers value on-time delivery, then on-time delivery becomes a lead indicator for a key performance driver such as customer retention. Lead indicators of customers may be on-time delivery, defects per shipment, cost and service. It is well recognised that if business units are to achieve long-run superior financial performance, they must create and deliver products and services that are valued by customers.

Customers care about three things in general. These are product's price, function and quality. Companies use the following performance measures among others, while considering the customer perspective:

(i) Customer satisfaction

(ii) Customer retention

(iii) Market share

(iv) Customer profitability

The customer perspective is the source of the revenue component for the financial objectives. Failure to deliver the right kinds of products and services to the targeted customers means revenue will not be generated.

(a) Core Objectives and Measures: Once the customers and segments are defined, core objectives and measures are developed. These are common to all the organisations. There are five key core objectives as follows:

(i) Increase in market share

(ii) Increase customer retention

(iii) Increase customer acquisition

(iv) Increase customer satisfaction

(v) Increase customer profitability

Possible core measures for these objectives are market share, growth of business from existing customers, percentage of repeating customers, number of new customers, ratings from customer satisfaction surveys and individual and segment profitability. Activity based costing is a key tool in accessing customer profitability.

(b) Customer Value: Measures are also needed to drive the creation of customer value to drive the core customers. Increasing customer value builds customer loyalty and increases customer satisfaction. Customer value is the difference between realisation and sacrifice. Realisation is what the customer receives and sacrifice is what the customer gives up. Realisation includes such attributes as product functionality, product quality, reliability of delivery, response time, image and reputation. Sacrifice includes attributes such as product price, time required to learn to use the product, operating cost, maintenance cost and disposal cost. The costs incurred by the customer after purchase are known as post-purchase cost.

The attributes associated with realisation and sacrifice provide the basis for the objectives and measures that will lead to improving the core outcomes. The objectives for the sacrifice side of the value equation are the simplest, i.e., decrease price and decrease post-purchase cost. Selling price and post-purchase costs are important measures of value creation. Decreasing these costs decreases customer sacrifice and increases customer value. Increasing customer value should impact favourably on most of the core objectives. Similar favourable effects can be attained by increasing realisation. Realisation objectives include the following:

(i) Improve product functionality

(ii) Improve product quality

(iii) Increase delivery reliability

(iv) Improve product image and reputation

Possible measures for these objectives includes the following:

(a) Feature satisfaction ratings

(b) Percentage of returns

(c) On-time delivery percentage

(d) Product recognition ratings

Of these objectives and measures, delivery reliability can be used to illustrate how measures can affect managerial behaviour, indicating the need to be careful in the choice and use of performance measures.

Delivery reliability means that goods are delivered on time. It is commonly used as operational measure of reliability. In order to measure on-time delivery, a firm sets delivery dates and then finds on-time delivery performance, by dividing the orders delivered on time by the total number of orders delivered. The goal is to achieve a ratio of 100 per cent.

C. Internal Business and Production Process Perspective

Business should concentrate on the improvement of only those areas, that have tactical relevance to a company's strategic direction namely innovation, operations, and after-sale services to customers. There is a cause and effect relationship between the learning and growth perspectives and the internal business and production process perspective. Employees who do the work are the best source of new ideas for better business processes. Supplier's relations are becoming increasingly important as more and more companies are outsourcing activities that are once done internally. Some of these increased reliance on supplies is derived from the use of activity based costing and management. Customers value receiving goods and services reliably on time. Suppliers can satisfy customers if they hold large amounts of inventory to ensure that goods are on hand. But holding lots of inventory leads to high inventory carrying and storage costs, inventory obsolescence and many other problems.

Process Perspective

The internal process perspective describes the internal processes needed to provide value for customers and owners. Processes are the means by which strategies are executed. Therefore, the process perspective entails the identification of the critical processes needed that affect customer and shareholder satisfaction. In order to provide the framework needed for this perspective, a process value chain is defined. It is made up of three processes as follows:

(i) **Innovation process:** It anticipates the emerging and potential needs of customers and creates new products and services to satisfy these needs. It represents the long-wave of value creation. The operations process produces and delivers existing products and services to the customers. It begins with a customer order and ends with the delivery of the product or service. It is short-wave of value creation. The post-sales service process provides critical and responsive services to customers after the product or service has been delivered. The objectives of the innovation process are:

- Increase the number of new products
- Increase percentage of revenue from proprietary products
- Decrease the time to develop new products

(ii) Operations process: The objectives of operation process are as follows:

- Increase process quality
- Increase process efficiency
- Decrease process time

Measures of process efficiency are concerned mainly with process cost and process productivity. Measuring and tracking process cost are facilitated by activity based costing and process value analysis.

(iii) Cycle time and velocity: Cycle time and velocity are two operational measures of responsiveness. Cycle time is the length of time, it takes to produce a unit of output from the time materials are received until the goods are delivered to finished goods inventory. Thus, cycle time is the time required to produce a product. Velocity is the number of units of output that can be produced in a given period of time. Incentives can be used to encourage operational managers to reduce manufacturing cycle time or to reduce velocity. A natural way to accomplish this objective is to tie up product costs to cycle time and reward operational managers for reducing product costs. Using the theoretical productive time available for a period, a value-added standard cost per minute can be computed as follows:

$$\text{Standard cost per minute} = \frac{\text{Cell conversion costs}}{\text{Minutes available}}$$

To obtain the conversion cost per unit, the standard cost per minute is multiplied by the actual cycle time used to produce the units during the period. By comparing the unit cost computed using the actual cycle time with the unit cost possible using the theoretical or optimal cycle time, a manager can assess the potential for improvement.

Illustration 6.1: A company has given the following data for one of its manufacturing cells:

Theoretical velocity: 40 units per hour

Productive minutes available (per year): 12,00,000

Annual conversion cost: ₹ 48,00,000

Actual velocity: 30 units per hour

Determine: (a) Actual conversion cost and (b) Ideal conversion cost.

Solution:

(a) Calculation of actual conversion cost per unit:

$$\text{Standard cost per minute} = \frac{48,00,000}{12,00,000} = ₹\,4$$

$$\text{Actual cycle time} = \frac{60\,\text{minutes}}{30\,\text{units}} = 2 \text{ minutes per unit}$$

Actual conversion cost (per unit) = ₹ 4 × 2 = ₹ 8

(b) Calculation of ideal conversion cost per unit:

$$\text{Theoretical cycle time} = \frac{60\,\text{minutes}}{40\,\text{units}}$$

$$= 1.5 \text{ minute per unit}$$

Ideal conversion cost = ₹ 4 × 1.5 = ₹ 6

(iv) Manufacturing Cycle Efficiency: Manufacturing cycle efficiency is a time-based operational measure which is calculated as follows:

$$\text{MCE} = \frac{\text{Processing Time}}{\text{Processing Time} + \text{Move Time} + \text{Inspection Time} + \text{Waiting Time} + \text{Other Non-value-added Time}}$$

Process time is the time it takes to convert materials into a finished product. The other activities and their times are viewed as wasteful. Therefore, the objective is to reduce those times to zero.

If this is accomplished, the value of MCF would be 1.00. As MCE improves, cycle time decreases. The MCE can improve by reducing waste, hence cost reduction is possible.

Illustration 6.2: 'B' Ltd. gives the following data for one of its manufacturing cells:

Theoretical velocity: 40 units per hour

Productive minutes available (per year) = 1,20,000

Annual conversion cost: ₹ 4,80,000

Actual velocity = 30 units per hour

Determine the MCE.

Solution:

$$\text{Standard cost per minute} = \frac{₹\,4,80,000}{1,20,000} = ₹\,4$$

$$\text{Actual cycle time} = \frac{60\,\text{minutes}}{30\,\text{minutes}} = 2 \text{ minutes per unit}$$

$\therefore$ Actual conversion cost = ₹ 4 × 2 = ₹ 8

$$\text{Theoretical cycle time} = \frac{60 \text{ minutes}}{40 \text{ units}} = 1.5 \text{ minutes per unit}$$

Ideal conversion cost = ₹ 4 × 1.5 = ₹ 6 per unit

$$\text{MCE} = \frac{\text{Processing Time}}{\text{Processing time + Waiting time}} = \frac{2}{2.5} = 0.80$$

Note: Actual cycle time is 2 minutes

Theoretical cycle time is 1.5 minutes

$\therefore$ Time wasted = 0.5 minute (2 – 1.5)

(v) **Post-sales Service Process:** The objectives of post-sales service process are increasing quality, increasing efficiency and decreasing process time. Service quality can be measured by first-pass yields where the first-pass yields are defined as the percentage of customer requests resolved with a single service cell. Efficiency can be measured by cost trends and productivity measures. Process time can be measured by cycle time where the starting point of the cycle is defined as the receipt of a customer request and the finishing point is when the customer's problem is solved. The objectives and measures for the process perspective are given below:

Objective	***Measures***
Increase service quality	First-pass yields
Increase service efficiency	Cost trends outputs/inputs
Decrease service time	Cycle time

D. Learning and Growth Perspective

In learning and growth objective, the goal is to determine what is necessary to achieve the objectives set in the other perspectives. Kaplan and Norton pointed out three categories into which objectives in this perspective normally fall as follows:

(i) Employees' capabilities

(ii) Information systems' capabilities

(iii) Motivation, empowerment and alignment.

For incentive purposes, the learning and growth perspective focuses on the capabilities of people. Managers would be responsible for developing employee capabilities. Key measures for evaluating manager's performance would be employee satisfaction, employee retention and employee productivity. A good incentive system rewards managers who promote high employee satisfaction, low employee turnover and high employee productivity. An environment that supports employees provides greater opportunities for improving internal business processes.

Implementing the balanced scorecard is an iterative process because targets, performance measures and even strategies change over time. People who are only comfortable with a single objective performance measure that never changes, such as return on investment, will probably find the balanced scorecard frustrating. On the other hand, using the balanced scorecard can provide a more realistic view about the complexities and trade-offs that organisations face today.

Following are the advantages of a balanced scorecard:

(i) The balanced scorecard brings to focus strategy and vision.

(ii) It facilitates communication and understanding.

(iii) It provides strategic feedback and learning and guards against traditional performance measures which yield substantial results.

(iv) The balanced scorecard guards against sub-optimisation. It also forces senior managers to consider all important operational measures together.

(v) The balanced scorecard brings together in a single management report, many of the seemingly disparate elements of a company's competitive agenda.

The learning and growth perspective defines the capabilities that an organisation needs to create long-term growth and improvement. It is concerned with three major enabling factors:

(a) Employee Capabilities: The core outcome measurements for employee capabilities are employee satisfaction ratings, employee turnover percentages and employee productivity. The lead measures or performance drivers for employee capabilities include hours of training and strategic job coverage ratios. As new processes are created, new skills are often demanded. Training and hiring are sources of these new skills. The percentage the employees needed in certain key areas with the requisite skills signals the capability of the organisation to meet the objectives of other perspectives.

(b) Employee Attitudes: Employee not only have the necessary skills but they should also have the freedom, motivation and initiatives to use those skills effectively. The number of suggestions per employee and the number at suggestions implemented per employee are possible measures of motivation and empowerment. Suggestions per employee provide a measure of the degree of employee involvement. On the other hand, suggestions implemented per employee signal the quality of the employee participation. This also signals the employees whether their suggestions are being taken seriously or not.

(c) Information Systems Capabilities: Increasing information system capabilities provides more accurate and timely information to employees so that they can improve process and effectively execute new processes. Measures are concerned with the strategic information availability. The objectives and measures for the learning and growth perspective are given below:

	Objectives	*Measures*
(i)	Increase Employee Capabilities	Employee Satisfaction Ratings Employee Turnover Percentage Employee Productivity Hours of Training Strategic Job Coverage Ratio
(ii)	Increase Motivation and Alignment	Suggestions Per Employee Suggestions Implemented Per Employee
(iii)	Increase Information Systems Capabilities	Percentage of process with real-time feed-back capabilities percentage of customer facing employee with online access customer and products information

Illustration 6.3: Zee Ltd. can produce 60 units per hour of a particular product. During this hours, move time and wait time take 30 minutes, while actual processing time is 30 minutes.

Required:

(a) Calculate the current MCE.

(b) Calculate the current cycle time.

(c) If the move time and wait time are reduced by 50 per cent, what is the new velocity?

(d) What is the new cycle time?

(e) What is the new MCE?

Answer:

(a) $$\text{MCE} = \frac{\text{Process Time}}{\text{Process Time} + \text{Wait Time}}$$

$$= \frac{30\text{ minutes}}{60\text{ minutes}} = 0.50$$

(b) Cycle time $= \frac{1}{\text{Velocity}} = \frac{1}{60}$ hour

= One minute

(c) New velocity $= \frac{60}{3/4\,\text{hour}} = 80$ units per hour

(d) Cycle time $= \frac{1}{80}$ hour $= 0.75$ minute

(e) Final MCE $= \frac{30}{30+15} = 0.67$

6.4 COMPONENTS AND MEASURES OF PERFORMANCE

There are several approaches to performance reporting. Each approach attempts to link organisational strategy to actions of managers and employees. One popular approach to performance reporting is the balanced scorecard. A balanced scorecard is a performance measurement and reporting system that strikes a balance between financial and operating measures, links performance to rewards, and gives explicit recognition to the diversity of organisational goals. Companies such as Champion International, AT and T, Allstate, and Apple Computer use the balanced scorecard to focus management's attention on items subject to action on a month-by-month and day-to-day basis.

One advantage of the balanced scorecard approach is that line managers can see the relationship between non-financial measures, which they often can relate more easily to their own actions, and the financial measures that relate to organisational goals. Another advantage of the balanced scorecard is its focus on performance measures from each of the following four components of the successful organisation. This enhances the learning process because managers learn the results of their actions and how these actions are linked to the organisational goals.

Components and Measures of Performance

Sr. No.	Components	Performance Measures Used to Monitor Achievement of the Responsibility Center In-charge
1	Financial Strength	Product Profitability, Earnings before Interest and Taxation (EBIT), Return on Investment (ROI), Residual Income (RI)
2	Customer Satisfaction	Market-share, Customer Satisfaction Scores, Customer Complaints etc.
3	Business Process Improvement	Cycle Time, Defects/Non-conformities, Activity Costs etc.
4	Organisational Learning	Training Time, Employees Turnover Ratio, Staff Satisfaction Score etc.

6.5 EVALUATION OF RESPONSIBILITY CENTRES

'Responsibility Centres' provide the basis for one such approach. A responsibility centre has been defined by the Chartered Institute of Management Accountants as 'a segment of the organisation where an individual manager is held reponsible for the segment's performance'.

There are three types: expense centres, profit centres and investment centres. Together, they form the basis for 'responsibility accounting', a system of accounting, ' that segregates revenues and costs into areas of personal responsibility in order to assess performance attained by persons to whom authority has been assigned'.

Thus, it can be applied at all levels, to group, division, sector, business or product. The important point is that performance reporting reflects managerial responsibility and appropriate adjustments are made for those items which fall outside that responsibility.

Profit responsibility performance can be reflected in figures relating profit to turnover. However, performance may be subject to the fairness of apportioned costs and transfer prices. Investment responsibility performance can be judged on the basis of return on investment or residual income (excess earnings over the cost of capital). In each case, the assets/capital included should be that over with the responsible management has control. It is also clear that assets must be valued on a consistent basis so that for like comparisons can be made between different investment responsibility centres. Historical cost valuations should be converted to current valuations by using index numbers. Working capital should be included as part of the total assets/capital employed calculation with stocks valued on a similar basis between divisions. When measuring the return, it is usual for the average capital employed/total asset figure for the period to be used (the calculation is earnings times 100, divided by investment [assets/capital employed]). This can be subdivided into profit margin (profit as a percentage of sales), and asset turnover (sales divided by investment [assets/capital employed]).

Cost of capital used in residual income calculations should be the cost of financing the business or division the investment responsibility for which is being assessed. This may be an average cost based on group experience or an amalgam of different costs. Residual income is a concept that has been used by accountants for four or more decades. Alfred Sloan, of General Motors Corporation, knew and used the principle in the 1920s. More recently, Stern Stewart, New York Consultancy Group has 'trade marked' the term EVA (Economic Value Added) for what amounts to the same thing. EVA, according to the book *The Quest for Value – the EVA Management Guide,* is simply the net operating profit after tax less the cost of capital (the weighted average cost of debt and equity) used in the business. Verity Perkins, a subsidiary of Lucas Verity, uses EVA to arrive at its investment decisions and performance measurement analysis and also to reward divisional managers and employees.

6.6 EXERCISES

1. What is performance measurement? Explain the steps involved in performance measurement.

2. What is a balanced scorecard? What are the four basic perspectives of the balanced scorecard?

3. The following measures belong to one of four perspectives:

   (a) Revenue from new products

   (b) On-time delivery percentage

   (c) Economic value added

   (d) Employee satisfaction

   (e) Cycle time

   (f) Pass yields

   (g) Strategic Job Coverage Ratio

   (h) Number of new customers

   (i) Unit product cost

   (j) Customer profitability

   Required:

   Classify each measures by perspective and suggest a possible strategic objective that might be associated with measure.

4. A manufacturing cell has the theoretical capability to produce 30,000 printers per quarter, but currently produces 15,000 units. The conversion cost per quarter is ₹ 1,35,000. There are 7,500 production hours available within the cell per quarter. In addition to the processing minutes per unit used, the production of printers uses five minutes of move time, six minutes of inspection time and four minutes of rework time.

   Required:

   (a) Compute the theoretical and actual velocities.

   (b) Compute the ideal and actual amounts of conversion cost assigned per printer.

   (c) Calculate MCE. How does MCE relate to the conversion cost per printer?

5. A manufacturing cell has the theoretical capability to produce 60,000 space heaters per quarter. The conversion cost per quarter is ₹ 6,00,000. There are 20,000 production hours available within the sale per quarter.

   Required:

   (a) Compute the theoretical velocity and the theoretical cycle time.

   (b) Compute the ideal amount of conversion cost that will be assigned per heater.

(c) If the actual time required to produce a heater is 30 minutes, compute the amount of conversion cost actually assigned to each heater.

(d) Calculate MCE.

(e) Calculate cycle time, velocity, MCE and conversion cost per unit and non-value-added costs are all measures of performance for the cell process.

6. Matter Ltd. manufactures a product that experiences the following activities:

Activity	*Hours*
Processing (two departments)	30
Inspecting	02
Rework	03
Moving (three moves)	08
Waiting for the second process	24
Storage (before delivery to customers)	31

Required:

(a) Compute the MCE for this product.

(b) A study lists the following root causes of the inefficiencies. Poor quality components from suppliers, lack of skilled workers and plant layout. Suggest a possible cost reduction strategy expressed as a series of if-then statements that will reduce MCE and lower costs.

(c) Is MCE a lag or a lead measure? If and when MCE acts as a lag measure, what lead measures would affect it?

Chapter

7

Audit

STRUCTURE:

7.1 Introduction

7.2 Definition of Auditing

7.3 Compulsory Audit

7.4 The Auditor

7.5 Internal Audit

7.6 Cost Audit

7.7 Efficiency Audit

7.8 Management Audit

7.9 Strategic Assessment of Cost and Managerial Performances

7.10 Exercises

7.1 INTRODUCTION

No business or institution can effectively carry on its activities without the help of proper records and accounts, since transactions take place at different points of time with numerous persons and entities. The effect of all transactions has to be recorded and suitably analysed to see the results as regards the business as a whole. Periodical statements of account are drawn up to measure the success or failure of the activities in achieving the objective of the organisation. This would be impossible without a systematic record of transactions. Financial statements are often the basis for decision making by the management and for corrective action so as to even closing down the organisation or a part of it. All this would be possible only if the statements are reliable; decisions based on wrong accounting statements may prove very harmful or even fatal to the business. For example, if the business has really earned a profit but because of wrong accounting, the annual accounts show a loss, the proprietor may take the decision to sell the business at a loss. Thus, from the point of view of the management itself, authenticity of financial statements is essential. It is more essential for those who have invested their money in the business but cannot take part in its management for example, shareholders in a company; such persons certainly need an assurance that the annual statements of accounts sent to them are fully reliable. It is auditing which ensures that the accounting statements are authentic. In today's economic environment, information and accountability have assumed a larger role than ever before. As a result, the independent audit of an entity's financial statements is a vital service to investors, creditors, and other participants in economic exchange.

Historically, the word 'auditing' has been derived from Latin word *'audire'* which means 'to hear'. In fact, such an expression conveyed the manner in which the auditing was conducted during ancient time. However, over a period of time, the manner of auditing has undergone revolutionary change. According to Dicksee, traditionally auditing can be understood as an examination of accounting records undertaken with a view to establishing whether they completely reflect the transactions correctly for the related purpose. But this is not the end of matter. In addition, the auditor also expresses his opinion on the character of the statements of accounts prepared from the accounting records so examined as to whether they portray a true and fair picture.

7.2 DEFINITION OF AUDITING

According to General Guidelines on Internal Auditing issued by the ICAI, "Auditing is defined as a systematic and independent examination of data, statements, records, operations and performances (financial or otherwise) of an enterprise for a stated purpose. In any auditing situation, the auditor perceives and recognises the propositions before him for examination, collects evidence, evaluates the same and on this basis formulates his judgement which is communicated through his audit report."

Spicer and Peglar define Audit as "An examination of the books of accounts and vouchers of a business as will enable the auditors to satisfy that the balance sheet is properly drawn up so as to give a true and fair view of the state of affairs of the business and whether the Profit and Loss Account gives a true and fair view of the Profit and Loss for the period, according to the best of his information and the explanations given to him and as shown by the books, and if not, in what respect he is not satisfied."

Thus, audit is a critical examination of the books of accounts and the financial statements drawn from them. An audit examination can be made by a person who is duly competent for this purpose. An audit examination is to be made on the basis of evidential documents. The object of audit examination is to enable the auditor to express his opinion as regards the truth and fairness of the financial statements.

An auditor may review the financial statements of an enterprise to ascertain whether they reflect a true and fair view of its state of affairs and of its working results. In another situation, he may analyse the operations of an enterprise to appraise their cost-effectiveness and in still another, he may seek evidence to review the managerial performances in an enterprise. In yet another type of audit, the auditor may examine whether the transactions of an enterprise have been executed within the framework of certain standards of financial propriety. However, the variations in the propositions do not change the basic philosophy of auditing, though the process of collection and evaluation of evidence and that of formulating a judgement thereon may have to be suitably modified.

According to AAS-1 on "Basic Principles Governing an Audit", "An audit is independent examination of financial information of any entity, whether profit oriented or not, and irrespective of its size or legal form, when such an examination is conducted with a view to expressing an opinion thereon." The person conducting this process should perform his work with knowledge of the use of the accounting statements and should take particular care to ensure that nothing contained in the statements will ordinarily mislead anybody. This he can do honestly by satisfying himself that:

1. The accounts have been drawn up with reference to entries in the books of account;
2. The entries in the books of account are adequately supported by underlying papers and documents and by other evidence;
3. None of the entries in the books of account has been omitted in the process of compilation and nothing which is not in the books of account has found place in the statements;
4. The information conveyed by the statements is clear and unambiguous;
5. The financial statement amounts are properly classified, described and disclosed in conformity with accounting standards; and
6. The statement of accounts taken as a whole, present a true and fair picture of the operational results and of the assets and liabilities.

The aforesaid definition is very authoritative. It makes clear that the basic objective of auditing, i.e., expression of opinion on financial statements does not change with reference to nature, size or form of an entity. The definition given in AAS-1 is restrictive since it covers financial information aspect only. However, the scope of auditing is not restricted to financial information only but, today; it extends to variety of non-financial areas as well. That is how various expressions like marketing audit, personnel audit, efficiency audit, production audit, etc. came into existence.

7.3 COMPULSORY AUDIT

Compulsory Audit in the case of companies was introduced by the Companies Act, 1956 with specific provisions as to maintenance of books of accounts, and Audit. Accordingly only, independent persons duly qualified and trained in the profession can act as statutory auditor in the case of a company. The scope of duties, rights and liabilities of the auditor and requirements as to annual accounts and the audit report have also been enlarged.

In 1949, Parliament enacted the Chartered Accountants Act which was vested the management and control of accounting profession in the members of the profession. Accordingly, the Institute of Chartered Accountants of India (ICAI) was set up under the Act in Delhi. The affairs of the ICAI are managed and controlled by a Council comprising elected representatives of Chartered Accountants and nominees of Central Government. The Council lays down standards of education, training, professional conduct and discipline. The ICAI has issued a number of statements on Auditing statements on Standard Auditing Practices (SAPs) and Accounting Standards (AS) for guidance of the members of the profession.

The Companies Act, 1956 also prescribes a cost audit in the case of specified companies to be conducted by a Cost and Works Accountant within the meaning of the Cost and Works Accountants Act, 1959. The Income-tax Act, 1961 has also made the audit of accounts of certain assesses compulsory.

7.4 THE AUDITOR

The person conducting audit is known as the auditor. He makes a report to the person appointing him after due examination of the accounting records and the accounting statement in the form of an opinion on the financial statements. The opinion that he is called upon to express is whether the financial statement reflects a true and fair view. Auditing, especially of companies and for public purposes, has become the preserve of persons having recognised professional training and qualification. In India, under the authority of the Companies Act, 1956, only Chartered Accountants are professionally qualified for the audit of the accounts of companies. Chartered Accountants are in a position to undertake auditing of almost any accounting aspect, unlike cost accountants whose sphere has been restricted to audit of the cost accounting records and statements.

7.5 INTERNAL AUDIT

Internal audit is defined as an exercise in managerial control by means of an independent appraisal by employees of the organisation. It is carried out by employees of the company. With the introduction of the Manufacturing and Other Companies (Auditor's Report) Order, 1988, establishing of an effective internal audit system has been made obligatory in the case of every specified company. Accordingly, the statutory auditor is required to state whether the internal audit system is commensurate with the size and nature of the business of the company. The objects of internal audit are as follows:

(a) To study and evaluate the adequacy and effectiveness of accounting, financial and operating controls.

(b) To ascertain the extent to which business assets are accounted for and safeguarded from losses.

(c) To evaluate the quality of performance in carrying out assigned responsibilities.

(d) To ascertain the degree of compliance with predetermined policies, plans and procedures.

(e) To ascertain the authenticity of accounting and other data compiled within the organisation.

(f) To furnish the members of management with the objective analysis, comments and recommendations as regards activities of the business so as to help them in efficient and effective discharge of their responsibilities.

Internal Auditing may be called as a special segment of the broad field of accounting. The techniques and methods of auditing are the same as in external auditing. However, the main concern of an internal auditor is to ensure that there is proper compliance with policies, rules and procedures of the enterprise such as good business practices, generally accepted accounting principles, laws of the land and government regulations. Internal auditing is a staff function. An internal auditor does not exercise direct authority over other persons in the enterprise whose work is reviewed and appraised by the internal auditor. The internal auditor is made answerable to a high ranking officials so that the scope of his activities is broadened and his findings and recommendations are duly considered and implemented.

Internal audit helps an organisation accomplish its objectives by bringing a systematic, disciplined approach to evaluate and improve effectiveness of risk management, control and governance process. Internal audit is an independent, objective assurance and consulting activity designed to add value and improve an organisation's operations. It helps an organisation accomplish its objectives by bringing a systematic, disciplined approach to evaluate and improve effectiveness of risk management, control and governance process. Therefore, internal audit, as a consultancy service is expected to provide inputs to the formulation and implementation of strategies. As an assurance service, it should conduct strategy audit and review management decisions, in addition to operational audit and financial audit.

The World Bank defines accountability as the obligation of power-holders to take responsibility and answer for their actions. It defines social responsibility as the broad range of actions and mechanism that citizens and their organisations can use to hold societal power-holders to account, as well as actions on the part of government, civil society, media and other societal actors that promote or facilitate these efforts.

7.6 COST AUDIT

Cost Audit is defined as the verification of correctness of cost records and check on the adherence to the cost accounting plan. It is the audit of cost records. It is an audit process for verification of the cost of manufacture or production of any article on the basis of accounts relating to utilization of material, labour and other items of cost maintained by the company with the accepted principles of cost accounting. Thus, Cost Audit is an audit of efficiency. It is mainly a preventive measure, a guide for management policy and decision, in addition to being a barometer of performance of a company.

The Government of India has taken steps to study the cost structure of certain basic industries such as coal, sugar, drugs, tyres, cement etc. and to administer the prices charged by these industries. Such control is aimed at assuring a fair price to the consumer and a fair return to the manufacturer. It also enables the government to adjust its tax and tariff policies in respect of these industries in the larger interests of society. Statutory Provisions as regard cost audit were introduced by the Companies (Amendment)Act, 1965. Section 209(1)(d) deals with provisions relating to cost records and Section 233 B with audit of cost accounts in the cases of specified industries.

Objectives of Cost Audit

The objectives of cost audit are:

1. Verification of cost accounts with a view to ascertain that those have been properly maintained and compiled according to the cost accounting system.
2. Ensure that the prescribed procedure of cost accounting are duly adhered to.
3. Detection of errors and frauds.
4. Determination of inventory valuation.
5. Facilitating the fixation of prices of goods or services.
6. Periodical reconciliation between cost accounts and financial accounts.
7. Ensuring optimum utilisation of human, physical and financial resources of the company.
8. Detection and correction of abnormal losses.
9. Inculcation of cost consciousness.
10. Advising management as regards the areas where performance calls for improvement.

The Central Government may, if it considers it necessary, direct that the audit of cost accounts kept by a company under Section 209(1)(d) shall be conducted by a cost accountant within the meaning of the Cost and Works Accountants Acts, 1959, in such manner as may be prescribed. Such direction may in relation to a company engaged in production, processing, manufacturing or mining activities, require, specified particulars relating to material, labour or other items of cost. The Central Government has from time to time framed rules regarding the particulars as to the books of account relating to cost, to be kept by a company.

7.7 EFFICIENCY AUDIT

Efficiency audit ensures application of the basic economic principles, i.e., resources flow into the most remunerative channels. The main purpose of efficiency audit is to ensure that:

(a) Every rupee invested in capital or in other resources gives the optimum returns and

(b) The planning of investment between the different functions and aspects is designed to give optimum results.

From the above point of view, cost audit can appropriately be called as an efficiency audit. Efficiency audit can be defined as a "systematic analysis of activities to assess the efficiency with which resources are utilised."

The purpose of efficiency audit is to control rising costs and inflation. As a prerequisite to the introduction of efficiency audit, the company has to develop basic measures of performance. Adherence to efficiency, audit norms will enable the company to sell its products in a competitive market. The audit of government companies conducted by the Comptroller and Auditor General of India can be regarded as a proprietary audit because the objective of such an audit is to bring to the notice of the administration lacunae in the rules and regulations and to suggest wherever possible ways and means for the execution of plans and projects with greater expedition, efficiency and economy. A system is a given setup wherein by its very operation output or information is provided. Systems are man-made. It is necessary to examine whether a system fulfils the purpose for which it is devised and if not decisions have to be taken to change the system so that better output can be obtained.

The following are evidences to prove that cost audit can be called as an efficiency audit:

1. The cost audit report reflects the installed and actual capacity utilised. It also analyses the reasons for shortfall in actual capacity utilisation.
2. The cost auditor is also expected to compare the consumption with standards. An analytical study of the consumption of raw materials per unit of production both in quantity and value is made.
3. A manufacturing firm should keep its plant and machinery in a good state so that the productivity of the machines is not allowed to deteriorate.
4. A sound financial management is reflected in the maintenance of minimum inventory of stores and spares.
5. A cost auditor is also expected to offer his comments on the budgetary control systems and internal audit systems prevailing in the organisation. A good control system is an instrument for achieving managerial objectives.
6. A cost auditor is expected to offer comments on fuller utilisation of installed capacity, cost of production, increased productivity, limiting factor causing production bottlenecks and improved inventory policies. So long as these matters are discussed with the management and accepted by them, they are bound to be practicable suggestions.

Thus, it can be established that cost audit is so well designed to bring out the efficiency aspect of the operations of a manufacturing unit.

7.8 MANAGEMENT AUDIT

Management Audit is "The comprehensive examination of an enterprise to appraise its organisational structure, policies and procedures in order to determine whether sound management exists at all levels, ensuring effective relationship with the outside world and internal efficiency." Management audit is concerned with review of the past performance to ascertain whether it is in tune with the objective, policies and procedures. It is a method used to evaluate the efficiency of management at all levels through the organisation. Therefore, it is also called as efficiency audit. It comprises the investigation of a business by an independent body from the highest executive levels downwards in order to ascertain whether sound management prevails throughout and to report as to its efficiency. The management auditor reports on performance of the management during a particular period and suggests ways to remedy the deficiencies including modification of objectives, policies etc.

There is no limitation as to the period to be covered for management audit. There is no legal compulsion as regards management audit. The management auditor reports to the management. The need for management audit has grown because business organisations have became too large and complex leading to faulty organisational structure, ineffective decision-making process and slow execution of policies and programmes. Management audit alone can be an effective instrument for a critical review of all aspects of management of an enterprise.

Scope and Objectives of Management Audit

The following are the important areas that come within the normal terms of reference of management audit:

(a) Whether the basic aims and objectives of the enterprise are being fulfilled in practice.

(b) Whether the company is being successful in adopting itself to the technological change.

(c) Whether management is efficient at all levels and the extent to which economies are possible.

(d) Whether the management structure is suitable.

(e) Whether the policies with regard to staff recruitment and training are adequate.

(f) Whether there is a proper communication system both upwards and downwards throughout the enterprise.

(g) Whether return on capital employed is adequate and its comparison with other companies in the same industry.

(h) Whether the company's share of the market is increasing and comparison with its main competitor.

(i) Whether its relationships with the outside world are effective and whether its corporate image is satisfactory.

Appointment of Management Auditor

Management Audit is not compulsory under the law and hence the company may appoint any person to undertake management audit in its case, though invariably professional accountants are preferred for the purpose. The scope of audit, the period to be covered, the time frame for the submission of audit report are as stipulated in the letter of appointment of the auditor.

Process of Management Audit

Diagrammatic presentation of the Management Audit process is given below:

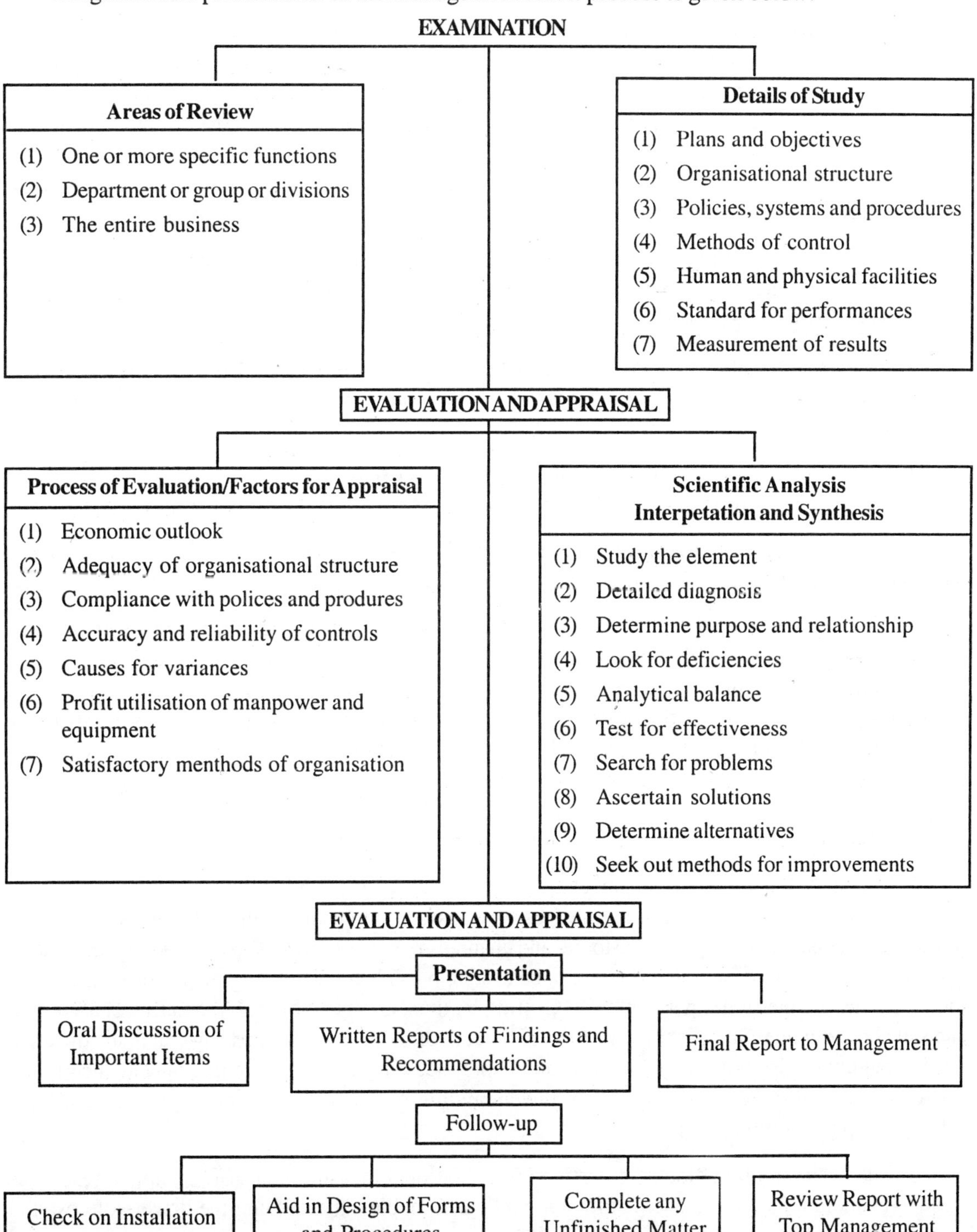

7.9 STRATEGIC ASSESSMENT OF COST AND MANAGERIAL PERFORMANCES

Cost Records and Cost Accounting Principles: The vital system for a responsive cost management in an enterprise is recording and reporting of cost influencing factors in a principles based approach also known as GACAP (Generally Accepted Cost Accounting Principles). In India, the Institute of Cost and Works Accountants in India is mandated for issuing Cost Accounting Standards and the Institute has already established a Cost Accounting Standards Board some years back. It has framed 12 CAS so far and identified 39 areas for CAS, that will provide business strategist, with the necessary tools and reporting mechanism, in performance measurement sphere.

Strategist Cost Management or Cost Management Strategy: It is fine differentiation as to whether one would concentrate on Managing Strategic Cost (the cost evolving out of different strategist) or Cost Management as a strategy in itself for an enterprise.

Whichever way we look, a business strategy cannot function without the help of the right kind of management tools that identifies and positions the cost in right proportion to the generation value that is sustainable in the long-run.

Whether cost management particularly strategic cost management is to be positioned at operational level or at the managerial level is a decision that clearly indicates a bottom-up approach.

Evaluating and Improving Cost in Organisations — International Good Practice Guidance Document released by the International Federation of Accountants:

1. The creation, operation, alteration and cessation of every action and function in an organisation – whether within the private, public or voluntary sector – all consume economic resources. Measuring, accumulating and assigning those resources to the organisation's various process and outputs allows the structure and operation of the organisation's various processes and outputs allows the structure and operation of the organisation to be explained, understood and improved costing, the accounting term that embraces these processes and expresses them using money as a common language lies at the heart of managerial accountancy and exercised managerial accountancy and exercised intelligently, is among the most powerful disciplines available to professional accountants in business (PAIB).

2. Costing contributes to an understanding of how profits and value are created and how efficiently and effectively operational processes transform input into output. It can be applied to resource, process, product/service, customer and channel-related information covering the organisation and its value chain. Costing information can be used to provide feedback on past performance and to motivate and change future performance. Costing is, thus, an essential tool in creating shareholder and stakeholder value. Given its importance and breadth of scope, it is unsurprising that many different costing methods exist, both in the literature and in practice. This can create confusion and uncertainty for managers and PAIB need a sufficient understanding of sound costing principles to be able to select and apply useful approaches.

3. The basic building blocks of costing are operational measurements of consumed resources (resources include people, space, equipment and consumables, these being the drivers of cost and

levers of change). Such measurements enable managers to draw conclusions and make judgement about why: (a) the organisation's result turned out as they did (performance evaluation), (b) what this means for the future (planning), and (c) the probable results of available courses of action (analysis of alternatives) all of which comprise essential information for effective decision-making. The principles in this International Good Practice Guidance (IGPG) support the application of judgement in providing good decision support. In turn, this calls for the professional accountant in business to clearly understand why cost information is to be used. For example, improving existing operational performance needs different treatment from that required to develop future strategy, although an ability to effectively relate managerial actions to their effects will be common to both objectives. The inclusion of measurement of resources in an explicit stage in the costing process can also help PAIBs to facilitate communication and interpretation of costing and profitability result, particularly for non-accountants.

4. Costing for decision support is valuable for performance improvement, value creation, "what if" analysis, and the effective and efficient application of an enterprise's resources and processes. However, the use of costs for external financial reporting for these decision support purposes can lead to misunderstanding. Examples of cost uses for financial reporting include the valuation of inventories, determination of transfer pricing amounts (for tax optimisation purposes) and segmental reporting. Such specific uses of cost assignment are usually mandated by jurisdictions and regulatory authorities, especially where cost assignment affects taxation or the determination of regulated pricing structures. The discipline applied to produce this type of output is usually called "cost accounting". Financial and tax accounting rules focus cost accounting on primarily historical results (i.e., what has already happened), an exception being when financial reporting standards include fair value-based calculations. The need for decision support usually requires deeper diagnostic insight into the causes of events (why they happened), a clear and direct connection to operations (to evaluate change options) and support to planning for desired future outcomes.

Strategic Cost Management Programme Steps

SCM Programme includes following five steps. These steps can be detailed out as follows:

1. **Focus:** Focus state starts with reviewing the different strategies of the company. Reviewing the strategies will lead to clear identification of performance gaps and this will help to bridge the gap by improving targets already set beforehand. Modifying the targets will lead to developed plan of action which will foster better internal communication within the organisation.

2. **Planning and Training:** Planning plays a crucial role in implementing strategic cost management programme. To implement the planning, a manager should gather very efficient team members and train them accordingly. Setting up of project management structure will facilitate the implementation of strategic cost management by clearly identifying the day-to-day activities, steering guidance and offering adhoc assistance.

3. **Fact Finding:** This stage includes the tasks such as data gathering, conducting interview, developing benchmarks, conducting customer surveys.

4. **Analysis and Recommendations for Changes:** Analysis of activities plays a crucial role in ascertaining the cost of the company. It can be done by various strategic cost management analytical tools, viz., cost driver analysis, activity based costing, selective business process re-engineering etc. An action plan for proposed change should address the following questions what, who, when how aspects of the activities.

5. **Implementation:** In implementation stage, the first task to be done is to define responsibilities and accountability of each individual and controlling, i.e., monitoring and corrective action should be taken at each stage of programme. And this is how the continuous improvement can be achieved. The third, fourth and fifth state in the above process indicates continuous improvement.

7.10 EXERCISES

1. What is auditing? What are the objectives of auditing?
2. What is cost audit? How does it differ from financial audit?
3. What is management audit? What are its objectives?
4. Explain the concept of efficiency audit.
5. What is internal audit? Explain the importance of internal audit as management control process.
6. Write short notes on the following:
   (a) Efficiency Audit.
   (b) Management Audit.
   (c) Cost Audit.
   (d) Internal Audit.
7. Explain the steps involved in Strategic Cost Management programme.
8. Explain the concept of Strategic Assessment of Cost and Managerial Performance.

❑ ❑ ❑

Chapter

Strategic Cost-Benefit Analysis

STRUCTURE:

8.1 Introduction

8.2 Strategic Cost-Benefit Analysis

8.3 Entrepreneurial Approach to Cost Management

8.4 Strategic Advantages

8.5 Long-term Perspectives of Cost Management

8.6 Exercises

8.1 INTRODUCTION

A strategy is a unified, comprehensive and integral plan that relates the strategic advantages of the firm to the challenges of the environment. Many organisations have alternatives for achieving their goals. Strategy is concerned with deciding which alternative is to be adopted to accomplish the overall objectives of the organisation. Strategy specifies how an organisation matches its own capabilities with the opportunities in the marketplace to accomplish its objectives. In formulating its strategy, an organisation should thoroughly understand its industry. Industry analysis focuses on the five forces, i.e., competitors, potential entrants into the market, equivalent products, bargaining power of customers and bargaining power of input suppliers. The collective effect of these forces shapes an organisation's profit potential. The profit potential, generally, decreases with greater competition, stronger potential entrants, products that are similar and more-demanding customers and suppliers.

Product differentiation is an organisation's ability to offer products or services perceived by its customers to be superior and unique relative to the products or services of its competitors. Pfizer has successfully differentiated its products in the pharmaceutical industry and Coca-Cola has also done the same thing in the soft drink industry. These companies have achieved differentiation through innovative products, R & D, careful development and promotion of their brands and the rapid push of products to the market.

Cost Leadership is an organisation's ability to achieve lower costs relative to competitors through productivity and efficiency improvements, elimination of waste and tight cost control. Cost leader in their respective industries include L & T (Engineering and Constructions), Hindustan Unilever Ltd. (Fast-moving consumer goods) and Maruti (Cars.) These companies provide products and services that are similar to but not differentiated from those of their competitors, but they are provided at a lower cost to the customers. Lower selling prices rather than unique products or services provide a competitive advantage for these cost leaders.

8.2 STRATEGIC COST-BENEFIT ANALYSIS

The Balanced Scorecard balances the use of financial and non-financial performance measures to evaluate short-run and long-run performance in a single report. It reduces the manager's emphasis on short-run financial performance, such as quarterly earnings. It is because the key strategic non-financial and operational indicators such as product quality and customer satisfaction, measure changes that a company is making for the long-run. The financial benefits of these long-run changes may not appear immediately in short-run earnings. However, given the company's strategy, strong improvement in non-financial measures indicate the creation of future economic value. For example, an increase in customer satisfaction is measured by customer surveys and repeat purchasesed signals, a strong likelihood of higher sales and income in the future.

The measures managers choose for each perspective relate to the action plans for furthering cost leadership strategy, to improve quality and reengineer processes. As a result of these actions, a company expects to reduce cut and downsize, eliminating excess capacity. However, management team may not want to cut personnel to the extent it would adversely affect employee morale and hinder future growth. To improve product quality, that is, reduce defect rates and improve yields in its manufacturing process, a company must maintain process parameters within tight ranges. To achieve this goal, it needs real-time data about manufacturing processes such as temperature and pressure and more effective process control methods. The company should also train its workers in quality management techniques to help them identify the causes of defects and ways to prevent them. Following this training, it needs to empower its workers to use their own initiative to make decisions and take actions that will improve quality.

Another element of strategy is to reengineer its order-delivery process. Reengineering is the fundamental thinking and redesign of business processes to achieve improvements in critical measures of performance, such as cost, quality, service, speed and customer satisfaction. A cross-functional team from the various departments can be reengineered to order the delivery process. The goal is to make the entire organisation more customer-focused and to reduce delays by eliminating the number of interdepartmental transfers. Under this system, a customer relationship manager is responsible for each customer and negotiates long-term contracts specifying quantities and prices. The customer relationship manager works closely with the customer and with manufacturing to specify delivery schedules. The experience of many companies in USA, indicates that the benefits from reengineering are most significant when it cuts across lines to focus on an entire business process. Thus, successful reengineering efforts involve changing roles and responsibilities eliminating unnecessary activities and tasks using information technology and developing employee skills.

8.2.1 Strategic Analysis of Operating Income

Managers need to evaluate the success of a strategy by linking the sources of operating income increases to the strategy. Operating income can increase simply because entire markets are expanding not because of company's strategy has been successful. Again changes in operating income may occur because of factors outside the strategy. For example, a company which has chosen a cost leadership strategy may find that its operating income instead resulted incidentally from some degree of product differentiation. A company may be successful in implementing its strategy and demonstrating that improvements in its financial performance and operating income over time resulted from achieving targeted cost savings and growth in market share. To be sure that the strategy has been successful, the company's management would like to see similar gains in subsequent years. The managers can also subdivide the changes in operating income into components that can be identified with product differentiation, cost leaderships or growth. Successful cost leadership or product differentiation generally increases market share and helps a company to grow.

Illustration 8.1: Wipro Ltd. implemented key elements of its strategy in 2010 and expected the financial consequences of these strategies to begin to appear in 2011. The company's data for 2010 and 2011 are given below:

Particulars	*2010*	*2011*
Units produced and sold	10 lakhs	11.50 lakhs
Selling price per unit (₹)	27	25
Direct materials (kg)	30 lakhs	29 lakhs
Material cost (per kg) (₹)	1.40	1.50
Processing capacity (units)	37.50 lakhs	35.00 lakhs
Conversion cost (₹)	160.5 lakhs	152.25 lakhs
Conversion cost per unit of capacity (₹)	4.28	4.35
R & D Employees	40	39
R & D costs (₹)	40 lakhs	39 lakhs

Additional Information:

1. Conversion costs for each year depend on production capacity and such costs do not vary with actual quantity. To reduce conversion costs, management would have to reduce capacity by selling some of the manufacturing equipment and by re-assigning manufacturing personnel to other tasks or laying them off.
2. At the start of each year, management uses its discretion to determine the amount of R & D work to be done. This work is independent of the actual quantity produced or sold.
3. The company's marketing and sales costs are small relative to the other costs. It has 10 customers each purchasing roughly the same quantities. Engineers from R & D work closely with customers to understand their needs regarding upgrades of the market. Its

cross-functional approach ensures that although marketing and sales costs are small, the entire organisation remains focused on increasing customer satisfaction and market share. Analyse the change in operating income of the company.

Solution:

Analysis of Change in Operating Income

Particulars	*2010*	*2011*
Revenues (₹)	270 lakhs	287.5 lakhs
Less: Costs:		
Direct material	42.00	43.5
Conversion	160.5	152.25
R & D costs	40.0	39.00
Total	242.5	234.75
Operating Income	27.50	52.75
Change in Operating Income	—	25.25

There is an increase in operating income in 2011. It is favourable. The company's strategy has gained an excess operating income of ₹ 25.25 lakhs in the year 2011.

8.2.2 Growth Component of Change in Operating Income

The growth component measures the change in operating income attributable solely to changes in prices of inputs. The price recovery component measures the change in output price compared with the changes in input prices. A company that has successfully pursued a strategy of product differentiation will be able to increase its output price faster than the increase in its input prices, boosting profit margins and operating income. It will show a large positive price recovery component.

The growth component of the change in operating income measures the increase in revenues minus the increase in costs from selling more units than the previous year assuming nothing else has changed. The growth component calculations use output prices, input prices, efficiencies and capacity relationships. The revenue effect of growth can be measured as follows:

$$\text{Revenue effect of growth} = \left(\text{Output sold in current year} - \text{Output sold in previous year}\right) \times \text{Selling price in previous year}$$

This component is favourable because the increase in output sold increases operating income.

The cost effect of growth measures how much costs would have changed in the current year if the company had produced increased units. In order to measure the cost effect of growth, managers distinguish variable costs such as direct material costs from fixed costs such as conversion costs and R & D costs. It is because units produced and sold increase, variable costs increase proportionately but fixed costs generally do not change. The cost effect of growth can be measured as follows:

$$\text{Cost effect of growth} = \left[\begin{array}{l}\text{Units of input} \\ \text{required to} \\ \text{produce in the} \\ \text{current year over} \\ \text{previous year}\end{array} - \begin{array}{l}\text{Actual units of} \\ \text{input used to} \\ \text{produce output} \\ \text{in the previous} \\ \text{year}\end{array}\right] \times \text{Input price in the previous year}$$

The net increase in operating income attributable to growth equals to revenue effect of growth and cost effect of growth.

Illustration 8.2: Chemplast Ltd. implemented key elements of its strategy in 2010 and expected the financial consequences of these strategies to begin to appear in 2011. The company's data for the year 2010 and 2011 are as follows:

Particulars	*2010*	*2011*
Units produced and sold	1,00,000	1,15,000
Selling prices (₹)	2.7	2.5
Direct materials (kg)	3,00,000	2,90,000
Direct material cost per kg (₹)	0.14	0.15
Manufacturing processing capacity	37,500	35,000
Conversion costs	1,60,500	1,52,250
Conversion cost per unit (₹)	4.28	4.35
R & D employees	40	39
R & D cost	40,000	39,000

Additional information:

1. Conversion cost for each year depends on production capacity.
2. At the beginning of each year, management uses it discretion to determine the amount of R & D work to be done.
3. The company uses a cross-functional team for its marketing and sales activities.

   You are required to:

   (a) Calculate the change in Operating Income

   (b) Revenue effect of growth and

   (c) Measure the cost effect of growth of the company.

Solution: (a) Analysis of Change in Operating Income

Particulars	*2010*	*2011*
Revenues (₹)	2,70,000	2,87,500
Less: Costs:		
Direct materials	42,000	43,500
Conversion costs	1,60,500	1,52,250
R & D costs	40,000	39,000
Operating Income	27,500	52,750
Change in Operating Income	25,250	

(b) Calculation of Revenue Effect

$= (1{,}15{,}000 - 1{,}00{,}000) \times 2.7$

$=$ ₹ 40,500

(c) Calculation of Cost Effect

(i) Materials $= (3{,}45{,}000 - 3{,}00{,}000 \times 0.14)$

$=$ ₹ $45{,}000 \times 0.14$

$=$ ₹ 6,300

(ii) Conversion cost = (Capacity Required – Actual Capacity) × Cost per unit

$= (37{,}500 - 37{,}500) \times 4.28$

$=$ ₹ 0

(iii) R & D costs = (Employees Required – Actual Employees) × Cost per employee

= (40 Employees – 40 Employees) × 1,000

= ₹ 0

(d) Increase in Operating Income Attributable to Growth:

		₹
Revenue effect of growth		40,500
Cost effect of growth:		
Materials	₹ 6,300	
Conversion costs	—	
R & D cost	—	6,300
∴ Change in Operating Income due to growth		34,200

8.2.3 Price Recovery Component of Change in Operating Income

The price recovery component of the change in operating income measures solely the effect of price changes on revenues and costs to produce and sell the increased production. It is assumed that the relationship between inputs and outputs continues in future. The calculation focuses on revenue changes caused by changes in the selling price. The revenue effect of the price recovery can be calculated as follows:

$$\text{Revenue effect of price recovery} = \left[\text{Selling price in current year} - \text{Selling price in previous year}\right] \times \text{Actual output in current year}$$

Cost effect of price recovery can also be calculated separately for variable costs and for fixed costs similar to the cost effect of calculating the effect of growth.

$$\text{Cost effect of price recovery} = \left(\text{Input price in current year} - \text{Input price in previous year}\right) \times \text{Units of input required to produce current year's ouput in previous year}$$

Illustration 8.3: Dynamic Ltd. implemented key elements of its strategy in 2010 and expected the financial consequences of these strategies to begin to appear in 2011. The company's data for the year 2010 and 2011 are given below:

Particulars	*2010*	*2011*
Units produced and sold	10,00,000	11,50,000
Selling price per unit (₹)	27	25
Direct materials (kg)	30,00,000	29,00,000
Direct materials cost per kg (₹)	1.40	1.50
Manufacturing Processing Capacity	37,50,000	35,00,000
Conversion costs (₹)	1,60,50,000	1,52,25,000
Conversion cost per unit (₹)	4.28	4.35
R & D Employees	40	39
R & D cost	40,00,000	39,00,000

Additional information:

1. Conversion cost for each year depends on production capacity.
2. At the beginning of each year, management uses its discretion to determine the amount of R & D work to be done.
3. The company uses a cross-functional team for its marketing and sales activities.

You are required to:

(a) Calculate the change in operating income

(b) Measure the revenue effect of price recovery

(c) Measure the cost effect of price recovery

(d) Calculate the change in operating income due to price recovery

Solution:

(a) Calculation of Change in Operating Income

Particulars	*2010*	*2011*
Revenues	2,70,00,000	2,87,50,000
Less: Costs:		
Direct materials	42,00,000	43,50,000
Conversion costs	1,60,50,000	1,52,25,000
R & D costs	40,00,000	39,00,000
Total cost	2,42,50,000	2,34,75,000
Operating Income	27,50,000	52,75,000
Change in Operating Income (₹)	25,25,000	

(b) Revenue Effect of the Price Recovery

= (SP in 2011 – SP in 2010) × Actual units of output sold in 2011

= (25 – 27) × 11,50,000

= ₹ 23,00,000 (unfavourable)

(c) Cost effect of Price Recovery

= (Input price in 2011 – Input price in 2010) × Units of input required

= (1.50 – 1.40) × 34,50,000

= ₹ 3,45,000 (unfavourable)

(d) Cost Effects of Price Recovery for Fixed Costs

(i) Conversion Costs = (4.35 – 4.28) × 37,50,000

= ₹ 26,500 (unfavourable)

(ii) R & D Costs = (Cost per Employee – Cost per Employee) × No. of Employees

= (1,00,000 – 1,00,000) × 40

= ₹ (Zero)

(e) Net Increase in Operating Income Attributable to Price Recovery

Revenue Effect of Price Recovery	₹ 23,00,000	
Cost Effect of Price Recovery:		
Direct material cost	₹ 3,45,000 U	
Conversion cost	2,62,500 U	
R & D costs	0	6,07,500
Change in Operating Income Due to Price Recovery		29,07,500 U

The price recovery analysis indicates that even as the prices of its inputs increased, the selling prices of 2011 decreased and the company could not pass on input price increase to its customers.

8.2.4 Productivity Component of Change in Operating Income

The productivity component of the change in operating income uses 2011 input prices to measure how costs have decreased as a result of using fewer inputs, a better mix of inputs and/or less capacity to produce 2011 output compared with the inputs and capacity that would have been used in 2010.

The productivity component calculations use 2011 Prices and output. It is because the productivity component isolates the change in costs between 2010 and 2011 caused solely by the change in quantities, mix and/or capacities of inputs. The cost effect of productivity for variable costs can be determined as under:

$$\text{Cost effect of productivity for variable costs} = \left[\begin{array}{c}\text{Actual units of input used to}\\ \text{produce}\\ \text{2011 output}\end{array} - \begin{array}{c}\text{Units of out put}\\ \text{required to}\\ \text{produce 2011}\\ \text{output in 2010}\end{array}\right] \times \begin{array}{c}\text{Input price}\\ \text{in 2011}\end{array}$$

The quality and yield improvements reduced the quantity of direct materials needed to produce output in the current year can be determined as under:

$$\text{Cost effect of productivity for fixed costs} = \left[\begin{array}{c}\text{Actual units}\\ \text{of capacity}\\ \text{in current year}\end{array} - \begin{array}{c}\text{Actual units of capacity}\\ \text{in previous year, if adequate}\\ \text{to produce in current year}\end{array}\right] \times \begin{array}{c}\text{Price per unit}\\ \text{of capacity in}\\ \text{current year}\end{array}$$

Illustration 8.4: Using the data in illustration 8.3:

(a) calculate cost effect of productivity

(b) change in operating income due to productivity.

Solution:

(a)(i) Cost effect of productivity for direct materials = (29,00,000 – 34,50,000) × 1.50

= 5,50,000 × 1.50

= ₹ 8,25,000 (Favourable)

(ii) Cost effect of conversion costs = (35,00,000 – 37,50,000) × 4.35

= ₹ (2,50,000 × 4.35)

= ₹ 10,87,500 (Favourable)

(iii) Cost effect of R & D costs = (39 Employees – 40 Employees) 10,00,000

= ₹ 1,00,000 (Favourable)

(b) Net increase in Operating Income attributable to Productivity:

Cost effect of productivity	₹
Direct Materials cost	8,25,000 F
Conversion costs	10,87,500 F
R & D Costs	1,00,000 F
Change in operating income due to productivity	20,12,500 F

Illustration 8.5: Following a strategy of product differentiation, WIL makes a high class machines. The company's data for the year ended on 31st March 2011 and 2012 are given below:

Particulars	*2011*	*2012*
Machines produced and sold	20,000	21,000
Selling price per machine (₹)	200	220
Direct materials (units)	60,000	61,500
Direct material cost per unit (₹)	20	22
Manufacturing capacity (units)	25,000	25,000
Conversion costs (₹)	10,00,000	11,00,000
Conversion cost per unit capacity (₹)	40	44
Selling and customer service capacity	30 customer	29 customers
Selling and customer service costs	36,000	3,62,500
Cost per customer of selling and customer service capacity	12,000	12,500

WIL produced no detective units and reduced direct material usage per unit of materials in 2012. Conversion costs in each year are tied up to manufacturing capacity. Selling and customer service costs are related to the number of customers that the selling and service functions are designed to support. The company had 23 customers in 2011 and 25 customers in 2012.

Required:

(a) Analyse the change in operating income

(b) Calculate the growth component of operating income

(c) Calculate the price recovery component of operating income

(d) Calculate productivity component of operating income

Solution:

(a) Anaylsis of Change in Operating Income

Particulars	*2011*	*2012*
Revenues (₹)	40,00,000	46,20,000
Costs:		
Direct materials	12,00,000	13,53,000
Conversion costs	10,00,000	11,00,000
Selling and customer service	3,60,000	3,62,500
	25,60,000	28,15,500
Operating Income	14,40,000	18,04,500
Change in Operating Income	3,64,500 F	

(b) Growth Component of Operating Income Change:

$$\text{Revenue effect of Growth} = \left(\text{Units sold in current year} - \text{Units sold in previous year}\right) \times \text{Selling price in previous year}$$

$$= (21{,}000 - 20{,}000) \times 200$$

$$= ₹\ (1{,}000 \times 200)$$

$$= ₹\ 2{,}00{,}000 \text{ (Favourable)}$$

$$\text{Cost effect of Growth for Direct Materials} = \left[\text{Units of input required to produce 2012 output in 2011} - \text{Actual units of input used to produce 2011 output}\right] \times \text{Selling price in previous year}$$

$$= \left(60{,}000 \times \frac{21{,}000}{20{,}000} - 60{,}000\right) \times 20$$

$$= (63{,}000 - 60{,}000) \times 20$$

$$= (3{,}000 \times 20)$$

$$= ₹\,60{,}000 \text{ (unfavourable)}$$

Cost effect of conversion cost = (25,000 – 25,000) × ₹ 20 = ₹ 0

Selling and Customer service costs = (30 customers – 30 customers) × 12,000 = ₹ 0

∴ Net increase in operating income attributable to growth

Change in operating income due to growth:

Revenue effect of growth		₹ 2,00,000 F
Cost effect of growth:		₹
Direct material cost	60,000	
Selling and Customer service costs	–	60,000
		1,40,000 F

(c) Price Recovery Component of Operating Income

(i) Revenue effect of Price Recovery = (220 – 200) × 21,000 units = ₹ 4,20,000 F

(ii) Cost effect of Price Recovery = (22 – 20) × 63,000

= ₹ (2 × 63,000) = ₹ 1,26,000

(iii) Cost effect of Price Recovery for conversion cost = (44 – 40) × 25,000 units

= ₹ (4 × 25,000) = ₹ 1,00,000 U

(iv) Cost effect of Price Recovery for Selling and Customer Service Costs

= (12,500 – 12,000) × 30

= ₹ (500 × 30) = ₹ 15,000 U

∴ Net increase in Operating Income attributable to price recovery:

	₹
Revenue effect of Price Recovery	4,20,000 F
Cost effect of Price Recovery:	2,41,000
Direct material cost	1,26,000 U
Conversion cost	1,00,000 U
Selling and Customer service	15,000
Change in Operating Income due to price recovery	1,79,000

(d) Productivity Component of Operating Income Change

$$\text{Cost effect of productivity for variable cost} = \left[\text{Actual units used to produce out put in 2012} - \text{Units of out put required to produce output}\right] \times \text{Input price in C.Y.}$$

= (61,500 – 63,000) × 22 = ₹ 33,000 F

(ii) Cost effect of Productivity for Conversion Cost = (25,000 – 25,000) × 40 = ₹ 0

(iii) Cost effect of Productivity for Selling and Customer Service Costs = (29 customers – 30 customers) × 12,500 = ₹ 12,500 F

Net increase in Operating Income Attributable to Productivity:

Cost effect of productivity:	₹
Direct material cost	33,000 F
Conversion cost	0
Selling and customer service	12,500 F
Change in operating Income due to productivity	45500 F

(e) A summary of Change in Operating Income between 2011 and 2012

Particulars	*Income Statement Amount for 2011* (₹)	*Revenue and Cost Effect of Growth Component* (₹)	*Revenue & Cost Effect of Price Recovery* (₹)	*Cost Effect of Productively Component* (₹)	*Income Statement for 2012* (₹)
Revenue	40,00,000	2,00,000 F	4,20,000 F	33,000 F	46,20,000
Costs	25,60,000	60,000 U	2,41,000 U	12,500 F	28,15,500
Operating Income	14,40,000	1,40,000 F	1,79,000 F	45,500 F	18,04,500

The analysis of operating income indicates that a significant amount of the increase in operating income resulted from WIL's successful implementation of its product differentiation strategy.

8.2.5 Partial Productivity Measures

Productivity measures the relationship between actual inputs used (both quantities and cost) and actual outputs produced. The lower the inputs for a given quantity of outputs or the higher the outputs for a given quantity of inputs the higher the productivity. Measuring productivity improvements over time highlights the specific input-output relationships that contribute to cost leadership. Partial productivity compares the quantity of output produced with the quantity of an individual input used. The partial productivity can be measured as follows:

$$\text{Partial productivity} = \frac{\text{Quantity of output produced}}{\text{Quantity of input used}}$$

The higher the ratio, the greater the productivity of the organisation.

For variable cost elements, productivity improvement measures the reduction in input resources used to produce output. For fixed cost elements, partial productivity measures the reduction in overall capacity over the period, regardless of the amount of capacity actually used in each period. An added advantage of partial productivity measures is that they focus on a single input. As a result, it is simple to calculate and easy to understand by operating personnel, managers and operators examine these numbers to understand the reasons underlying productivity changes, i.e., better training to workers, lower labour turnover, better incentives, improved methods or substitution of materials for labour. However, partial productivity focuses on only one input at a time rather than on all inputs simultaneously. Managers cannot evaluate the effect on overall productivity. Manufacturing conversion capacity partial productivity increases while direct materials partial productivity decreases. Total factor productivity is a measure of productivity that considers all inputs simultaneously. Thus, total factor productivity is the ratio of the quantity of output produced to the costs of all inputs based on current period prices. It is measured as follows:

$$\text{Total Factor Productivity} = \frac{\text{Quantity of output produced}}{\text{Costs of all inputs used}}$$

Total Factor Productivity considers all inputs simultaneously and the trade-offs across input based on current input prices. TFP is intrically tied to minimising total cost of production which is the financial objective of an organisation.

Illustration 8.6: Atul Ltd. implemented key elements of its strategy in 2010 and expects the financial consequences of these strategies in 2011 and 2012. The company's data for the two years are given below:

Particulars	***2011***	***2012***
Units produced and sold (lakhs)	10	11.50
Selling price per unit (₹)	27	25
Direct materials (kg)	30 lakhs	29 lakhs
Direct material cost per kg (₹)	1.40	1.50
Manufacturing processing capacity (kg)	37.5 lakhs	35 lakhs
Conversion costs (₹)	160.5 lakhs	152.25 lakhs
Conversion cost per unit (₹)	4.28	4.35
R & D Employees	40	39
R & D Costs (₹)	40 lakhs	39 lakhs

Your are required to determine:

(a) Partial Productivity and

(b) Total Factor Productivity:

Solution:

(a) Partial Productivity $= \dfrac{\text{Quantity of output produced}}{\text{Quantity of input used}}$

(i) Direct materials productivity $= \dfrac{11.50}{29.00} = 0.397$ units per kg

(ii) Manufacturing conversion capacity $= \dfrac{11.50}{35.0} = 0.329$

(iii) R & D $= \dfrac{11{,}50{,}000}{39} =$ ₹ 29,487

(iv) Comparable partial productivity based on 2011 Input:

Direct materials $= \dfrac{11{,}50{,}000}{34{,}50{,}000} = 0.333$

Manufacturing conversion cost $= \dfrac{11{,}50{,}000}{37{,}50{,}000} = 0.307$

R & D $= \dfrac{11{,}50{,}000}{40} =$ ₹ 28,750

Percentage change from 2011 to 2012:

Direct materials $= \dfrac{0.397 - 0.333}{0.333} \times 100 = 19.2\%$

Mfg. conversion cost $= \dfrac{0.329 - 0.307}{0.307} \times 100 = 7.2\%$

R & D cost $= \dfrac{29{,}487 - 28{,}750}{28{,}750} \times 100 = 2.6\%$

(b) Calculation of Total Factor Productivity

$$\text{TFP} = \frac{\text{Quantity of output produced}}{\text{Cost of all inputs used}}$$

$$= \frac{11{,}50{,}000}{(2900000 \times 1.5) + (35{,}00{,}000 \times 4.35)(39 \times 1{,}00{,}000)}$$

$$= \frac{11{,}50{,}000}{2{,}34{,}75{,}000}$$

= 0.0489 units of input per rupee input cost.

8.3 ENTREPRENEURIAL APPROACH TO COST MANAGEMENT

Over the last two decades, worldwide competitive pressures, deregulation, growth in the service industry and advances in information and manufacturing technology have changed the nature of our economy and caused many manufacturing and service industries to dramatically change the way in which they operate. These changes have promoted the development of innovative and relevant cost management practices. Moreover, the focus of cost management systems has been broadened to enable managers to better serve the needs of the customers and manage the firm's business processes that are used to create customer value. A company can establish a competitive advantage by providing more customer value for less cost than its competitors. In order to secure and maintain a competitive advantage, managers seek to improve time-based performance, quality and efficiency.

Global Competition

Vastly improved transportation and communication systems have led to a global market for many manufacturing and service firms. Now, both large and small firms are affected by the opportunities offered by global competition. Investment and management consultants can communicate with foreign offices instantly. Improved transportation and communication in conjunction with higher quality products that carry lower prices have increased the competition for all the firms. This new competitive environment has increased the demand not only for more cost information but also for more accurate cost data. Thus, cost information plays a vital role in reducing cost, improving productivity and assessing product-line profitability

Growth of Service Sector

The service sector of the economy has increased in importance. The service sector now comprises approximately three-fourth of the US economy and employment. It is about 60 per cent of India's economy. Many services among them are software services, entertainment services and travel and tourism are exported. Deregulation of many services has increased competition in the service industry. Many service organisations are scrambling to service. The increased competition has made managers in this industry more conscious of the need to have accurate cost information for planning, controlling, continuous improvement and decision-making. Thus, changes in the service sector have added to the demand for innovative and relevant cost management information.

Impact of Information Technology

Three significant advances relate to information technology. One is intimately connected with computer integrated applications. With automated manufacturing, computers are used to monitor and control operations. A considerable amount of useful information can be collected and managers can be informed about what is happening within an organisation. It is now possible to track products, continuously as they move through the factory and to report such information as units produced materials used, scrap generated and product cost. The outcome is an operational information system that fully integrates manufacturing with marketing and accounting data. The second major advance supplies the required tools. It is the availability of personal computers, online analytic programmes and decision support systems. The personal computer serves as a communication link to the company's information system and manages with the capability to use that information. The ability to enhance the accuracy of product costing is now available. Because of these advances, cost accountants have the flexibility to respond the managerial needs for more complex product costing. The third major advance is the emergence of electronic commerce. Internet trading allows buyers and sellers to come together and execute transactions from diverse locations and circumstances. It allows a company to act as a visual organisation thus reducing overhead. The emergence of Electronic Data Interchange and supply chain management has increased the importance of costing activities in the value chain and determining the cost to the company of different suppliers and customers.

Manufacturing Environment

Manufacturing management approaches such as the theory of constraints and just-in-time have followed firms to increase quality, reduce inventories, dominate waste and reduce costs. Automated manufacturing has produced similar outcomes. The impact of improved manufacturing technology and cost management has been significant. Product costing systems, control systems, inventory management, cost structure and many other accounting practices have been affected. The theory of constraints is a method used to continuously improve manufacturing and non-manufacturing activities. It is a thinking process that begins by recognising that all resources are finite. The most critical limiting factor called constraint becomes the focus point of attention. The performance can be improved by managing this constraint. It must be identified and exploited to manage the constraint. The constraint should be elevated in order to improve the performance. The process can be repeated until the constraint is busted. A demand-pull system, just-in-time, manufacturing strives to produce a product only when it is needed and only in the quantities demanded by customer. JIT manufacturing reduces inventories to much lower levels than those found in conventional systems, increases the emphasis on quality control and produces fundamental changes in the way production is organised and carried out. JIT manufacturing also focuses on continued improvement by reducing inventory costs and dealing with other economic problems. Thus, changing from traditional manufacturing set-up to JIT manufacturing allows the firm to focus more on quality and productivity and at the same time allows a more accurate assessment of costs to produce goods.

Computer Integrated Manufacturing

Automation of the manufacturing environment allows firms to reduce inventory, increase productive capacity, improve quality and service, decrease processing time and increase output. Automation can also produce a competitive advantage for a firm. The implementation of an automated manufacturing facility follows JIT and response to the increased needs for quality and shorter response time. Automation means installation of a computer integrated machines manufacturing system. It implies that the products are designed through the use of a computer-assisted design system and a computer-assisted engineering system to test the design. The product is manufactured using a computer-assisted manufacturing system and an information system connects the various automated components. Flexible manufacturing systems are capable of producing a bunch of products from start to finish using robots and other automated equipments under the control of a mainframe computer.

Customer Orientation

The cost management system should track information relating to a wide variety of activities important to customers. It includes product quality, delivery, performance, environmental performance, etc. Customers now count the delivery of the product or service as part of the product. Companies have to compete not only in technological and manufacturing terms but also in terms of the speed of delivery and response. The accounting department creates cost reports for production managers. The Accounts departments that are cost-driven assess the value of the reports to be sure that they communicate significant information in a timely and readable fashion.

New Product Development

A high proportion of production costs are incurred during the development and design stage of the new products. The effects of product development decisions on other parts of the value chain are now widely acknowledged. It has produced a demand for more sophisticated cost management procedures relating to new product development. This includes the procedures such as target costing and activity based costing management. Target costing encourages managers to assess the overall cost impact of product designs over the product's life cycle and provides incentives to make design changes to reduce costs. Activity based management identifies the activities produced at each stage of the development process and assesses their costs.

Total Quality Management

The two fundamental principles that govern a state of manufacturing excellence are continuous improvement and elimination of waste. Manufacturing excellence is the key to survival in today's world-class environment. A philosophy of total quality management has replaced the acceptable quality attitudes of the past. Managers strive to create an environment that may enable organisations to produce defect-free products and services. The emphasis on quality applies to services as well as products. Pursuing an objective of improving quality promises major benefits. Cost management supports this objective by providing crucial information concerning quality related activities and quality costs. Managers should know which quality related activities add value and which ones do not add value. They should also know what quality costs are and how they change over time. Producing products and services that actually perform according to specifications and with little waste are the twin objectives of the firm's today.

Time as Competitive Element

Time is a crucial element in all phases of the value chain. The firms can reduce time to market by redesigning products and processes by eliminating waste and by eliminating non-value-added activities. They can also reduce the time spent on delivery of products or services, reworking a product and other unnecessary movements of materials and sub-assemblies. The overall objective is to increase customer responsiveness. The rate of technological innovation has increased for many industries. The life of a product can be quite short. Thus, the time and product life-managers should respond quickly and decisively to changing market conditions. Information to allow them to accomplish this goal must be available. There is a correlation between time and cost and it is the part of the cost management system.

Improved Efficiency

Cost is a critical measure of efficiency. Trends in costs over time and measures of productivity changes can provide important measures of the efficiency of continuous improvement decisions. For this purpose, value and costs must be properly defined, measured and accurately assigned. Activity based costing is a new approach to cost accounting that provides more accurate and meaningful cost assignments. Production of output should be related to the inputs required and the overall financial effect of productivity changes should be calculated. Activity based costing and profit-linked productivity measurement are responsive to these demands. Dramatic increase in efficiency can be realised by analysing underlying activities and processes and eliminating those that do not add value and enhancing those that add value to the firm.

8.4 STRATEGIC ADVANTAGES

The most important strategic elements for a firm are its long-term growth and survival. Strategic decision-making is choosing among alternative strategies with the goal of selecting a strategy, that provides a company with reasonable assurance of long-term growth and survival. The key to achieving this goal is to gain a competitive advantage. Strategic cost management is the use of cost data to develop and identify superior strategies that will provide a sustainable competitive advantage.

Competitive advantage is creating better customer value for the same or lower cost than offered by competitors or creating equivalent value for lower cost than offered by competitors. Customer value is the difference between what a customer receives and what the customer gives up. What a customer receives is more than simply the basic level of performance provided by a product. It is called the total product. The total product is the complete range of tangible and intangible benefits that a customer receives from a purchased product. Thus, customer realisation includes basic and special product features service, quality, instructions for use, reputation, brand name and other factors which are important for customers. Customer sacrifice includes the cost of purchasing the product, the time and effort acquiring and learning to use the product and post-purchase cost which includes cost of using, maintaining and disposing of the product. Increasing customer value to achieve a competitive advantage is tied closely to judicious strategy selection.

Strategic Positioning is the process of selecting the optimal mix of the three general strategic approaches. This mix is selected with the objective of creating a sustainable competitive advantage. The objective of strategic cost management is to reduce costs while strengthening the chosen strategic position. Competitive advantage is tied to costs. For example, an organisation may be providing the same customer value at a higher cost than its competitors. By increasing customer value for specific customer segments and at the same time, decreasing costs, the organisation might reach a stage where it is providing greater value of the same or less cost than its competitors, thus creating a competitive advantage.

Management Accountants continually face resource allocation decisions, such as whether to purchase a new software package or hire a new employee. The cost benefit approach should be used in making these decisions. Resources should be spent if they are expected to better attain company goals in relation to the expected costs of those resources. The expected benefits from spending should exceed the expected costs. The expected benefits and costs may not be easy to quantify. However, the cost benefit approach is useful for making resource allocation decisions.

Corporate Strategy

Corporate strategy means determination of the business in which firm competes and allocates resources among the business units. It involves the formulation of strategy as a whole. It is concerned with being in the right business. The firm takes a conscious decisions to compete in certain businesses by choosing the right mix of businesses. Thus, the corporate strategy has more to do with where to compete. Strategic alternatives revolve around the issue of whether or not to pursue the existing business line so as to improve the efficiency of the firm. There are four grand corporate strategic alternatives:

(i) **Stability Strategy:** It means firms have to hold on to their current position in the product market. It is followed by those firms which are satisfied with their present position. These firms concentrate on the same products in the same markets.

(ii) **Growth Strategy:** A growth strategy is one which the enterprise pursues when it increases its level of objectives upward in significant increment much higher than an exploration of its past achievement level. The most frequent increase indicating a growth strategy is to raise the market share and sales upwards significantly. The firm has to enter into new markets, introduce new product lines and serve additional market segments.

(iii) **Retrenchment Strategy:** It involves dropping of some of the activities in a particular business. It may include totally getting out of some of the business of the firm. It is suitable during recession or in case of economic crisis. A firm may also drop some of its functions, products or markets. There is a need for redefining the priorities of the business.

(iv) **Combination on Strategy:** A firm can use a combination of strategies depending upon the situation. It may adopt a stable strategy in the case of a few businesses or products and a growth strategy in the case of others.

Business Unit Strategies

Business Unit Strategies are those which deal with the creation and sustenance of competitive advantage in each of the industries in which a firm is engaged. It is dependent upon its mission namely the overall objectives of a business and it is competitive advantage, that is, manner in which a business unit should compete in the industry to which it belongs in order to accomplish its mission.

In multi-product or multi-geographical area companies, strategic business units (SBUs) are created to manage effectively each of the products or a group of products. Separate SBUs are created each focusing on specific products like toiletries, beverages, ice-creams, laundry products, and cosmetics. Each SBU is managed independently as if it is a separate company by itself with clearly defined products/markets. Each SBU formulates for itself a clearly defined strategy. Each SBU has allocated resources in the form of physical, human and financial depending upon its activities and contributions made by it to the organisation. The advantages of strategies are as follows:

(i) The management of the organisation is efficient.

(ii) There is proper recognition of the Strategic Business Unit.

(iii) The SBUs provide motivation to employees.

(iv) The efficiency of the organisation is higher.

(v) It helps to provide better customer services.

(vi) It also facilitates innovation and create new ideas, products and markets.

(vii) It helps to improve the corporate image.

8.5 LONG-TERM PERSPECTIVES OF COST MANAGEMENT

The management accountants should understand the functions of business's value chain from manufacturing to marketing and from distribution to customer service. It is important because the companies are involved in international business. Definitions of product cost vary. The company's internal accountants have moved beyond the traditional manufacturing cost approach to a more inclusive approach. This new approach to product costing may take into account the costs of the value chain activities defined by initial design and engineering, manufacturing, distribution, sales and service. An individual who is well trained in the various definitions of cost and who understands the shifting definitions of cost from the short run to the long run can be invaluable in determining the type of information is relevant in decision-making.

Individual with ability to think cross-functionally can shift perspectives, expanding their understanding of problems and their solutions. Japanese automakers got their idea for JIT manufacturing from Taiichi Ohio's 1956 trip to the United States. He visited American automobile factories and supermarkets. The impressive array of goods in the supermarkets and their constant turnover led to Ohio's comprehension of the way that grocery customers pulled products through the stores. That understanding led to Toyota's attempt to pull parts through production precisely when and where needed.

Today, cost accountants cannot measure manufacturing costs in a traditional way. They have to relate cost management to marketing management and financé. When we take the systems approach to the company, we can see that these disciplines are interrelated. A decision affecting one affects the other. Many manufacturing companies engage in frequent trade leading the practice of encouraging wholesalers and retailers to buy more products than they can quickly resell. As a result, inventories become bloated and the wholesalers and retailers stop purchasing for a time. This look like a marketing problem but it is not, at least not entirely, when selling stops, the production also stops. As a result, trade-loading companies like Proctor & Gamble found themselves with wild swings in production. Sometimes, the factories were producing around the clock to meet demand for the product, other times, the factories were idle and workers were laid off. In effect, the sales were costing the companies millions of rupees of added production costs.

The Systems Approach

The systems approach for the modern companies is a database or relationship accounting approach. The transactions are effected and supporting documents are also accumulated. These documents contain a wealth data. For example, purchase order may show the type, amount and cost of the materials to be purchased as well as the date and the individual who has requested the materials. This purchase is then recorded into the journal and only the date, account and amount are retained. This results into elimination of useful information. The database or relationship accounting system preserves information. All information relating to a transaction is entered into a database in the systems approach. The moving force behind this shift from an external report-based accounting system to a relationship based accounting system is the widespread availability of technology. Powerful personal computers and networked systems make the accounting system available to a wide variety of users within the company. The development and adoption of powerful ERP programmes have moved the concept of an integrated database from the realm of theory to reality. This has forced a shift in perspective. An ERP system integrates many information systems into one enterprise-wide system. This directly impacts the costing systems such as activity based costing. An ERP system provides access to timely information both financial and non-financial about many organisational units and processes.

Flexibility: An understanding of the structure of the business environment in which the company operates is an important input in designing a cost management system. A primary distinction is to be made between manufacturing and service firms. There many be some overlapping because some manufacturing firms emphasise service to customers while some service firms emphasise the quality of their product.

Behavioural Impact: The cost management information system can shape the business. The cost information is not neutral. It does not stand in the background merely reflecting what has happened in an unbiased way. Today's Accountant should be an expert at valuing things. This includes methods of costing and achieving quality of differentiating between value-added and non-value-added activities and measuring and accounting for productivity. Thus, it is crucial that owners, managers and accountants should be aware of the signals that are being sent out by the accounting information system and ensure that correct signals should be sent to the organisation.

8.6 EXERCISES

1. Explain the Strategic Cost Benefit Analysis.
2. What is the Entrepreneurial approach to Cost management?
3. What are the strategic advantages of cost management?
4. What is the long-term perspective of cost management?
5. Write short notes on:
   (a) Analysis of change in operating income
   (b) Total Factor Productivity
   (c) The Systems Approach
6. Bombay Dyeing Ltd. sells cloth. The company's strategy is to offer a wide selection of clothes and excellent customer service and to charge premium price. The data relating to the year ended on 31st March are given below:

Particulars	*2011*	*2012*
Cloth purchased and sold (meters)	40,000	40,000
Average selling price (₹)	60	59
Average cost per meter (₹)	40	41
Selling and customer service capacity (meters)	51,000	43,000
Selling and customer service costs (₹)	3,57,000	2,96,700
Selling and customer service capacity cost per meter (₹)	7	6.90
Purchasing and Administrative capacity (designs)	980	850
Purchasing and Administrative cost (₹)	2,45,000	2,04,000

Total selling and customer service costs depend on the number of customers that the company has created capacity to support and not the actual number of customers that the company serves. Total purchasing and administrative costs depend upon purchasing and administrative capacity. Purchasing and administrative costs do not depend on the actual number of distinct clothing designs purchased. The company purchased 930 distinct designs in 2011 and 820 distinct designs in 2012. At the start of 2012, the company planned to increase operating income by 10% over the operating income in 2011.

You are required to:

(a) Analyse the change in operating income.

(b) Calculate the growth, price recovery and productivity components of changes in operating income.

(c) Does the strategic analysis of operating income indicate Bombay Dyeing was successful in implementing its strategy in 2012.

7. An analysis of Limca's operating income changes between 2011 and 2012 showed the following:

Operating income for 2011	₹ 16,00,000
Add: Growth component	60,000
Less: Price recovery component	– 50,000
Add: Productivity component	1,80,000
Operating income for 2012	₹ 17,90,000

The industry market size for the company's product did not grow. In 2012, input prices did not change and the company reduced the prices of its products.

Required:

(a) Has the company gained in operating income in 2012 consistent with the strategy?

(b) Explain the productivity component. Does it represent savings in only variable costs, only fixed costs or both?

8. Bharat Gears Ltd., operates in a very competitive market. Its strategy is to produce a quality product at a low cost. It produces no defective products. The company reports the following data for the past two years of operations:

Particulars	*2011*	*2012*
Units produced and sold	4,00,000	5,50,000
Direct Materials (kg)	4,50,000	6,30,000
Direct material cost per kg (₹)	1.20	1.25
Manufacturing labour hours	7,500	10,100
Wages per hour (₹)	20	25
Manufacturing capacity in units	6,00,000	5,82,000
Processing costs (fixed) (₹)	10,38,000	10,18,500
Fixed Manufacturing cost per unit (₹)	1.73	1.75

You are required to:

(a) Compute the partial productivity ratios for 2012.

(b) How much productivity has improved overall in 2012?

❑ ❑ ❑

Abbreviations

M&A	—	Mergers and Acquisitions
SCM	—	Strategic Cost Management
SBU	—	Strategic Business Unit
CBR	—	Cost-Benefit Ratio
NPV	—	Net Present Value
EIPR	—	Economic Internal Rate of Return
SCBA	—	Social Cost Benefit Analysis
UNIDO	—	United Nations Industrial Development Organisation
COECD	—	Centre for Organisation of Economic Co-operation and Development
IRR	—	Internal Rate of Protection
DRC	—	Domestic Resource Planning
BPR	—	Business Process Reengineering
ERP	—	Enterprise Resource Planning
TQM	—	Total Quality Management
PAT	—	Perform, Achieve and Trade Scheme
ABC	—	Activity Based Costing
R&D	—	Research and Development
ABM	—	Activity Based Management
MCE	—	Manufacturing Cycle Efficiency

JIT	—	Just in Time
SBU	—	Strategic Business Unit
ICAI	—	Institute of Chartered Accountants of India
SAP	—	Standard Auditing Practices
GACAP	—	Generally Accepted Cost Accounting Practices
IGPG	—	International Good Practice Guidance
PAIB	—	Professional Accountants in Business